D1526413

Traditional Musicians of the Central Blue Ridge

Traditional Musicians of the Central Blue Ridge

*Old Time, Early Country, Folk and
Bluegrass Label Recording Artists,
with Discographies*

by

Marty McGce

<small>WITH A FOREWORD BY</small>
Bobby Patterson

<small>CONTRIBUTIONS TO SOUTHERN APPALACHIAN STUDIES, 3</small>

McFarland & Company, Inc., Publishers
Jefferson, North Carolina, and London

Library of Congress Cataloguing-in-Publication Data are available

British Library Cataloguing-in-Publication data are available

ISBN 0-7864-0876-6 (softcover : 50# alkaline paper)

Manufactured in the United States of America

McFarland & Company, Inc., Publishers
  Box 611, Jefferson, North Carolina 28640
    www.mcfarlandpub.com

To my mother and father,
who instilled in me traditional values
and a love for the Blue Ridge region,
its people and its music

Acknowledgments

I would like to extend my sincere gratitude and appreciation to the following individuals, without whose encouragement and assistance this book would have never been completed:

The fine folks at the William Leonard Eury Appalachian Collection of Appalachian State University (Boone, N.C.), the Blue Ridge Heritage Institute and Museum at Ferrum (Va.) College (especially Susan Stephenson and Roddy Moore), and the Southern Folklife Collection at the University of North Carolina at Chapel Hill; Gary and Pam Mitchem; Katy Taylor; Rita Scott; Jimmy and Sue Trivette; Ginny Tobiassen; Mack Powers and Sandy Lemly; Eric Ellis; Drake Walsh; Ward Eller; Bobby Patterson; Dan Seeger; Dale Morris; Gene Earle; Marshall Wyatt; Gary Poe; Herb Key; Willard Gayheart; Scott Freeman; Ernest and Scotty East; Joe Hallford and Russell Easter; Paul Sutphin; Verlen and Larry Clifton; Art Menius, "B" Townes, Nancy Watson and the other kind folks at MerleFest; and last, but not least, my supportive wife Jackie, my daughters Caitlin and Olivia, and my Mom and Dad.

I couldn't have done it without you. God bless you all!

Contents

Foreword
by Bobby Patterson

My public involvement in traditional music really began in the 1960s when Kyle and Percy Creed bought a parcel of land in the Coleman section of Carroll County, Virginia. The local community store which had been the center focus for many years was owned by Lewis and Nancy Melton. It was put up for sale and Kyle, being a vigorous entrepreneur, bought it from the Meltons. It didn't take long for everyone around the area to get acquainted with the Creeds. My family and I were among several hundred who became good friends of the Creeds. I was single, living with my parents, John and Ruby Patterson, and was accepted by Kyle just like one of his family, almost like a son that Kyle and Percy never had. (They did have two daughters: one lived in California and the other near Richmond, Virginia.) This acquaintance turned into a great friendship that would last a lifetime.

String music was the main ingredient that brought us so tightly together. Kyle was a good fiddler and clawhammer banjo player. My father was also a good fiddler and clawhammer banjo player. I could play bluegrass banjo, mandolin and guitar so this turned every visit with either Kyle or my parents into a musical jamboree. We would meet and play till midnight while Mama and Percy caught up on the latest gossip. It was great!

Kyle kept talking to me about his musician friends in North Carolina and how we were going to go there and play some music with them. Our first trip was to Fred Cockerham's home in Low Gap. There I met Fred and his wife Eva, and was immediately embraced by this kind and gentle couple who had been down their road of hardships and joys. Fred was blind from an untreated eye disease in his later life but this didn't affect his ability to play. Paul Sutphin was there playing the guitar and he had a smile from ear to ear and a funny story to tell between tunes. This music session lasted till almost midnight and there are no words to describe this electric charge we all felt during this get-together.

The next session in Carolina was with Ernest East at his home in Pine

Ridge. Again this gathering was just as electrifying as Fred's but Ernest played the fiddle with more of a tightness to his bowing and noting. In my mind he was more of a square dance fiddler than Fred. I was soaking up all this music that I had never heard before and making new friends that would later become recording artists on both Mountain and Heritage record labels as well as County and Rounder Records.

After Ernest's session there came the biggest of all at Tommy Jarrell's home in Mount Airy. This one was the ultimate with Tommy, Kyle, Fred, Ernest, Paul and Verlen Clifton. If that combination and caliber of musicians couldn't make a convert out of you, then there's no hope left. All of them were great old-time musicians in their own way and were just beginning to emerge on a musical scene that would trigger a resurgence of old-time music as never seen before. Tommy was then accustomed to playing sitting down with his knees almost touching each other and playing with very little volume. I remember Kyle and I talking on the way home about Tommy's low volume playing. All this would change a few years later when Tommy's recording career started. This session brought in all the Jarrells from Mount Airy, friends and neighbors and another load of friendships that would last as long as life itself. I can never forget the bond we all shared and felt for each other. This bond and electric charge that I am referring to can only be understood by those who have experienced an informal musical gathering in a small home or apartment with personalities like these people and musicianship of such a high level.

It wasn't long after we started playing together that Kyle began to get more serious about his music. He told me that I was instrumental in getting him to playing again after a long dry spell before moving to Coleman, and that he wanted to revive his old band, the Camp Creek Boys. When he did revive the band, I became the banjo player, even though I played bluegrass style; he was the fiddler and we would use other local musicians to fill the gaps. Fiddlers' conventions were our main events to play and compete in. Blue ribbons and trophies soon lined the walls of Kyle's home. He kept the biggest majority of the mementos because he was the individual who won the most. When the band won trophies he shared them with the band members. I have several that he insisted I take home because Kyle was a good-hearted man. He wanted his recognition but also wanted his band members to feel they were just as important.

The Camp Creek Boys were enjoying a winning stint that would soon be challenged by a rule change at all conventions. This change concerned what an old-time band could consist of and what style the banjo had to play to be considered part of an old-time band. Kyle would immediately come to my rescue when anyone suggested that I was playing bluegrass banjo instead of old-time or clawhammer. He would say, "That's not bluegrass, it's old-time, the way he plays." However, the rules were changed and the band had to make the necessary changes to compete. This is when I started playing more guitar and branched off into other bluegrass bands.

We were still very close, so close in fact that in 1972 we formed our own record label, Mountain Records. Our first recording took place in a small recording studio built by Kyle, my father and myself, just behind my parents' home.

Kyle and I had agreed that I would build the studio and he would furnish the equipment. Work began in 1971 and was completed in the same year. This building became the most visited spot on the Coal Creek Road. From 1972 until the guest register was moved to a new studio in 1979 it had seen musicians from all over the globe: Germany, Japan, Australia, the Netherlands, Switzerland and beyond, not to mention the local musicians and relatives of both our families. Music sessions or "jams" were held every spare minute Kyle and I had.

It was under these conditions our very first commercial recording was made. On the night of the recording, my parents, Percy, Andrea Freeman (Dave Freeman's wife), James Lindsey, Artie Carlson and others were setting around the room trying to be very quiet during the cutting of the tapes. It was one big happy gathering of family and friends with jokes between cuts. The album was titled *Kyle Creed, Bobby Patterson and the Camp Creek Boys: Square Dance Time—Blue Ridge Style,* catalog number Mountain 301. Two other albums were released by Kyle Creed, myself and the Camp Creek Boys: *Mountain Ballads,* banjo and fiddle tunes with some friends and Thomas Norman on vocals, Mountain 303; and one on Leader Sound Ltd., from England, titled *Fiddle and Banjo Tunes Recorded in Galax, Virginia* (Led 2053).

After our first release the next project we undertook was the now-legendary recording *June Apple* with Tommy Jarrell playing fiddle and Kyle playing clawhammer banjo together with Audine Lineberry playing bass and me playing guitar. This one was recorded like the previous one except we were the only audience. Our recordings were made like a live performance. If we didn't like a cut or the way it was mixed, we all had to play it again, over and over until we got it right. *June Apple* became the standard by which all old-time recordings were judged, and some still consider it the best old-time recording ever made.

I had ties with local bluegrass bands and Kyle was more devoted to old-time, so we split our partnership of Mountain Records on March 31, 1973. I spent most of a day considering what to name a new record label before settling on Heritage Records. Kyle remodeled one of the rooms in his store building and put his recording equipment in and continued to record a total of fourteen releases for the Mountain label. Over the years there have been more than a hundred releases on the Heritage label, including gospel and bluegrass.

This new reference book by Marty McGee will allow readers to learn more about the lives and recordings of Tommy, Kyle, Fred, Ernest and dozens of others. Marty has provided a valuable service to researchers, collectors and those holding a general interest in traditional music from the Central Blue Ridge.

Bobby Patterson
Galax, Virginia
Fall 1999

Preface

My passion for old-time and bluegrass music began when I discovered a dusty box of old 78 rpm records that had belonged to my grandmother. It was as if a new world of music opened up before me when I dropped the phonograph's needle onto those well-worn vinyl grooves. The records were scratchy and lo-fi, but the music was passionate, spirited and full of life. Listening for the first time to the Carter Family, Jimmie Rodgers, the Carolina Tar Heels, Uncle Dave Macon, Fiddlin' John Carson, Henry Whitter, Vernon Dalhart, and Gid Tanner and His Skillet Lickers, something clicked. This music was the real deal, my ears were telling me.

My curiosity aroused, I soon checked out Harry Smith's famously bootlegged and still-influential *Anthology of American Folk Music*, and was blown away by this sometimes odd and foreign but always fascinating collection of songs. Two of the *Anthology* songs were performed by the Carolina Tar Heels, whose leader, Dock Walsh, I learned, raised up his family just a few miles from where I was born and reared in western Wilkes County, N.C.

Perhaps my scholarly pursuit of ancient tones began in earnest when I found an eight-track tape of *The Essential Doc Watson*, recorded by my father years ago from LPs owned by his brother. Doc picked the guitar as I'd never heard it picked before, or since. Better still, Doc lived just about ten miles up the road in Deep Gap, N.C.

Brimming with "hometown" pride, I set out to find who else besides Dock and Doc had made records and also called the central Blue Ridge Mountains their home. I wanted to know who these people were, what were the key events in their lives, where they lived and worked, and how their music was recorded and released. Having found no comprehensive source that held the answers to all of my questions, I decided to compile such a reference myself. My background as a local newspaper reporter turned out to be a great advantage in my gathering of the facts.

Since this was a reference book, I needed to establish some criteria for inclusion in the work. I decided to include all known musicians who were

5

natives of or lived primarily in the northwestern North Carolina counties of Alleghany, Ashe, Avery, Surry, Watauga, and Wilkes. I defined the Central Blue Ridge as also including the adjacent Virginia counties of Carroll and Grayson. In looking at traditional music from northwestern North Carolina, one must not exclude the Carroll-Grayson area (whose epicenter is Galax, the self-proclaimed "old time music capital of the world") because they share not only a similar musical style but also many common pickers who might have lived in one state and worked in the other or who made music with neighbors just across the state line. Good music knows no political boundaries, anyway.

Now that I had pinpointed my geography, I chose to focus on those musicians whose work had been released on a major commercial label such as Folkways, Rounder, County, Rebel, Sugar Hill, Marimac, Hay Holler and Heritage. For purposes of this study all of the 78 rpm labels from the 1920s and 1930s are considered "major," regardless of distribution or sales. Finally, I've used the term "traditional" to encompass most forms of acoustic string-based music: old time, early country, folk and bluegrass are the primary genres covered herein.

The format is the same for all entries: Following a biographical synopsis, all of the performer's released works are listed in chronological order. For each recording I've attempted to list the label and catalog number on which it was released, the date and place of the recording, the technical staff involved in the recording, the guest musicians who participated, and any unusual information about the recording. I have included both primary recordings featuring the artist and anthologies on which a song or two by the performer appeared.

A chronological overview of the contributions made by Central Blue Ridge traditional musicians from the late 1920s to the late 1990s is provided in the Introduction.

It is hoped that this book will in some small way help to preserve what traditional musicians of the Central Blue Ridge have achieved. Their music is timeless, edifying and certainly worthy of preservation so that future generations might enjoy such a rich and moving part of their mountain heritage. In the Foreword to this work Bobby Patterson (who has probably contributed more to the Galax traditional music scene than any other person in the past forty years) talks about the tight bond and "electric charge" he felt when jamming with such old-time music stalwarts as Tommy Jarrell and Kyle Creed. I know exactly what he means: I get chills every time I hear Tommy "rocking the bow," Wade Ward "frailing," Kilby Snow "slurring" or Doc Watson "pickin' one" with Merle or Richard. This music endures because, to so many, it's music that truly matters.

Introduction

The Central Blue Ridge, taking in the mountainous regions of northwestern North Carolina and southwestern Virginia, is an area well-known for its musical traditions. The early mountain folk of the South were carriers of oral traditions of folk tale, folk dance and ballad, brought with them from their homelands in England, Scotland and Ireland. Left in relative isolation in the mountains and backwoods of Appalachia, these pioneers developed a strong folk culture and staunchly held on to and passed down to future generations their fiddle and banjo tunes and ballads.

In the introduction to *The Songs of Doc Watson*, folklorist Ralph Rinzler wrote, "Western North Carolina has long been recognized as one of the richest repositories of folk song and lore in the southeastern United States." Indeed, English folksong scholar Cecil Sharp found the Central Blue Ridge to be a rich terrain as he was collecting ballads and folksongs between 1916 and 1918. In the liner notes to *The Doc Watson Family Tradition*, A.L. Lloyd writes, "The northwest corner of North Carolina is still probably the busiest nook in the United States for domestic music, singing, fiddling, banjo-picking, and it's no accident that when Cecil Sharp was collecting songs and ballads in the Appalachians (in 1916) it was precisely this small area that yielded the greatest harvest."

During the early 1920s, phonograph companies began to develop markets for string band music, or as some called it, "hillbilly" music. Henry Whitter of Fries, Virginia, was the Central Blue Ridge's first musician to record when he traveled uninvited to New York City in March 1923 to record "The Wreck on the Southern Old 97" and "Lonesome Road Blues" for OKeh Records. Along with his fiddling partner, G.B. Grayson, Whitter recorded about 40 songs from 1927 to 1930, many of which remain influential and prime examples of old-time music. Ashe County native Grayson was the posthumous recipient of the International Bluegrass Music Association's Award of Merit in 1996.

One of the stalwarts of old-time music, Ernest V. (Pop) Stoneman of Carroll County, Virginia, began his extensive recording career, like Whitter, in New York City for OKeh in September of 1924. That recording is recognized as the first with autoharp. Stoneman went on to record over 200 sides for Edison, Gennett, Victor and Vocalion, and served as patriarch of the Stoneman Family, one of the most enduring bluegrass bands of the 1960s. Pop was posthumously inducted into the Autoharp Hall of Fame in 1994. (He was preceded into the Hall a year earlier by another Central Blue Ridge legend, John Kilby Snow.)

The "hillbilly" musical scene exploded in the mid–1920s, as musicians from the Central Blue Ridge were recruited to make records at various locations in the South where record companies had established provisional studios. The influential string band Carolina Tar Heels was formed in 1925; the Wilkes County–based group subsequently made over 40 sides for Victor Records. The Hill Billies, an early old-time string band, radio and vaudeville act that toured up and down the East Coast, was organized by John Rector of Galax, Virginia, in 1925. Another group that toured the East Coast vaudeville circuit during the late 1920s and early 1930s was H.M. Barnes' Blue Ridge Ramblers, which recorded on the Brunswick label.

In the late 1920s, the Red Fox Chasers, organized in 1927 by Paul Miles, recorded nearly 50 sides, mostly for the Gennett and Champion labels. Other Central Blue Ridge bands that recorded around 1927 and 1928 include Da Costa Woltz's Southern Broadcasters, Frank Blevins and His Tar Heel Rattlers, Holland Puckett, J.P Nester and Norman Edmonds.

The Great Depression severely crippled the market for commercial 78 rpm recordings, but Central Blue Ridge musicians found new means of exposure through radio broadcasts and field recordings made by collectors of folklore. In 1934 Fields Ward of Grayson County, Virginia, formed the Ballard Branch Bogtrotters, a legendary band also made up of his father Crockett, brother Sampson, uncle Wade (later on), Alec (Uncle Eck) Dunford and Dr. W.P. Davis. The Bogtrotters recorded over 150 songs for John Lomax and the Library of Congress between 1937 and 1942. During this time Lomax also recorded E.C. and Orna Ball of Rugby, Virginia, who would in the 1970s record numerous albums for the Prestige, Atlantic, County and Rounder labels.

Radio, record and film stars Lulu Belle and Scotty (both of whom were raised in the Central Blue Ridge) were the nation's leading husband-and-wife team of the 1930s, 1940s and 1950s. For some twenty years they starred on the *National Barn Dance* show from WLS Chicago and were also featured on *Boone County Jamboree* over WLW Cincinnati from 1938 to 1940. A band that gained a significant radio market in Pennsylvania, Maryland and Delaware during this same time was the North Carolina Ridge Runners, made up of displaced Ashe (N.C.) Countians Ola Belle Campbell, Shorty Smith, Slick Miller, Elmer Elliott and Bryan Dolinger.

Ola Belle, her brother Alex and Sonny Miller later formed the New

River Boys and Girls in 1948. Later including such Central Blue Ridge musicians as John Jackson and Ted Lundy, the band would play throughout Pennsylvania, Maryland and Delaware into the 1970s.

Central Blue Ridge musicians were involved in the formative days of bluegrass music's "holy trinity": Bill Monroe's Blue Grass Boys, Lester Flatt and Earl Scruggs' Foggy Mountain Boys, and Ralph and Carter Stanley's Clinch Mountain Boys. Fiddler Art Wooten of Sparta, N.C., was the first Blue Grass Boy ever hired by Monroe. After two stints with Monroe, Wooten joined the Stanley Brothers in 1948. He fiddled with the Clinch Mountain Boys until 1952. After a stint with Monroe, Wilkes County (N.C.) native Jim Shumate fiddled on Flatt and Scruggs' first recording session in 1949. Shumate was the recipient of a North Carolina Folk Heritage Award in 1995.

The 1950s saw the emergence of bluegrass as a distinct and vital musical genre. An early, regional bluegrass band based in Wilkes County, N.C., the Church Brothers put out records on the Blue Ridge and Rich-R-Tone labels but never really gained the nationwide acclaim that they deserved.

In 1951 Alex Campbell, his sister Ola Belle and her husband Bud Reed established a bluegrass music park called the New River Ranch near Rising Sun, Maryland. Many Central Blue Ridge musicians would play at New River before its total destruction in a 1958 blizzard. The following year Galax, Virginia, native Ted Lundy formed the Southern Mountain Boys with Fred Hannah in Wilmington, Delaware. The Southern Mountain Boys went on to record four acclaimed albums (1973–1978) for Rounder.

In 1958 Alan Lomax recorded the Galax-based Mountain Ramblers for his "Southern Folk Heritage" series on Atlantic Records, catapulting the Ramblers to near legendary status among mountain bluegrass bands. Under various lineups led by guitarist James Lindsey, the Ramblers dominated area fiddlers' conventions in the late 1950s and throughout the 1960s.

Mount Airy (N.C.) native Larry Richardson and his bluegrass banjo hit the spotlight in the 1950s, as he played with the Lonesome Pine Fiddlers, Carl Sauceman and Happy Smith before joining up with the Blue Ridge Boys in the mid–1960s.

The 1960s was notable for the "rediscovery" of many Central Blue Ridge artists that had recorded in the 1920s, 1930s and 1940s. Due in large part to the folk music revival that was sweeping the country, artists such as Clarence Ashley, the Carolina Tar Heels, the Camp Creek Boys, Fields and Wade Ward, and Tommy Jarrell were thrust into the national limelight and visited by outsiders who sought tutelage and guidance. The Camp Creek Boys—featuring such notables as Fred Cockerham, Kyle Creed, Ernest East, Paul Sutphin, Verlen Clifton and Ronald Collins—were actually formed in the 1930s but gained considerable attention and influence during the 1960s.

Another master from the Round Peak area of North Carolina, Tommy Jarrell, was visited and recorded by Alan Jabbour in the mid–1960s, sparking an extensive recording career on the County, Mountain and Heritage labels. Many aspiring fiddlers made the pilgrimage to Mount Airy to learn from Jarrell in the 1970s.

The folk music revival also led to the "discovery" of the Central Blue Ridge's most acclaimed and decorated musician, Arthel (Doc) Watson of Deep Gap, N.C. Ralph Rinzler and Eugene Earle, while in the area to record Clarence Ashley, were struck by the flatpicking of Watson. Thus began an extensive recording career (for Folkways, Vanguard and Sugar Hill, among other labels), five Grammy Awards and countless other accolades on the local, state and national levels.

Another folk singer from the mountains of Watauga County, Frank Proffitt, recorded over 120 songs for folklorists Anne and Frank Warner, including "Tom Dooley," the unofficial ballad of the Central Blue Ridge. Featured on Folkways and Folk-Legacy Records, Proffitt was also a noted luthier. Another acclaimed craftsman of musical instruments, fiddler Albert Hash, taught the tricks of the trade to Wayne Henderson in the 1960s; for eight years the two played together in the Virginia-Carolina Boys. In the 1970s Hash's Whitetop Mountain Band was featured on Mountain and Heritage albums.

On the bluegrass front in the 1960s, the Mount Airy–based Easter Brothers (formerly the Green Valley Quartet) recorded some standout bluegrass gospel albums on King, Commandment and County. In the 1970s and 1980s their success continued on the Old Homestead, Rebel, Life Line and Morningstar labels. The Virginia Mountain Boys, led by fiddler Glen Neaves, recorded four albums for Folkways, performed on a popular radio program out of WBOB Galax and make good showings at local fiddlers' contests.

The 1970s brought continued success to several Central Blue Ridge bands. Organized by Paul Sutphin in 1971, the Smokey Valley Boys went on to win top band honors seven times at Union Grove. Not surprisingly, three members of the band—fiddler Benton Flippen, guitarist Sutphin and mandolinist Verlen Clifton—would eventually win North Carolina Folk Heritage Awards. Another band that dominated fiddlers' conventions around this time, L.W. Lambert and the Blue River Boys, played in 1980 at New York's Lincoln Center.

Organized in 1971 by fiddler and luthier Whit Sizemore, the Shady Mountain Ramblers made multiple recordings, toured extensively and won numerous fiddlers' contests. Another Galax-based band, the Highlanders, led by Willard Gayheart, Jimmy Zeh and Bobby Patterson, put out multiple albums on the Princess and Heritage labels. Jimmy Arnold of Fries, Virginia, had four released on Rebel between 1974 and 1983.

Ashe County native Bob Paisley and the Southern Grass, formed in 1979, cut numerous albums and traveled internationally, touring Europe four times and playing in Japan in 1986. Wilkes County's David Johnson, in 1985, performed on his fourth Folkways release, this time with his father Billie Ray and grandfather Bill. This third generation multi-instrumentalist formed Dixie Dawn, a well known regional band, in 1981, and was a popular Nashville session player in the 1990s.

The Konnarock Critters, an old-time string band, was formed in 1986 by siblings Brian and Debbie Grim. The Critters made their major label debut in 1997 on Marimac.

In a preview of accolades bestowed upon Round Peak old-time musicians, Ernest East won the Brown-Hudson Folklore Award, given by the North Carolina Folklore Society, in 1988. In 1990 East (and Benton Flippen) were further recognized with a North Carolina Folk Heritage Award.

The critical and commercial success of traditional music originating in the Central Blue Ridge continued in the 1990s. Mount Airy native Ronnie Bowman joined the Lonesome River Band in 1990; five LRB and two solo releases followed, topping the bluegrass charts and winning multiple industry awards for Bowman and the band.

Challenging Bowman and the Lonesome River Band at the top of the charts were James King and his band, who were named the IBMA's "Emerging Artists of the Year" in 1997; the following year saw their third release on the Rounder label. King, of Cana, Virginia, is also a member of the supergroup Longview, winner of multiple IMBA awards in 1998.

Ric-O-Chet (later called Last Run) released two chart-climbing albums on Rebel in the mid–1990s. Another critically acclaimed group, Big Country Bluegrass, signed a long-term deal to record for the Hay Holler label. Another Hay Holler artist, Wayne Henderson, received a National Heritage Fellowship Award from the National Endowment for the Arts in 1995.

On the old-time front in the 1990s, the Iron Mountain String Band, featuring banjoist Enoch Rutherford, released one of the best folk recordings of 1992, according to a list picked by the Library of Congress. The New Ballard's Branch Bogtrotters won an unprecedented four straight first prizes in the old-time band competition (1993–1996) at the Galax Old Fiddlers' Convention.

As noted by many experts and documented for prosperity in recorded song, the Central Blue Ridge has enjoyed an unusually rich musical heritage which continues to evolve, grow and prosper into the 21st century. Unrivaled in tradition, unequaled in acclaim and unprecedented in influence, this area can claim to have contributed as much to the musical landscape of Americana as any other region in the United States, if not more.

The Musicians

Jimmy Arnold

Acclaimed bluegrass fiddler-banjoist-guitarist Jimmy Arnold was born on June 11, 1952, in Fries, Virginia. After hearing his friends practicing music next door, Arnold first learned to play the guitar, but soon picked up on the banjo. At the age of 12 he founded a bluegrass band called the Twin County Partners. Other members of the group were his cousin Tommy Arnold on mandolin and friend Wes Golding on guitar.

The Twin County Partners grew quite popular in Carroll County, leading to appearances on local television shows and the recording of a single on Stark Records. Upon their disbandment in 1965, Arnold began performing at music festivals all over the South.

After graduating from high school, Arnold accepted an invitation by studio musician Joe Greene to play in Nashville. After that stint he again teamed up with Wes Golding to form the Virginia Cut-Ups, whose other members were Wayne Golding and Joe Edd King. The Cut-Ups cut an album for Latco Records in 1971.

Arnold worked with many bands over the next few years (including Keith Whitley and the New Tradition), but did not stay long with many because of a drinking problem. Between 1974 and 1983 Arnold released four albums on the Rebel label, but none was a commercial success, and he left the music scene in 1984.

Arnold opened a tattoo parlor in North Carolina, but soon started abusing drugs and using the parlor as a front for narcotics distribution. In 1985 he was arrested on drug charges and served a brief jail sentence. Upon his release from prison he was the artist in residence at Martin Community College, which soon led to his performing in public again. In 1992 Arnold became a member of a Pentecostal church and went completely sober. However, his body was irreparably damaged from drugs, and he died of heart failure on December 26, 1992.

Discography

Strictly Arnold (Rebel 1538; released 1974)
Guitar (Rebel 1565; released 1977)
Rainbow Ride (Rebel 1603; released ca. 1980)
Southern Soul (Rebel 1621; released 1983; produced and mixed by Jimmy Arnold and
  Peter Bonta; engineered by Bonta; arranged by John Hartford and Charlie Moore;
  also features Mike Auldridge on Dobro, Roy Self on bass, Tim Callahan on
  rhythm guitar and Jeff Scheneman on drums)

Clarence (Tom) Ashley

Clarence Earl McCurry was born September 29, 1895, to Rosie-Belle
(née Ashley) and George McCurry, an accomplished fiddler, in Bristol, Tennessee. Two years later Rosie-Belle, Clarence and the Ashley family moved
back to Ashe County, where her mother Maddy Robeson had married Enoch
Ashley shortly after the Civil War. In 1899 the Ashley family settled in Mountain City, Tennessee, and set up a boarding house. Clarence, whom everyone
called Tommy, later changed his name to Tom McCurry Ashley.

At the age of 8 Ashley learned to play a "peanut banjo" given to him by
his grandfather. Ashley left school at 10 to work odd jobs around Mountain
City. When he was 12 Ashley picked up the guitar and learned to pick it.
About four years later he joined Doc White Cloud's medicine show that was
then camped in Mountain City. It was during his summers on the circuit that
he taught the musical and comedic ropes to lifelong friend Roy Acuff, later
the great country singing star of the 1940s. Ashley would not give up the medicine show circuit for good until 1943.

In 1914 Ashley married Hettie Osborne, a native of Ashe County. They
settled in Shouns, Tennessee, just outside of Mountain City, and Ashley made
a living by "busking"—singing in the streets, near carnivals, and outside of
mines on pay day. Ashley sometimes traveled with musician neighbors such
as fiddler Gilliam Banmon Grayson and mandoliner Ted Bare. The trio met
frequent collaborator Hobart Smith at a week-long carnival in Saltville, Virginia, around 1918.

Ashley then sang and picked the guitar with two different pairs of mandolin and fiddle playing sisters: the Cook Sisters from Boone, North Carolina, and the Greer Sisters. He later formed a band called the West Virginia
Hotfoots with Dwight and Dewey Ball from Wilkes County. Ashley played
guitar on several 1931 recordings with the Blue Ridge Mountain Entertainers (joining fiddler Clarence Greene, harmonica player Gwen Foster, auto-
harp-harmonica player Will Abernathy and lead guitarist Walter Davis).

In 1931 Ashley also played with the Haywood County Ramblers, a Victor

Clarence Ashley (left) performing with Doc Watson at a Friends of Old Time Music event in the early 1960s (photo by Dan Seeger/Southern Historical Collection, Wilson Library, The University of North Carolina at Chapel Hill).

recording group. It was during a recording session with Byrd Moore and His Hot Shots that Ashley was invited to perform a few of his "lassy-makin'" tunes (those learned at molasses-making time back home). The A&R man was so impressed with Ashley's rendition of "The Coo Coo Bird"—during which Ashley used his odd "sawmill" banjo tuning—that he arranged for Ashley to record more solo records in New York City.

In 1925 Ashley met Dock Walsh at a fiddlers' contest in Boone, and soon after the Carolina Tar Heels were formed (*see also* the Carolina Tar Heels entry). Ashley left the band in 1929 but in 1933 recorded some fine white blues duets with Gwen Foster for Vocalion. Poor record sales, though, led to hard times in the mid to late 1930s and an end to touring. During the early 1940s he had occasion to work with Charlie Monroe (during which time he met Lester Flatt and Tex Isley) and the Stanley Brothers.

Ashley had all but given up his singing and banjo picking when he was "rediscovered" by Ralph Rinzler at the Union Grove Old Time Fiddlers' Convention in April 1960. Ashley was recorded at his home in September of that year, and these new sides were issued in two volumes by Folkways as *Old Time Music at Clarence Ashley's*. In March 1961 he gave a concert in New York that was sponsored by the Friends of Old Time Music. Ashley and his group of musical friends then played at the University of Chicago Folk Song Festival in February 1962. In March of that year the group played a three-week engagement at the Ash Grove in Los Angeles, California, with Jean Ritchie. Subsequent shows in 1962 took place at the University of California at Los Angeles, the University of Wisconsin and Carnegie Hall. In 1963 Ashley was featured at the country's largest and best folk festivals: Newport, Chicago, Monterey and Philadelphia. In 1966 he even toured overseas in England.

Ashley lived on his 75 acres of land in Shouns with wife Hettie and his three children until his death on June 2, 1967.

Discography

"The Coo Coo Bird"/"Dark Hollar Blues" (Columbia 15489-D; recorded October 1929)

"Naomi Wise"/"Little Sadie" (Columbia 15522-D; recorded October 1929)

"The House Carpenter"/"Old John Hardy" (Columbia 15654-D; recorded October 1929)

"Haunted Road Blues"/"My Sweet Farm Girl" (Conqueror 7939; under "Tom Ashley"; recorded December 1931)

"The Fiddler's Contest"/"Over at Tom's House" (Conqueror 8103; under "Tom Ashley"; recorded December 1931)

"You're a Little Too Small"/"Four Nights' Experience" (Gennett 6404; under "Thomas C. Ashley"; Champion 15525 under pseudonym of "Oscar Brown"; Challenge 391; recorded January 1928)

"Four Nights' Experiences" (Challenge 405; under pseudonym of "Tom Hutchinson")

Anthology of American Folk Music, Vol. 1: Ballads (Folkways FA 2951; released 1952; reissued on CD as Smithsonian/Folkways SFW 40090 in 1997; edited by Harry Smith; Clarence Ashley performs "The House Carpenter")

Anthology of American Folk Music, Vol. 3: Songs (Folkways FA 2951; released 1952; reissued on CD as Smithsonian/Folkways SFW 40090 in 1997; edited by Harry Smith; Clarence Ashley is featured on "The Coo Coo Bird")

Old Time Music at Clarence Ashley's (Folkways 2355; released 1961; edited and annotated by Ralph and Richard Rinzler; discography by Eugene Earle; includes lyrics and bibliographic references; Ashley contributes nine original compositions: "East Tennessee Blues," "Claude Allen," "Richmond Blues," "The Old Man at the Mill," "The Haunted Woods," "Maggie Walker Blues," "God's Gonna Ease My Troublin' Mind," "The Louisiana Earthquake" and "Honey Babe Blues")

Old Time Music at Clarence Ashley's, Volume Two (Folkways 2359; released 1963; recorded July 1961 in Saltville, Virginia, February 1962 in Chicago, Illinois, and April 1962 in Los Angeles, California, by Eugene Earle, Mike Seeger, Ed Kahn and Ralph Rinzler; edited by Richard and Ralph Rinzler; notes by Ralph Rinzler; discography by Eugene Earle and Ralph Rinzler; includes lyrics and bibliographic references; Ashley is credited with three original songs: "Walking Boss," "My Home's Across the Blue Ridge Mts." and "The Coo-Coo Bird" [arrangement])

Friends of Old Time Music (Folkways 2390; released 1964; live performances from concerts staged in New York by the Friends of Old-Time Music; edited by Peter Siegel and John Cohen; notes by Siegel; recorded by Siegel, Cohen, Ralph Rinzler, Michael Seeger, Jerry Goodwin and Ed Kahn; Ashley plays "Dark Holler Blues" with Doc Watson)

Galax Va. Old Fiddlers' Convention (Folkways FA 2435; released 1964; recorded by Lisa Chiera, Michael Eisenstadt, Alice Schwebke and Brian Sinclair in Galax, Virginia, 1961-63; six-page brochure by Lisa Chiera; Ashley performs "Whoa Mule")

Old Time Music at Newport (Vanguard VRS-9147/VSD-79147; released 1964; recorded at Newport, Rhode Island, in 1963; liner notes by Stacey Williams; Clarence (Tom) Ashley is featured on "Coocoo Bird," "House Carpenter" and "Little Sadie"; Ashley, Clint Howard, Fred Price and Doc Watson perform "Amazing Grace" [with Jean Ritchie] and "The Old Account Was Settled Long Ago")

Old Time Classics: A Collection of Mountain Ballads (County 502; released 1964; edited by David Freeman; consists of commercial 78 rpm recordings made from 1926 to 1930; Clarence Ashley performs "Dark Holler Blues")

Folk Box (Elektra EKL-9001; released 1964; Ashley sings "Coo Coo [Bird]" and "Sally Ann")

Clarence Ashley and Tex Isley Play and Sing American Folk Music (Folkways 2350; released 1966; recorded in Shouns, Tennessee, by Ralph Rinzler ca. 1966; annotations by Jon Pankake; highlights include "The House Carpenter," "Rude and Rambling Man" and "May I Sleep in Your Barn Mister?"; Larry "Tex" Isley, from Spray [now Eden], N.C., accompanies Ashley on guitar and autoharp; Isley recorded with Charlie Monroe in 1946 and 1950)

Folk Go-Go (Verve/Folkways FV 9011; released in 1970s; Ashley performs "Coo Coo [Bird]" and "Free Little Bird")

A Fiddlers' Convention in Mountain City, Tennessee (County 525; released 1972; three-page insert booklet by Joe Wilson; consists of 12 commercial 78 rpm recordings made from 1925 to 1930; Clarence "Tom" Ashley is featured on "Dark Holler Blues" and "Old John Hardy")

White Country Blues, 1928-36: A Lighter Shade of Blue, Vol. 1 (Columbia Legacy CT47920; released 1993; Ashley is featured on "Haunted Road Blues")

Doc Watson and Clarence Ashley: The Original Folkways Recordings: 1960-1962 (Smithsonian/Folkways CD SF-40029/30; 1994 reissue of Folkways 2355 and 2359, with 20 additional unreleased selections)

Old-Time Mountain Ballads (County 3504; released 1996; annotated by Charles Wolfe; Clarence Ashley performs "Dark Hollow Blues")

Close to Home (Smithsonian/Folkways SF 40097; released 1997; recorded by Mike Seeger at Tom Ashley's home near Shouns, Tennessee, on April 13, 1961; Ashley performs "Pretty Fair Damsel")

WITH BYRD MOORE AND HIS HOT SHOTS

"Careless Love"/"Three Men Went A-Hunting" (Columbia 15496; recorded October 23, 1929, in Johnson City, Tennessee)

"Frankie Silvers"/"The Hills of Tennessee" (Columbia 15536; recorded October 23, 1929, in Johnson City, Tennessee)

A Collection of Mountain Songs (County 504; released 1965; edited by David Freeman; consists of commercial 78 rpm recordings made from 1927 to 1930; Byrd Moore and His Hot Shots perform "Careless Love")

The String Bands, Vol. 2 (Old Timey 101; released 1965; edited by Chris Strachwitz; liner notes by Strachwitz; consists of 16 commercial 78 rpm recordings made from 1922 to the 1950s; Byrd Moore and His Hot Shots are featured on "Three Men Went A-Hunting")

Ballads and Songs (Old Timey 102; released 1965; edited by Chris Strachwitz; liner notes by Toni Brown; consists of 16 commercial 78 rpm recordings made from 1925 to 1939; Byrd Moore and His Hot Shots perform "Frankie Silvers")

WITH GWEN FOSTER (AS ASHLEY AND FOSTER)

"Times Ain't What They Used to Be" (Vocalion 02554; recorded September 1933)

"Greenback Dollar" (Okeh 02554)

"Bay Rum Blues"/"Sideline Blues" (Vocalion 02611; recorded September 1933)

"The Old Armchair"/"Frankie Silvers" (Vocalion 02647; recorded September 1933)

"Let Him Go, God Bless Him"/"Faded Roses" (Vocalion 02666; recorded September 1933)

"One Dark and Stormy Night"/"Down at the Old Man's House" (Vocalion 02750; [Gwen Foster]; recorded September 1933)

"Baby, All Night Long"/"My Sweet Farm Girl" (Vocalion 02780)

"Ain't No Use to High Hat Me"/"Go 'Way and Let Me Sleep" (Vocalion 02789; recorded September 1933)

"My North Carolina Home"/"Sadie Ray" (Vocalion 02900; recorded September 1933)

Oh My Little Darling: Folk Song Types (New World NW 245; released 1977; edited by Jon Pankake, who provides a six-page insewn brochure; comprises commercial 78s and field recordings made from 1923 to 1939; Tom Clarence Ashley and Gwen Foster perform "Haunted Road Blues")

Tennessee Strings (Rounder 1033; released 1979; edited by Charles Wolfe; liner notes by Charles Wolfe; consists of 16 commercial 78 rpm recordings made in the 1920s and 1930s; Tom Ashley and Gwen Foster are featured on "Times Ain't What They Used to Be")

The Cold-Water Pledge, Vol. 2: Songs of Moonshine and Temperance Recorded in the Golden Age (Marimac 9105 [cassette]; released 1984; edited by Pat Conte; contains brief insert leaflet; booklet by W.K. McNeil sold separately; consists of 19 commercial 78 rpm recordings made from 1925 to 1937; Ashley & Foster perform "Bay Rum Blues")

WITH THE BLUE RIDGE MOUNTAIN ENTERTAINERS

"I Have No Lovin' Mother Now"/"Bring Me a Loaf from the Sea" (Melotone 12425; recorded December 1931)

"Washington and Lee Swing"/"Goodnight Waltz" (Conqueror 7942; recorded December 1931)

WITH WALTER DAVIS
"Crooked Creek Blues"/"Drunk Man Blues" (Melotone 12538; recorded December 1931)

WITH CLARENCE GREENE
"Penitentiary Bound"/"Short Life of Trouble" (Conqueror 8149; recorded December 1931)

AS ASHLEY AND ABERNATHY
Going Down the Valley: Vocal and Instrumental Styles in Folk Music from the South (New World NW 236; released 1977; Ashley and Abernathy perform "Corrinne [Corrina]")

E.C. (Estil) and Orna Ball

Old-time gospel singer and guitarist Estil C. Ball was born on October 1, 1913, in Rugby, Virginia. He began to play guitar at the age of 12, on an instrument given to him by his sister. Growing up, Estil was influenced by the records of the Carter Family, Riley Puckett, Jimmie Rodgers and Merle Travis. His first band was the Rugby Gully Jumpers, named after Paul Warmack's string band whose radio broadcasts on the Grand Ole Opry were quite popular at the time. Estil and his wife, the former Orna Reedy (born 1907), were recorded in 1937 and 1941 by John A. Lomax for the Library of Congress after he met them at the fiddlers' convention in Galax.

Equally adept at finger picking and flat picking, Ball was a consistent winner of guitar and folksinging awards at local fiddlers' conventions, and was a regular performer for local dances, jamborees and radio stations. In the early 1940s he organized a band called the Appalachian Ramblers, who performed on the radio at Marion, Virginia. In addition to his wife, the band consisted of fiddler Roy Russell and mandolin player Blair Reedy, Orna's brother.

E.C. and his wife Orna ran a general store and service station in Grassy Creek (Ashe County, North Carolina), just a few miles from where Estil was born. Orna's first instrument was the banjo, which she used to play in string bands. She was also proficient with the mandolin, guitar and accordion.

In the 1960s and 1970s E.C. & Orna Ball and the Friendly Gospel Singers performed primarily gospel music in public and recorded extensively for the Prestige, Atlantic, County and Rounder labels. The Friendly Gospel Singers included Orna singing alto, Charles Hodges of West Jefferson on tenor, and Charles Harless of West Jefferson on bass. The quartet had a weekly gospel program over WKSK in West Jefferson that lasted for 19 years. In addition, E.C. and Orna had another weekly gospel program out of WHHV in Hillsville, Virginia. They were accompanied on occasion by Blair Reedy on mandolin and Gary Reedy (Blair's son) on guitar.

E.C. and Orna Ball traveled all over the country playing music at festivals and gatherings, and over the years held down a regular radio program on WKSK in West Jefferson, N.C. (Blue Ridge Heritage Archive).

Estil Ball's Merle Travis–influenced style of guitar picking—richly evident in such instrumentals as "Sugarfoot Blues" and his own "Crazy Fingers"—was unique in traditional gospel singing. E.C. Ball died in July 1978; Orna Ball died January 21, 2000.

Discography

Anglo-American Ballads (Library of Congress AFS L1; released 1943 [78 rpm] and 1956 [LP reissue]; collected and recorded by Alan & Elizabeth Lomax, Herbert Halpert, Charles Seeger, Charles Draves, and John A. & Bess Lomax; recordings made from 1934 to 1941; 21-page booklet by Alan Lomax, with an introduction by Wayne Shirley; Estil C. Ball performs "Pretty Polly," a song he learned from a commercial Victor recording of 1925)

Anglo-American Shanties, Lyric Songs, Dance Tunes and Spirituals (Library of Congress AFS L2; released 1943 [78 rpm] and 1956 [LP reissue]; collected and recorded by Alan Lomax [with Elizabeth Lomax or Pete Seeger], Charles Todd, Robert Sonkin and Herbert Halpert; recordings made 1937–1941; 13-page booklet by Alan Lomax [introduction by Wayne Shirley]; E.C. Ball plays "Jennie Jenkins")

Play and Dance Songs and Tunes (Library of Congress AAFS L9; released 1943 [78 rpm] and 1959 [LP reissue]; edited by B.A. Botkin; recordings made from 1936 to 1942; eight-page insert by B.A. Botkin; Estil C. Ball backs up Blair C. Reedy on syncopated guitar on "Bile Dem Cabbage Down")

Sounds of the South (Atlantic SD-1346; released 1960; rereleased 1993 as 7-82496-2; recorded by Alan Lomax with Shirley Collins in 1959; four-page booklet by Lomax; E.C. Ball performs "Farmer's Curst Wife" on SD-1346; on 7-82496-2 he is featured on "Cabin on the Hill," "Devil and the Farmer's Wife," "Father, Adieu," "Father, Jesus Loves You," "Lonesome Valley," "Please Let Me Stay a Little Longer," "Tribulations," "Wayfaring Stranger" and "When I Get Home [I'm Gonna Be Satisfied]")

Blue Ridge Mountain Music (Atlantic SD-1347; released 1960; recorded by Alan Lomax with Shirley Collins in 1959; four-page booklet by Lomax; E.C. and Orna Ball contribute "Jennie Jenkins")

White Spirituals (Atlantic SD-1349; released 1960; recorded and edited by Alan Lomax in 1959; four-page booklet by Lomax; Estil C. Ball performs "Father Adieu," "Father, Jesus Loves You," "Please Let Me Stay a Little Longer," "The Poor Wayfaring Stranger" and "Tribulations"; Estil C. Ball and Blair Reedy play "When I Get Home"; Estil and Orna Ball, Lacey Richardson and Blair Reedy are credited on "The Cabin on the Hill" and "Lonesome Valley")

American Folk Songs for Children (Atlantic SD-1350; released 1960; recorded and edited by Alan Lomax in 1959; four-page booklet by Lomax; E.C. Ball performs "Paper of Pins")

Ballads and Breakdowns from the Southern Mountains: Southern Journey 3 (Prestige International INT 25003; released 1961 [reissued as Rounder 1702 *Southern Journey, Vol. 2: Ballads and Breakdowns*, 1997]; collected and recorded by Alan Lomax with Shirley Collins and Anne Lomax in 1959 and 1960; produced by Kenneth S. Goldstein; annotated by Alan Lomax; E.C. Ball is credited for "Poor Ellen Smith")

Bad Man Ballads: Southern Journey 9 (Prestige International INT 25009; released 1961 [reissued as Rounder 1705 *Southern Journey, Vol. 5: Bad Man Ballads—Songs of Outlaws and Desperadoes* in 1997]; collected and recorded by Alan Lomax with Shirley Collins and Anne Lomax in 1959 and 1960; produced by Kenneth S. Goldstein; 11-page booklet by Alan Lomax; Estil C. Ball performs "Pretty Polly")

E.C. Ball and the Friendly Gospel Singers (County 711; released 1967; recorded and produced by Charlie Faurot; jacket notes by Charles Faurot)

E.C. Ball (Rounder 0026; released 1973; recorded in Grassy Creek, N.C., by R.N. Drevo and Bruce Kaplan; edited by Mark Wilson; jacket notes by Bruce Kaplan; with Orna Ball and the Friendly Gospel Singers)

High Atmosphere (Rounder 0028; released 1974; collected and recorded by John Cohen in Virginia and North Carolina in 1965; produced by Mark Wilson and John Cohen; nine-page booklet by Cohen and Wilson; Estil C. Ball performs "Warfare" and, with Wade Reedy, "Old Jimmy Sutton")

Fathers Have a Home Sweet Home (Rounder 0072; released 1976; recorded in Rugby, Virginia, in 1976 by Mark Wilson; brief liner notes by "Rounder Collective"; with Orna Ball, Blair Reedy and Elsie Reedy)

Old Mother Hippletoe: Rural and Urban Children's Songs (New World NW 291; released 1978; edited by Kate Rinzler and Bess Lomax Hawes; eight-page sewn-in notes by Kate Rinzler; Estil C. Ball performs "Bobby Halsey")

Traditional Music on Rounder: A Sampler (Rounder SS-0145; released 1981; collected and recorded by Jim Carr, et al.; produced by Mark Wilson; liner notes by Mark Wilson; E.C. and Orna Ball are featured on "No Tears in Heaven")

Rounder Old-Time Music (Rounder 11510; released 1988; E.C. and Orna Ball perform "Father Have a Home Sweet Home")

E.C. Ball with Orna Ball & the Friendly Gospel Singers (Rounder 11577; released 1996 [reissue of Rounder 0026]; recorded at Grassy Creek, N.C., by R.N. Drevo and Bruce Kaplan; includes as a bonus seven songs from a WKSK (West Jefferson, N.C.) radio show from May 6 and 12, 1972, provided by E.C. Ball; "Black Mountain Rag" recorded January 16, 1975, by Bob Marsh at WKSK; edited by Mark Wilson; notes by Bruce Kaplan and Mark Wilson)

The Land of Yahoe: Children's Entertainments from the Days Before Television (Rounder 8041; released 1996; produced and annotated by Mark Wilson; E.C. Ball performs "Bile 'Em Cabbage Down" and "Fox"; E.C. and Orna Ball play "Little Moses")

E.C. Ball and Orna: Through the Years—1937–1975 (Copper Creek CCCD-0141; released 1997; introduction by John Lomax; liner notes by Kip Lornell; consists of 24 songs, some of which were taken from Starday and County releases of the 1950s and 1960s, and live recordings made by Kip Lornell and Joe Wilson from WAMU in Washington in 1975)

Southern Journey, Vol. 1: Voices from the American South—Blues, Ballads, Hymns, Reels, Shouts, Chanteys and Work Songs (Rounder 1701; released 1997; recorded and produced by Alan Lomax with Shirley Collins; Estil C. Ball performs "Pretty Polly")

Southern Journey, Vol. 6: Sheep, Sheep, Don'tcha Know the Road?—Southern Music, Sacred and Sinful (Rounder 1706; released 1997; recorded and produced by Alan Lomax with Shirley Collins; E.C. Ball, with Lacey Richardson, performs "Tribulations")

A Treasury of Library of Congress Field Recordings (Rounder 1500; released 1997; selected, annotated and produced by Stephen Wade)

Close to Home (Smithsonian/Folkways SF 40097; released 1997; recorded by Mike Seeger at Estil and Orna Ball's home near Rugby, Virginia, in August 1957; the Blue Ridge Buddies [also includes Blair Reedy] perform "Three Nights Drunk" and "Jimmie Sutton")

H.M. Barnes' Blue Ridge Ramblers

This string band toured the East Coast vaudeville circuit during the late 1920s and early 1930s. H.M. "Hank" Barnes led the group and handled their bookings through the Loew's chain of theaters, but was not himself a musician.

The Ramblers' lineup in the late 1920s included three fiddlers: Frank E. (Dad) Williams, Fred Roe and Jim Smith. Jack Reedy, who frequently played with the Hill Billies and Ashe Countian Frank Blevins, was the band's banjoist. Other members included Frank Wilson and Russell Jones on steel guitar, Harry Brown on mandolin, Henry Roe on guitar and Lonnie Austin on piano. The early 1930s saw new band members, including sisters Jennie and Pauline Bowman, banjoist Bob Culp, comedian Kyle Roop, clogdancers the De Forrest Sisters, and a 16-year-old "boy wonder" called Spark Plug.

The Blue Ridge Ramblers regularly appeared at theaters and hotels in

The members of H.M. Barnes' Blue Ridge Ramblers (personnel unknown) all pose with banjos in the late 1920s (Clarence H. Greene/Blue Ridge Heritage Archive).

North Carolina, West Virginia, Virginia, Maryland, and New England. They once played for an entire week in New York City, where they recorded for Brunswick on January 28 and 29, 1929.

Discography

"Golden Slippers"/"Old Joe Clark" (Brunswick 313; recorded January 28, 1929, in New York City)

"Repasz Band March"/"Our Director March" (Brunswick 361; Melotone 18022; recorded January 28, 1929, in New York City)

"Lineman's Serenade"/"Goin' Down the Road Feelin' Bad" (Brunswick 327; recorded January 28, 1929, in New York City)

"Who Broke the Lock on the Hen-House Door?"/"She'll Be Comin' Round the Mountain When She Comes" (Brunswick 310; Brunswick 1027; Supertone 2052/2093; recorded January 28, 1929, in New York City)

"Blue Ridge Ramblers' Rag"/"Flop Eared Mule" (Brunswick 346; Supertone 2093; recorded January 28, 1929, in New York City)

"Honolulu Stomp"/"Three O'Clock in the Morning" (Brunswick 463; recorded January 29, 1929, in New York City)

"Echoes of Shenandoah Valley"/"Mandolin Rag" (Brunswick 397; recorded January 29, 1929, in New York City)

[Title Unknown] (County 548; H.M. Barnes' Blue Ridge Ramblers perform "Mandolin Rag")

Early Mandolin Classics, Vol. 1 (Rounder 1050; released 1989; H.M. Barnes' Blue Ridge Ramblers perform "Echoes of the Shenandoah Valley")

Big Country Bluegrass

Big Country Bluegrass plays authentic, hard-core, traditional bluegrass music that has become known to many as the "Galax" or "Round Peak" style of 'grass. All of its members live in communities along the Virginia–North Carolina border near Galax.

Tommy and Teresa Sells formed Big Country Bluegrass in the late 1980s. Tommy plays mandolin and handles most of the emcee work. His wife Teresa plays rhythm guitar and sings lead and tenor. Larry Pennington, formerly of the High County Ramblers, handles banjo duties and sings lead, baritone and tenor. Jeff Michael saws on the fiddle and does most of the lead singing.

Members of Hay Holler recording artists Big Country Bluegrass are (left to right) Jeff Michael, Tommy Sells, Teresa Sells, Alan Mastin and Larry Pennington (courtesy Dale Morris).

Michael can also play the mandolin, guitar and clawhammer banjo. Alan Mastin mans the acoustic bass.

After self-producing four recordings, Big Country Bluegrass signed a long-term recording contract with Hay Holler Records of Blacksburg, Virginia, on February 1, 1997. In addition to three Hay Holler recordings under their belt, the group plays at numerous fiddlers' conventions, capturing their share of individual and band honors, as well as performing at major festivals up and down the East Coast. In June 1999 Big Country Bluegrass won a nationwide talent search sponsored by Martha White, earning the right to play at the world-famous Grand Ole Opry in Nashville, Tennessee.

Discography

60th Annual [Galax] Old Fiddlers' Convention (Heritage HRC-C-712; released in 1997; Big Country Bluegrass performs "I'm on My Way Back to the Old Home"; Larry Pennington picks "Cumberland Gap")

Big Country Bluegrass (Hay Holler HH-1336; released April 8, 1997)

Up in the High Country (Hay Holler HH-1340; released May 1998)

Life's Highway (Hay Holler HH-1343; released May 1999)

Frank Blevins and His Tar Heel Rattlers

Frank Blevins was born February 25, 1912, in Smyth County, Virginia. At a very early age Frank moved with his family to Lansing in Ashe County, North Carolina. By the age of 9 Frank was fiddling like his father, Avery Blevins. Frank's older brother, Ed, played banjo and guitar, and by 1926 they were regularly making music together at social events around Ashe County.

Between 1926 and 1929 the Blevins Brothers played professionally around northwestern North Carolina, southwestern Virginia and eastern Tennessee. Frank Miller, a neighbor and banjoist, sometimes played with them. Miller first learned to play on a homemade fretless banjo when he was 12. He met his musical mentor, Charlie Poole, while cutting timber near Beckley, West Virginia.

In 1927 Fred's brother-in-law, John Richardson (a sales agent for Gibson instruments and both Victor and Columbia records), wrote a letter to the Columbia Phonograph Company recommending Fred and the Blevins Brothers as potential recording artists. (Richardson wrote a similar letter that led to the same results—a tryout at Columbia—for the Carolina Night Hawks.) A Columbia representative auditioned the three musicians at Phillips Music Store in West Jefferson, North Carolina, and offered them a contract.

Frank Blevins (left) and Ed Blevins in Marion, Va., in 1930 (courtesy Marshall Wyatt).

On November 8, 1927, they arrived in Atlanta, Georgia, to record for the Columbia Record Company. In the midst of a practice session the Columbia stenographer exclaimed, "I ain't never heard such a rattlin' bunch!" which inspired Columbia's artist-and-repertoire man, Frank B. Walker, to choose "Frank Blevins and His Tar Heel Rattlers" to appear on the group's record labels. The band played six songs during their session, including two of Frank's original numbers, "I've Got No Honey Babe Now" and "Old Aunt Betsy." They were paid $450 for this session, a considerable sum for the day.

Their contract called for a second recording session in Atlanta the following April. In the meantime the group made an extensive two-month tour of West Virginia coal camps as Frank Blevins and the Tar Heel Rattlers. In January of 1928 Columbia issued the band's first record, "Old Aunt Betsy" and "Fly Around My Pretty Little Miss."

Fred Miller, banjoist with Frank Blevins' band, in Ashe County, N.C., circa 1930 (courtesy Marshall Wyatt).

In mid–April the Rattlers headed back to Atlanta, accompanied in separate cars by two other Ashe County groups: the North Carolina Ridge Runners and the Carolina Night Hawks. On April 17 the Rattlers recorded four more songs. Eventually three records by Frank Blevins and His Tar Heel Rattlers were issued on Columbia's hillbilly series, using six of the ten songs recorded by the group at their two sessions. Their records did not sell in large numbers but are considered prime examples of traditional Southern music.

When the Depression hit, the Blevins brothers moved to Marion, Virginia, to work at a furniture factory. In Smyth County the brothers played music part-time with such local musicians as Jack Reedy and Corwin Matthews. Billed as the Southern Buccaneers, the quartet played many theaters in West Virginia and participated in the 1933 White Top Folk Festival in Grayson County, which was attended by First Lady Eleanor Roosevelt, who presented Frank Blevins with two blue ribbons.

In the early 1940s Frank Blevins all but gave up the fiddle after, in the span of two years, his brother Ed died of blood poisoning and Jack Reedy died of a heart attack. Frank worked for several furniture companies in Smyth County and West Jefferson, Ashe County, until 1965, when he started managing his own plant in Greenville, Tennessee, with the help of his two sons.

Discography

"Old Aunt Betsy"/"Fly Around My Pretty Little Miss" (Columbia 15210-D; Clarion 5142-C; Velvet Tone 7101-V ["Old…"; rev. by the Blue Ridge Highballers]; Velvet Tone 7103-V ["Fly…"; rev. by the Blue Ridge Highballers]; recorded in Atlanta, Georgia, on November 8, 1927)

"Sally Aim [Ann]"/"I've Got No Honey Babe Now" (Columbia 15765-D; recorded in Atlanta, Georgia, on November 8, 1927; considered to be the most collectable of Blevins' 78 rpm recordings)

"Don't Get Trouble in Your Mind"/"Nine Pound Hammer" (Columbia 15280-D; recorded in Atlanta, Georgia, on April 17, 1928)

Ballads and Breakdowns of the Golden Era (Columbia CS 9660; released 1968; liner notes by Richard Nevins; consists of studio recordings made from 1926 to 1931; Frank Blevins and the Tar Heel Rattlers perform "Fly Around My Pretty Little Miss")

It'll Never Happen Again: Old Time String Bands, Vol. 1 (Marimac 9110 [cassette]; released ca. 1985; edited by Bill Dillof; contains discographical data; consists of 20 commercial 78 rpm recordings made from 1927 to 1937; Frank Blevins and the Tar Heel Rattlers are featured on "I've Got No Honey Babe Now" and "Sally Aim [Ann]")

Goin' Up Town: Old Time String Bands, Vol. 2 (Marimac 9111 [cassette]; released ca. 1985; edited by Bill Dillof; contains discographical information; consists of 20 commercial 78 rpm recordings made from 1924 to 1937; Frank Blevins and His Tar Heel Rattlers perform "Don't Get Trouble in Your Mind" and "Old Aunt Betsy")

Music from the Lost Provinces (Old Hat CD-1001; released 1997; produced, booklet notes and graphic design by Marshall Wyatt; Frank Blevins & His Tar Heel Rattlers perform "Nine Pound Hammer," "Fly Around My Pretty Little Miss," "Don't Get Trouble in Your Mind," "I've Got No Honey Babe Now," "Old Aunt Betsy" and "Sally Ann")

Frank Bode

Frank Bode was born in 1939 in Greensboro, N.C. When Frank was 9 his father, a native of New York City, died, and Frank moved to his mother's hometown, Dobson, the county seat of Surry County, to live with his grandparents. He grew up in Dobson and took up an interest in playing traditional music.

The Toast String Stretchers in Galax, Virginia, in 1995: (bottom row, left to right) Paul Brown, Terri McMurray, Barbara Poole, (top row, left to right) Ginger Bode, Verlen Clifton and Frank Bode (courtesy Larry Clifton).

Just after finishing school, Bode married into a musical family. His wife played the guitar; her mother played the banjo; and her father played the mandolin and other instruments. In the 1980s Bode played guitar and sang in the Smokey Valley Boys, an award-winning old-time string band. He continues to live in Toast, just outside of Mount Airy, and is currently a member of the Toast String Stretchers alongside his wife Ginger.

Discography

Appalachia—The Old Traditions—Vol. 2 (Home-Made Music LP002; released 1983; collected, recorded and edited by Mike Yates in Virginia and North Carolina, 1979-80 and 1983; three-page booklet by Mike Yates; Robert Sykes and the Surry County Boys perform "Black-Eyed Susie" and "Paddy on the Turnpike")

Been Riding with Old Mosby (Folkways FTS 31109; released 1986; recorded in Toast, N.C., in September 1984 by Eric Davidson and Ellen Victoria; annotated by Ellen Victoria and Eric Davidson; Frank Bode (guitar, vocals) with Tommy Jarrell (fiddle) and Paul Brown (banjo); the title of the album comes from a line in "My Home's Across the Blue Ridge Mountains" that refers to General John Singleton Mosby, the "Grey Ghost of the Confederacy," a guerrilla cavalry leader in the Shenandoah Valley)

Robert Sykes and the Surry County Boys (Heritage 057; released in 1986; recorded by Paul Brown and Lew Bode [12 of 14 tracks were recorded during radio sessions at WPAQ in Mount Airy, N.C.]; mastered by Bobby Patterson; jacket notes by Paul Brown; features Frank Bode on guitar and Paul Brown on banjo)

===

The Bogtrotters *see* Fields Ward

===

Ronnie Bowman

Award-winning singer and guitarist Ronnie Bowman was born in Mount Airy, N.C., on July 9, 1961. Ronnie took up guitar as a teenager and sang with his parents and four sisters in a family group called the Bowman Gospel Singers. Bowman's first full-time music gig was when he played for a year with Allen Mills in Lost & Found in the early 1980s. During a party at Mills' house, Tim Austin heard Bowman sing and offered him a spot in the Lonesome River Band in 1990. Bowman first played bass in the band, which was formed in 1982 by rhythm guitarist Austin.

Banjoist Sammy Shelor of Meadows of Dan, Virginia, also joined LRB in 1990. Austin, the last remaining original member of the group, left the band in 1995, allowing tenor singer/mandolin player Don Rigsby and guitarist/vocalist Kenny Smith to come aboard that same year and cement LRB's current lineup.

The Lonesome River Band's breakthrough album was 1992's *Carrying the Tradition*, which was number one for six months on the bluegrass charts and won the International Bluegrass Music Association's "Album of the Year" award. The critical acclaim and awards continued with the releases of *Old Country Town* (1994, which supplanted *Carrying the Tradition* at the top of the bluegrass charts), *One Step Forward* (1996) and *Finding the Way* (1998). LRB was named "Vocal Group of the Year" in 1997 and "Band of the Year" in 1998 by the Society for the Preservation of Bluegrass Music in America.

Bowman's best-selling, chart-topping debut 1994 solo album, *Cold Virginia Night*, earned him multiple awards from the SPBGMA and the IBMA, including best album and vocalist of the year. He released a followup solo project, *The Man I'm Tryin' to Be*, in 1998, and in 1998 and 1999 was named the IBMA's "Male Vocalist of the Year." A cut off the album, "Three Rusty Nails," was designated as IBMA "Song of the Year" in 1999.

Discography

Cold Virginia Night (Rebel 1704; released 1994; produced by the Lonesome River Band; engineered by Tim Austin, Ronnie Bowman and Dan Tyminski; guest musicians include Alison Krauss, Del McCoury, Tony Rice, Kim Gardner, Ron McCoury, Rickie Simpkins and Jason Carter)

The Man I'm Trying to Be (Sugar Hill SHCD-3880; released 1998; produced by Ronnie Bowman and Dan Tyminski; engineered by Tim Austin, Gary Paczosa, Dan Tyminski and Bill VornDick; guest musicians include Jerry Douglas, Tony Rice, Ricky Skaggs, Sam Bush, J.D. Crowe and Vince Gill)

WITH THE LONESOME RIVER BAND

Carrying the Tradition (Rebel 1690; released 1992; produced, engineered and mixed by the Lonesome River Band; liner notes by Alison Krauss; guest musicians include Krauss, Kim Gardner, Bobby Hicks and Steve Thomas)

Old Country Town (Sugar Hill SHCD-3818; released 1994; arranged, produced, engineered and mixed by the Lonesome River Band; guest musicians include Stuart Duncan, Aubrey Hylton and Rickie Simpkins)

Mounty Airy, N.C., native Ronnie Bowman thumps out a bass line as the Lonesome River Band performs on the Watson Stage at the 1999 MerleFest (photo by the author).

One Step Forward (Koch 3848; released 1996; produced by the Lonesome River Band; engineered by Tim Austin, Sammy Shelor, Brent Truitt and Scott Bolen; mastered by David Glasser)

Saturday Night ... Sunday (Rebel 1660; released 1997)

Finding the Way (Sugar Hill SHCD-3884; released 1998; produced by Jerry Douglas; engineered by Brent Truitt and Ben Surratt; guest musicians include Jerry Douglas [Dobro, Wisenhorn guitar], Jason Carter [fiddle] and Randy Howard [fiddle])

Rafe Brady

An influential old time fiddler, Rafe Brady was born on October 17, 1913, and raised around Mount Airy in Surry County. At age 14 he traveled with a medicine show throughout the South, playing music and acting. Dubbed "The Cherokee Kid" because of his uncanny ability to portray Indians, Brady was influenced by the fiddling of G.B. Grayson, whom he met while with the shows.

Also quite skilled as a guitarist and vocalist, Brady backed up Ernest V. (Pop) Stoneman during a tryout for Bluebird Records. Brady asked for and received an audition as well, which led to him signing a recording contract. However, Brady never returned to the Bluebird studio to record.

An experienced veteran of radio and school house shows, Brady played with the Southern Pioneers, Roy Hall and the Blue Ridge Entertainers, Jay Hugh Hall and the Happy Go Lucky Boys and the Salt and Peanuts Band. In the early 1950s he moved to New Jersey and played occasionally at truck stops and night clubs. Brady moved back to the Blue Ridge in the late 1960s, working and living in Bassett, Virginia, until he retired. In his later years he lived in the Laurel Fork section of Carroll County, Virginia. Rafe Brady died in March 1987.

Discography

Cherokee Rose (Heritage XXXII; released 1981; recorded in Galax, Virginia, in 1980 by Bobby Patterson and Dale Morris; produced by Fred Williams; jacket notes by Dale Morris; also features Ron Mullennex, Tom Mylet, Jimmy Edmonds, Bobby Patterson and Dale Morris)

Otis Burris

Old-time and bluegrass fiddler Otis Burris was born on November 7, 1917, near Elk Creek in western Grayson County, Virginia. His father, James, and his mother, Nonnie May (Roberts), were farmers and musicians. In 1926, when Otis was 8, he attended his first fiddlers' convention at the Independence, Virginia, courthouse.

Burris' fiddling was heavily influenced by that of Fiddlin' Arthur Smith, whom he first heard on the *Grand Ole Opry* in 1932. During World War II Burris served in the Navy and was stationed in the Philippines. He and a guitar player from Mount Airy, N.C., often performed aboard ship for officers and crew. Burris was put in the orchestra for 14 weeks, despite not knowing how to read music.

After his discharge from the Navy, Burris returned to Galax (where his family had moved in 1934) and joined the Blue Ridge Buddies, whose band members included Kelly Lundy, Larry Richardson, Ernest Joines and Ivery Melton. Burris later played with Ernest and Henry Dean, brothers who sang and played the guitar. In 1949 Burris got a job at the Edgewood Arsenal near Bel Air, Maryland. He stayed in the area about three years, playing with musicians such as Porter Church and Bob Goff, and with other transplants from his home area such as the Dean brothers and Sonny Miller.

Burris returned to Galax in 1952 and in 1962 joined the Mountain Ramblers, a famed mountain bluegrass band that in 1959 had been recorded by Alan Lomax for Atlantic Records. Burris played regularly with the Ramblers until 1967, helping the group dominate Galax-area fiddlers' conventions. He continued to play sporadically until bad health forced him to quit fiddling altogether in the early 1980s. Burris was convinced to begin playing again in 1986, though, by former Rambler mandolinist James Lindsey. The group Otis Burris & Fortune, in the late 1980s, also included Eldridge Montgomery, Alice Gerrard and Wendell Cockerham.

Otis Burris died on September 20, 1989, but the Burris family musical tradition has been carried on in the 1990s by James, Joey and Robbie Burris, all nephews or grandchildren of Otis Burris and members of the New River Old Time Boys and, later, the Haywood Ramblers. James captured first place in old time fiddle at the 1995, 1998, and 1999 Galax Old Fiddlers' Conventions, and Joey took top honors in clawhammer banjo at Galax in 1999.

Discography

Otis Burris and Fortune (Heritage 073C; released 1989; features 16 tracks)

WITH THE MOUNTAIN RAMBLERS
Virginia Breakdown (County 705; released 1967; the Mountain Ramblers perform "Fortune," "Red Apple Rag," "Richmond Cotillion" and "Sail Away Ladies" with Otis Burris on fiddle)

Sen. Robert Byrd

Robert C. Byrd, a U.S. senator and old-time musician, was born November 20, 1917, in North Wilkesboro (Wilkes County), North Carolina. His father was a furniture worker, and his mother died in the great flu epidemic of 1918, when Robert was still a baby. Robert was raised by an aunt and uncle in Stotesbury, West Virginia. Robert began to play the fiddle at age 12, and by his teens was playing square dances. After World War II, following work as a butcher and welder, Robert and his wife, Erma Ora (James), bought a grocery store in Sophia, West Virginia.

In 1946 Byrd ran successfully for a seat in the lower house of the West Virginia State Legislature. After a second term, he went to the State Senate for two years. In 1952, "Fiddlin' Bob" was elected to the U.S. Congress, where he served three terms. In 1958 he won a seat in the U.S. Senate and was reelected in 1964, 1970, 1976, 1982, 1988 and 1994. He has been majority and minority floor leader and received national fame for his success in channeling federal tax dollars into the state of West Virginia.

Byrd played for various parties and functions in Washington and made a national television guest appearance on the *Grand Ole Opry*. He recorded several reels of tape for Alan Jabbour and the Library of Congress in July 1975 and December 1977, and made an album of traditional music and songs for County Records in February 1978. In the 1980s, Byrd often twin-fiddled around the nation's capital with well-known bluegrass sideman Joe Meadows. Byrd penned the foreword to Ivan Tribe's 1984 book *Mountaineer Jamboree: Country Music in West Virginia.*

Discography

U.S. Senator Robert Byrd: Mountain Fiddler (County 769; released October 1, 1978; highlights among the 14 tracks include "Cumberland Gap," "Forked Deer," "Don't Let Your Sweet Love Die" and Kris Kristofferson's "Come Sundown"; Byrd is backed by the Country Gentlemen: James Bailey on banjo, Spider Gilliam on bass, and Doyle Lawson on guitar)

The Camp Creek Boys *see* Kyle Creed, Fred Cockerham

Alex Campbell & Ola Belle [Reed]

Alex and Ola Belle Campbell were two of 13 children born to Ella Mae (Osborne) and Arthur Campbell, a school teacher who turned to music and formed his own band with his brother Doc and sister Ellen, called the New River Boys and Girls, in 1910. Ola Wave Campbell (she later changed her name to Ola Belle) was born in Lansing (Ashe County), North Carolina, on August 17, 1916. Her brother Alex was born in 1922. The Campbell family owned a general store on the banks of the New River that also sold record players. As a child Ola Belle learned from her Uncle Dockery Campbell to play clawhammer banjo on a borrowed instrument. She taught Alex to play guitar when he was 10 years old.

TOP ROW
LEFT TO RIGHT
DEACON BRUMFIELD
TED LUNDY
JOHN JACKSON
EARL WALLACE

FRONT ROW
ALEX CAMPBELL
OLA BELLE REED

Alex Campbell and Ola Belle Reed (bottom row) formed the New River Boys and Girls in 1948. Pictured on the top row are (left to right) Deacon Brumfield, Ted Lundy, John Jackson and Earl Wallace (Southern Historical Collection, Wilson Library, The University of North Carolina at Chapel Hill).

In 1934 Arthur Campbell, whose finances were ruined by the Depression, had to uproot his family and move to Chester County, Pennsylvania, and then to Cecil County, Maryland. In 1936 Ola was invited to join the North Carolina Ridge Runners, one of the first hillbilly bands of the Delaware-Maryland area, and whose band members included Ashe County natives Arthur "Shorty" Smith and Lester "Slick" Miller. Ola sang with this band from 1936 to 1948.

Alex served in World War II, in the same unit as Grandpa Jones. After the German surrender Campbell and Jones broadcast live at a 100,000-watt Munich radio station as Grandpa Jones and His Munich Mountaineers. They continued their live show from April to December 1945. Upon returning from the war Alex joined the North Carolina Ridge Runners. In 1948 Ola, Alex and Sonny Miller (Slick Miller's cousin) formed the New River Boys and Girls. In 1949 the Campbells reformed the band to include Deacon Brumfield (Dobro), John Jackson (fiddle), Ted Lundy (five-string bass) and Earl Wallace (string bass). The New River Boys would play throughout the tri-state area through the 1970s.

In 1951 Alex, Ola Belle and her husband Bud Reed (they met in 1945 and were married on February 19, 1949) established the New River Ranch near Rising Sun, Maryland. This music park was the first to bring big-name bluegrass and country stars to the area, and it operated until totally destroyed by a blizzard in 1958.

In 1949, Ola Belle and Alex began what would become a long and influential career in radio broadcasting. Their "Campbell's Corners" program was eventually expanded to three hours and lasted for ten years, until 1960. The Campbells then moved to Oxford, Pennsylvania, and were featured on radio shows on WCOJ (Coatesville, Pennsylvania) and WBMO (Baltimore, Maryland). From 1962 to 1966 they could be heard all up the eastern U.S. seaboard (even into Canada) over WWVA in Wheeling, West Virginia. Alex and Ola Belle operated a very successful Oxford grocery and record store called Campbell's Corner (named after their father's grocery store which was started in Lansing, N.C., in 1918) that specialized in mail order sales of country and gospel music. The store and the radio show ran successfully for 24 years, until 1984.

Alex worked as an independent disc jockey out of his Campbell's Corner store for over 40 years. One of radio's top pitchmen, he bought time and broadcast by remote control from his store. Alex retired in 1984 but in the early 1990s still kept busy on radio WGCB in Red Lion, Pennsylvania, and helped out at Sunset Park.

Ola Belle Reed did radio work for over 40 years. She frequently performed her Appalachian ballads, banjo, bluegrass, country and western, and gospel tunes at festivals with her husband Bud and son David (the trio began performing regularly together in 1969). In July 1972 she was one of the musicians who represented Maryland at the Smithsonian Folk Festival in Washington, D.C. She also recorded 75 songs for the Library of Congress, and was a featured performer at President Jimmy Carter's inaugural ceremonies. Ola Belle Reed played at the 1982 World's Fair in Nashville, Tennessee, and in 1986 she was awarded the prestigious National Heritage Fellowship Award. In 1988 she was given the International Bluegrass Music Association's Award of Merit for making "significant contributions to the field of bluegrass music and its development."

Discography

Sixteen Radio Favorites (Starday SLP 214; released 1963)
Travel On (Starday SLP 342; released 1965)
Ola Belle Reed (Rounder 0021; released 1973; collected and recorded by Gei Zantzinger in Devault, Pennsylvania, in the fall of 1972; executive produced by Gei and Ruth Zantzinger; produced by Ken Irwin, Marian Leighton and Bill Nowlin [the Rounder Collective]; includes liner notes; also features Bud Reed [harmonica, banjo, guitar], David Reed [banjo, guitar], Alan Reed [banjo, guitar] and John

Miller [fiddle]; Ola Belle Reed sings lead vocals and plays the banjo and guitar; "High on a Mountain" has been covered by Del McCoury & the Dixie Pals and Marty Stuart, among others)

1st Annual Brandywine Mountain Music Convention (Heritage 006; released 1975; Ola Belle Reed performs "Ruben" and "Undone in Sorrow")

My Epitaph: A Documentary in Song and Lyric (Folkways FA 2493; released 1976; recorded by King Street Recording Company; produced by Kevin Roth, who provides a seven-page booklet; features David Reed and Bud Reed; also included are lengthy selections from a 1976 interview)

All in One Evening (Folkways FA 2329; released 1977; produced by Kevin Roth; Ola Belle and Bud Reed perform "Bonaparte's Retreat," "Foggy Mountain Top," "Ole Belle's Blues," "Sweet Evalina" and "Tear Down the Fences")

Ola Belle Reed and Family (Rounder 0077; released 1977; produced by Kevin Roth; liner notes and 2-page leaflet by David Whisnant; features Bud Reed and David Reed; seven of fourteen tracks are original compositions by Ola Belle Reed, who plays clawhammer banjo on the recording)

The Old-Time Banjo in America (Kicking Mule KM 204; released 1978; produced and annotated by Art Rosenbaum; Old Belle Reed performs "Boat's Up the River" and "My Honey, Where You Been So Long?")

Traditional Music on Rounder: A Sampler (Rounder SS-0145; released 1981; collected and recorded by Jim Carr, et al.; produced by Mark Wilson; liner notes by Mark Wilson; Ola Belle Reed performs "The Train That Carried My Girl from Town")

Rounder Old-Time Music (Rounder 11510; released 1988; Ola Belle Reed plays on "You Led Me to the Wrong")

Third Annual Farewell Reunion (Rounder 0313; released 1994; Ola Belle Reed performs "Boat's Up the River")

Land of Yahoe: Children's Entertainments from the Days Before Television (Rounder 8041; released 1996; produced and annotated by Mark Wilson; Ola Belle Reed is featured on "Chewing Gum," "Little Birdie" and "The Miller's Will")

Blue Ribbon Banjo (Easydisc 7001; released 1996; compiled by Ken Irwin; Ola Belle Reed performs "Boat's Up the River")

The North Carolina Banjo Collection (Rounder 0439; 2-CD set released 1998; produced by Bob Carlin; Ola Belle Reed performs "Going to Write Me a Letter")

Carolina Night Hawks

The Carolina Night Hawks, an old-time string band comprised of four Ashe Countians, made but one recording for the Columbia Phonograph Company, traveling to Atlanta, Georgia, in April of 1928 to perform "Governor Al Smith for President," an original song promoting Smith's bid for the Democratic nomination.

Donald (Tommy) Thompson, the group's banjoist and the author of the song, was born in Laurel Springs in 1901. He learned to pick the banjo when he was 7 years old, and started to play the violin when he was 10. A graduate of Jefferson High School (he composed the school song for the class of 1922), Thompson was a schoolteacher for many years.

The Carolina Night Hawks, circa 1928: (clockwise from top right) Charles Miller, Lester Miller, Howard Miller and Ted Bare (not pictured: Donald Thompson) (courtesy Marshall Wyatt).

Mandolinist and high tenor Ted Bare grew up near Big Ridge in Ashe County. He studied medicine for two years before deciding to pursue music full-time. Also proficient on the piano, Bare began playing music with Charles and Howard Miller in the mid–1920s.

Charles Miller was born in 1887 along Stagg Creek, near Comet, N.C. His father, Monroe Miller, taught him to fiddle a number of traditional mountain songs. At age 24, Charles married Hattie Barr of Horse Creek. Their son, Howard, born in 1912, began playing the fiddle when he was just a toddler. When Howard's skills exceeded his father's, Charles switched to guitar.

In 1927 the group was formed when Bare recruited Thompson to join the band, which he called the Carolina Night Hawks. They were soon practicing with the Millers. The group soon built up a repertoire of more than 100 fiddle tunes, old-time songs, waltzes and pop songs and performed all over Ashe and Alleghany counties at private homes, schoolhouses, box suppers, square dances, cake walks and corn shuckings.

A local phonograph dealer, John Richardson, wrote the Columbia Phonograph Company and recommended that they record the Night Hawks. A Columbia talent scout traveled to West Jefferson to hear the band, and agreed to send the quartet to Atlanta to make recordings. On April 17, 1928, the Carolina Night Hawks recorded four songs: "Butcher's Boy," "Nobody to Love," "A Stern Old Bachelor" and "Governor Al Smith for President." Each man was paid $100 plus expenses.

Columbia released "Governor Al Smith for President" on June 10, 1928; on the reverse side of the disc was "The Sidewalks of New York" by Al Craver, better known as Vernon Dalhart. Smith did receive the nomination, but lost handily to Republican Herbert Hoover in November.

The Night Hawks' one record failed to attract any national spotlight, but they did continue to play throughout Ashe County, where they remained popular for a few years. Their brief heyday had ended, though, by 1930.

Thompson quit the band and soon entered Appalachian State Teacher's College in Boone. After graduating, he continued his career as a schoolteacher and principal, later earning a master's degree in education from the University of North Carolina at Chapel Hill. In the 1960s he began playing the fiddle again on a regular basis with guitarist Charlie Cox and banjoist Edison Nuckolls. This association lasted eight years, after which he and his wife Ola Triplett retired to Boone, N.C. He died in 1999.

Bare and the Millers continued as a trio and soon toured West Virginia. Bare later served as a cook in the U.S. Army, got into furniture making, briefly toured with Carl Story and His Rambling Mountaineers in the late 1940s, made moonshine whiskey back in Ashe County, and operated his own photography studio in West Jefferson throughout most of the 1950s. He died in Hudson, N.C., of heart failure at age 67.

Donald Thompson in 1991 with the banjo he played at his 1928 recording session with the Carolina Night Hawks (courtesy Marshall Wyatt).

Charles Miller worked as a carpenter and cabinet maker after his music career. He died of heart disease in Blowing Rock, N.C., in 1976. His son, Howard, was profoundly influenced by blind fiddler G.B. Grayson, whom he met in the 1930s. In the 1950s he turned his attention to instrument making and became known for his finely crafted fiddles, mandolins and dulcimers. In the 1980s Howard resumed fiddling, backed by his son, Harold Dean Miller, on guitar. On June 15, 1990, Howard Miller died of cancer at home in West Jefferson.

Discography

"Governor Al Smith for President" (Columbia 15256-D; recorded in Atlanta, Georgia, on April 17, 1928)

The Cold-Water Pledge, Vol. 2: Songs of Moonshine and Temperance Recorded in the Golden Age (Marimac 9105 [cassette]; released 1984; edited by Pat Conte; contains brief insert leaflet; booklet by W.K. McNeil sold separately; consists of 19 commercial 78 rpm recordings made from 1925 to 1937; the Carolina Night Hawks perform "Governor Al Smith for President")

Music from the Lost Provinces (Old Hat CD-1001; released 1997; produced, booklet notes and graphic design by Marshall Wyatt; the Carolina Night Hawks are featured on "Governor Al Smith for President")

The Carolina Tar Heels

A successful and influential 1920s string band, the Carolina Tar Heels made over 40 sides for Victor Records. The group was one of many

The Carolina Tar Heels, in a photo taken sometime around 1930: (left to right) Clarence (Tom) Ashley, Dock Walsh and Gwin Foster (Southern Historical Collection, Wilson Library, The University of North Carolina at Chapel Hill).

"rediscovered" in the 1960s during the folk music revival that swept the country.

Doctor Coble Walsh, often known as "Dock," was born July 23, 1901, in Wilkes County. A banjoist and singer, Walsh had been recorded as a soloist for Columbia in 1925 and 1926. In 1926 he met harmonica and guitar player Gwin (sometimes spelled "Gwen" or "Gwyn") Stanley Foster (born December 25, 1903) around the mills of Gastonia. The pair added a couple of musicians (one of whom was Dave Fletcher of Mount Holly, N.C.) to form a full string band and auditioned for Ralph S. Peer in 1927. Peer, however, signed up only Walsh and Foster and called them the Carolina Tar Heels.

Three Victor recording sessions were made before Walsh and Foster split up in late fall of 1927, due primarily to differing musical tastes and the physical distance between Dallas and Wilkesboro. Walsh replaced Gwin Foster with old friend Garley Foster (no relation), a talented harmonica player and whistler. Born January 10, 1905, in Wilkes County, Garley Foster sometimes billed himself as "the Human Bird."

Banjoist and singer Clarence (Tom) Ashley joined the band in the fall of 1928. Ashley had already recorded on his own and with Byrd Moore, displaying his superb banjo skills and singing ability. But during the 17 songs he recorded as a Carolina Tar Heel Ashley played only the guitar and sang. The Carolina Tar Heels traveled to Atlanta in October 1928 and recorded

Look Who's Coming!

The Original

CAROLINA TAR HEELS

VICTOR AND COLUMBIA RECORDING ARTISTS
— RADIO ARTISTS —

DOC. WALSH
The Banjo King of The Carolinas
WITH
GARLEY FOSTER
The Human Bird

ARTISTS IN THE RENDITION OF POPULAR NUM-
BERS THAT TOUCH THE HEART. MAKE YOU
LAUGH OR PUT A TICKLE IN YOUR FEET

GARLEY FOSTER

DOC WALSH

HONEST-TO-GOODNESS STRING MUSIC OF THE HILLS

You'll Be Pleased

Mr. Foster will really entertain you with
his mockery of many, many birds, including Red Bird, Canary Bird, Mocking Bird,
Wren, Pewee, Owls, Hawks, etc. Also
imitation of a saw mill in operation.
You'll marvel at the unusual talent Foster
will display in this program of music with
his guitar and harmonica. Nothing used
in these imitations except the voice well
trained. An exceptional program. If in
doubt come and hear him!

THE HUMAN BIRD

Southern Songs

Doc. Walsh will entertain you with Hawaiian music on the Banjo. Old time
Southern Songs mingled with the latest
Broadway Hits will be sung as only Doc.
and Foster can sing them. A program
of music and songs played and sung by
Foster and Doc that will please everyone.
Don't miss this unusual program of high
class entertainment.

It's Your Time For A Good Time!

PLACE

TIME

ADMISSION

Adults:_____ Children:_____

A handbill used to publicize an upcoming performance by the Carolina Tar Heels,
promising "honest-to-goodness string music of the hills" (courtesy Drake Walsh).

A reunion of sorts happened in 1962 when (from left) Garley Foster, Dock Walsh and Drake Walsh recorded a number of old Carolina Tar Heels songs for a Folk-Legacy album (courtesy Drake Walsh).

eight sides for the Victor company. They recorded eight additional numbers for Victor in the spring of 1929, driving north to Camden, New Jersey.

Ashley left the band shortly after the 1929 session. Walsh did another solo session for Victor in late September 1929, and he and Foster later issued a few records under the Pine Mountain Boys name. Walsh enlisted the talents of original member Gwin Foster for his last studio session, in Atlanta in 1932. The duo was forced to bill themselves as "The Original Carolina Tar Heels" because an entirely separate band called the Carolina Tarheels were performing at the time over WSB radio in Atlanta.

In 1962 researchers Gene Earle and Archie Green discovered Walsh and Garley Foster and recorded them (along with Dock's son, Drake, who had learned much of the Tar Heels' repertoire) for release on a Folk Legacy album (FSA-24). This recording features remakes of some of the Tar Heels' old 78s and a few original compositions. Gwin Foster died in Dallas, N.C., on November 25, 1954; Dock Walsh died on May 28, 1967; Clarence Ashley passed on June 2, 1967; and Garley Foster died on October 5, 1968.

Discography

"There Ain't No Use Workin' So Hard"/"I'm Going to Georgia" (Victor 20544; recorded in Atlanta, Georgia, on February 19, 1927)

"Bring Me a Leaf from the Sea"/"Her Name Was Hula Lou" (Victor 20545; recorded in Atlanta, Georgia, on February 19, 1927)

"When the Good Lord Sets You Free"/"I Love My Mountain Home" (Victor 20931; recorded in Charlotte, North Carolina, on August 15, 1927)

"Shanghai in China"/"The Bulldog Down in Sunny Tennessee" (Victor 20941; recorded in Charlotte, North Carolina, on August 11, 1927)

"My Mama Scolds Me for Flirting"/"Goodbye, My Bonnie, Goodbye" (Victor 21193; recorded in Charlotte, North Carolina, on August 11 and 15, 1927)

"Farm Girl Blues"/"Washing Mama's Dishes" (Victor 23516; recorded in Memphis, Tennessee, on November 19, 1930)

"The Hen House Door Is Always Locked"/"Your Low-Down Dirty Ways" (Victor 23546; recorded in Memphis, Tennessee, on November 19, 1930)

"Got the Farm Land Blues"/"Back to Mexico" (Victor 23611; recorded in Memphis, Tennessee, on November 19, 1930)

"Nobody Cares If I'm Blue"/"Why Should I Care" (Victor 23671; recorded in Atlanta, Georgia, on February 25, 1932)

"She Shook It on the Corner"/"Times Ain't Like They Used to Be" (Victor 23682; recorded in Atlanta, Georgia, on February 25, 1932)

"You're a Little Too Small"/"Peg and Awl" (Victor 40007; recorded in Atlanta, Georgia, on October 11, 1928)

"Lay Down Baby, Take Your Rest"/"Roll On, Boys" (Victor 40024; recorded in Atlanta, Georgia, on October 11, 1928)

"There's a Man Goin' Around Takin' Names"/"I Don't Like the Blues No-How" (Victor 40053; recorded in Atlanta, Georgia, on October 11, 1928)

"Rude and Rambling Man"/"Oh, How I Hate It" (Victor 40077; recorded in Camden, New Jersey, on April 3, 1929)

"Who's Gonna Kiss Your Lips, Dear Darling?"/"My Home's Across the Blue Ridge Mountains" (Victor 40100; recorded in Camden, New Jersey, on April 3, 1929)

"Somebody's Tall and Handsome"/"The Train's Done Left Me" (Victor 40128; recorded in Camden, New Jersey, on April 3 and 4, 1929)

"Hand in Hand We Have Walked Along Together"/"The Old Gray Goose" (Victor 40177; recorded in Camden, New Jersey, on April 3 and 4, 1929)

"Can't You Remember When Your Heart Was Mine?"/"I'll Be Washed" (Victor 40219; recorded in Atlanta, Georgia, on October 11, 1928)

Anthology of American Folk Music, Vol. 1: Ballads (Folkways FA 2951; released 1952; reissued on CD as Smithsonian/Folkways SFW 40090 in 1997; edited by Harry Smith; the Carolina Tar Heels are featured on "Got the Farm Land Blues" and "Peg and Awl")

Old Time Music at Clarence Ashley's, Volume Two (Folkways 2359; released 1963; recorded July 1961 in Saltville, Virginia, February 1962 in Chicago, Illinois, and April 1962 in Los Angeles, California, by Eugene Earle, Mike Seeger, Ed Kahn and Ralph Rinzler; edited by Richard and Ralph Rinzler; notes by Ralph Rinzler; discography by Eugene Earle and Ralph Rinzler; includes lyrics and bibliographic references; Ashley, Garley Foster and Dock Walsh combine their talents (along with Doc Watson) on the track "My Home's Across the Blue Ridge Mts." [written by Ashley])

The Carolina Tar Heels (Folk-Legacy FSA-24; released 1965; recorded by Archie Green and Eugene Earle in Taylorsville, N.C., in 1961-62; 33-page booklet by Green and Earle; the 17 songs feature Dock Walsh, Drake Walsh and Garley Foster)

A Collection of Mountain Songs (County 504; released 1965; edited by David Freedman; consists of commercial 78 rpm recordings made from 1927 to 1930; the Carolina Tar Heels perform "Your Low Down Dirty Ways")

The String Bands, Vol. 2 (Old Timey 101; released 1965; edited by Chris Strachwitz; liner notes by Strachwitz; consists of 16 commercial 78 rpm recordings made from 1922 to the 1950s; the Carolina Tar Heels perform "Lay Down Baby, Take Your Rest")

Southern Dance Music, Vol. 2 (Old-Timey LP 101; released 1965; the Carolina Tar Heels perform "Lay Down Baby, Take Your Rest")

The Railroad in Folksong (RCA Victor LPV 532; released 1966; edited by Archie Green; liner notes by Archie Green; consists of 16 studio recordings made from 1926 to 1940; the Carolina Tar Heels are featured on "The Train's Done Left Me")

Mountain Blues (County 511; released ca. 1966; edited by David Freeman; consists of 12 commercial 78 rpm recordings made in the 1920s and 1930s; the Carolina Tar Heels are featured on "Farm Girl Blues")

Early Rural String Bands (RCA Victor LPV 552; released 1968; edited by Norm Cohen; liner notes by Norm Cohen; consists of 14 studio recordings made from 1922 to 1949; the Carolina Tar Heels perform "Bring Me a Leaf from the Sea")

The Carolina Tar Heels (GHP [West Germany] LP 1001; released 1969; reissued as Old Homestead OH 113 in 1978; edited by Gerd Hadeler; consists of 14 commercial 78s recorded from 1927 to 1931; liner notes by Norm Cohen; the first Tar Heels reissue, on the now long-defunct German label GHP)

Can't You Remember the Carolina Tar Heels? (Bear Family [West Germany] BF 15507; released 1975; edited by Richard Weize; comprised of 16 commercial 78s recorded from 1927 to 1931; annotated brochure by Richard Weize)

Folk Music in America, Vol. 2: Songs of Love, Courtship... (Library of Congress LBC-02; released 1978; the Carolina Tar Heels perform "You Are a Little Too Small")

Folk Music in America, Vol. 13: Songs of Childhood... (Library of Congress LBC-13; released 1978; the Carolina Tar Heels contribute "Go Tell Aunt Rhody")

The Church Brothers

The Church Brothers and Their Blue Ridge Ramblers was an early, regional bluegrass band from North Wilkesboro, N.C. Influenced by Flatt & Scruggs and Bill Monroe's ubiquitous band of the mid–1940s, the Church Brothers were extremely popular locally and were among the most recorded of the parochial groups, being associated with Blue Ridge Records and Rich-R-Tone Records.

The Church brothers—Bill, Edwin and Ralph—grew up in the Mount Pleasant community near Ferguson, N.C. Their father, Albert (whose wife was Bessie), played both fiddle and banjo. William Cears (Bill), born September 8, 1922, and the oldest of ten children, was the first to take up an instrument: the guitar. Edwin Ralph was born July 29, 1925, and Arthur Ralph was born on June 28, 1928.

Bill and a friend/coworker, mandolinist Otis Hamby, began performing early as a duet, appearing on the "Farm and Fun Time" radio show in Asheville. They shared the bill with the Morris Brothers (Wiley and Zeke) and with Carl Story. Later, at a Mount Airy fairgrounds talent show in 1939, Roy Hall saw the boys play and hired them on the spot for $50 a week apiece to join his popular group, the Blue Ridge Entertainers.

During summer recess, Bill and Otis went to Roanoke, Virginia, and played on the radio every day from 6:30 to 7:00 A.M. and noon until 1 P.M. In the afternoons they packed their instruments and headed out for a show date somewhere in the area.

Two years later, in 1941, Bill Church found himself in the U.S. Army. At this time his younger brothers, Edwin and Ralph, were playing music with another local boy, Drake Walsh (son of old-time banjoist Dock Walsh, the founding member of the Carolina Tar Heels). Edwin soon followed his older brother into the armed services. Upon Bill's and Edwin's discharges from the

An early (late 1940s) version of the Church Brothers and the Blue Ridge Ramblers included (clockwise from top left) Elmer Bowers, Drake Walsh, Ward Eller, Gar Bowers, Bill Church and Ralph Church (courtesy Ward Eller).

army around 1946, they formed their own group, with Bill on guitar, Edwin on fiddle, Ralph on mandolin, their first cousin Ward Eller (born May 24, 1930) on guitar, and Drake Walsh on banjo—the nucleus of the first Church Brothers band. They called themselves the Wilkes County Entertainers and had a Saturday morning show on local radio station WILX out of North Wilkesboro. The arrival of banjoist James Garfield (Gar) Bowers (who later played and recorded with Bill Monroe) allowed Walsh to switch to fiddle, and James' youngest brother Elmer also joined the group as its bass fiddler.

In 1948 the band switched over to station WKBC in North Wilkesboro, which would be their radio home for the remainder of their career. At this time the group also adopted the name of the Church Brothers and Their Blue Ridge Ramblers.

While Bill was away in the service, his brothers met Drusilla Adams (born September 9, 1934), a songwriter who was looking for a band to record her songs. Adams would write much of the Church Brothers' material and make business contacts for the group, booking them into new places outside Wilkes County. Adams was the person who made sure that everything was set up properly and running smoothly. For a while they were a regular feature at local schoolhouses in Blowing Rock and Boone, Watauga County, on Friday nights, appearing on radio once or twice each Saturday.

In 1950 the Church Brothers signed a five-year contract with Jim Stanton to have the band's first record released on Rich-R-Tone Records of Johnson City, Tennessee. Later in the year the group held their first recording session, cutting eight sides with Johnny McKinley Nelson on banjo and John Ralph Pennington on bass. Nelson was born June 21, 1931, in Caldwell County, N.C., and was introduced to the Church Brothers by Ward Eller, whom he worked with at the Caldwell Furniture Company in Valmead. Pennington was born March 2, 1923, in Alleghany County, but moved to Wilkes County as a child.

The first Church Brothers release was "A Sweeter Love Than Yours I'll Never Know"/"I'm Lonely for You" on RRT 1009. A second record followed, and a third after a followup recording session on October 27, 1951. Delays in releasing the other records, though, prompted Drusilla's father, Noah Adams (1896–1958), to sign on as the band's business manager and form a new label, Blue Ridge Records. Drusilla handled promotion and A&R duties.

The Church Brothers backed Jim Eanes on Blue Ridge's first release, "Missing in Action," a Korean War ballad that proved to be a regional country hit. Shortly thereafter, Drusilla Adams traded the Eanes masters to Stanton's Rich-R-Tone in return for the remaining Church Brothers masters, which would be issued on the new Blue Ridge label. The Church Brothers continued, however, to occasionally back up solo artists such as Buffalo Johnson on Rich-R-Tone.

The Church Brothers' first Blue Ridge session was held at WKBC Radio

Flanking songwriter-promoter Drusilla Adams are the early 1950s members of the Church Brothers: (left to right) Johnny Nelson, Ward Eller, Ralph Church, Edwin Church, Bill Church and Ralph Pennington (courtesy Ward Eller).

sometime in 1951. A second session took place in 1952, of which some sides were cut at WPAQ Radio in Mount Airy. Between early 1950 and late 1952, the Church Brothers had a total of eight sides released on Blue Ridge and six on Rich-R-Tone. Three unissued masters later appeared on album releases, with Bill Church writing one song and Johnny Nelson contributing an original instrumental.

Following Johnny Nelson's death in a car accident on January 28, 1953, the band decided to gradually stop performing. Bill Church stayed on at his day job in South Carolina, returning to Wilkes County only for occasional bookings. Soon after, Ward Eller joined the U.S. Army. Over the next couple of years, the Church Brothers became more and more tied to their farms and families, with music taking a back seat to other responsibilities.

Drusilla Adams married in 1958—the same year that her father died—and the Blue Ridge label was soon sold and its catalogue of masters transferred to a group of investors including Bill Clifton and Don Owens, a bluegrass enthusiast and radio personality in Washington, D.C. Owens' efforts to jumpstart the label were short-lived, as he was tragically killed in an automobile accident on April 21, 1963. The company was purchased in the late 1980s by Rounder Records.

The members of the Church Brothers remained active musically into the late 1990s. Ward Eller, a retired school principal, has been a regular Saturday night feature at the North Wilkesboro V.F.W. since 1947. Drake Walsh plays with Southland, an old-time musical duo featuring Floyd Williams, Jr. Walsh and Williams' fathers played together in a string band called the Four Yellowjackets in 1926-27.

Discography

"A Sweeter Love Than Yours I'll Never Know"/"I'm Lonely for You" (Rich-R-Tone 1009; recorded ca. winter 1950 in Johnson City, Tennessee)

"We'll Meet Up There"/"I Know My Name Will Be Called Up There" (Rich-R-Tone 1017; recorded ca. winter 1950 in Johnson City, Tennessee)

"Day Dreaming"/"I Don't Know What to Do" (Rich-R-Tone 1019; recorded on October 27, 1951, in Johnson City, Tennessee)

"Darling Brown Eyes"/"Someone Else Is Loving You" (Blue Ridge 101; recorded ca. winter 1950 in Johnson City, Tennessee, and ca. 1951 in North Wilkesboro, North Carolina)

"Broken Vows and a Broken Heart"/"Way Down in Ole Caroline" (Blue Ridge 209; recorded ca. 1951 and late 1952 in North Wilkesboro, North Carolina; released February 9, 1953)

"No One to Love Me"/"You're Still the Rose of My Heart" (Blue Ridge 609; recorded ca. winter 1950 in Johnson City, Tennessee, and ca. 1951 in North Wilkesboro, North Carolina)

"An Angel with Blue Eyes"/"When Jesus Calls You Home" (Blue Ridge 1208; recorded May 1952 in Mount Airy, North Carolina)

The Church Brothers: The Early Days of Bluegrass, Volume 8 (Rounder 1020; released 1978; mastered by John Nagy (The Mixing Lab), from the tapes and 78s of Pete Kuykendall; jacket notes by Walter V. Saunders (Bluegrass Unlimited) and "The Rounder Folks"; highlights among the 15 tracks include the Flatt & Scruggs standard "Roll in My Sweet Baby's Arms" and the Church Brothers original "You're Still the Rose of My Heart")

Traditional Bluegrass: The Church Brothers and Their Blue Ridge Ramblers (GHP [of Cuxhaven, Germany] 900; released in 1968; produced by Gerd Hadeler; contains 14 Church Brothers masters and two songs with vocals by Buffalo Johnson)

Fred Cockerham

Fred Cockerham, born on November 3, 1905, and a native of the Beulah section of Surry County, was an accomplished old-time fiddler and clawhammer banjoist. He was one of seven children born to Elias and Betty Jane Cockerham. As a youth Fred was influenced by his uncle, Troy Cockerham, who used only two fingers to note with on the fiddle, and Mal Smith, a local banjo player who taught Fred his signature piece, "Roustabout." Although part of a talented musical family, Fred was the only one to pursue a musical career. Providing early musical guidance were the legendary Charlie Lowe (b. February 1878; d. March 1964) and Cockerham's protégé, Tommy Jarrell (who was five years his senior).

Cockerham spent most of his life working as a musician, playing and singing in numerous old-time bands and a wide range of dances, conventions and festivals all over North Carolina and Virginia. Radio also played a significant role in his musical career and development, providing a source of

The lineup of the Camp Creek Boys in 1966 included (bottom row, left to right) Paul Sutphin, Verlen Clifton, G.F. Collins, (top row, left to right) Fred Cockerham, Kyle Creed and Ernest East (courtesy Larry Clifton).

regular employment and exposing him to new styles and genres of music. Cockerham was particularly influenced by the fiddling of Arthur Smith, whom he heard over WSM's *Grand Ole Opry* show and at fiddlers' contests.

When he was a teen Cockerham played with Charlie Lowe and the Round Peak Band. The other band members (who later reunited as the Camp Creek Boys) were Kyle Creed, Paul Sutphin, Lawrence Lowe (Charlie's son) and Ernest East and his two older brothers. Cockerham's first professional band was the Ruby Tonic Entertainers, who performed an hour-long program on WBT Radio in Charlotte and at concerts throughout North Carolina and Virginia. After this group disbanded Cockerham joined Fiddling Slim and the North Carolina Ramblers, a group that broadcast out of High Point, N.C., and played every Saturday night at the Dan River Park Dance Hall.

Cockerham took second place at the 1934 Galax Fiddlers' Convention, and the next year he took first prize. After moving to Galax, Virginia, Cockerham also played with the Royal Hawaiians from about 1937 to 1940. This group was made up of Cockerham, Fields Ward, his brother Sampson (Simp) Ward, and Herbert Higgins, the mandolin player for the Ruby Tonic Entertainers.

In the early 1940s Cockerham had an early morning half-hour radio show over WFMR in High Point. During World War II Cockerham took jobs building Quonset huts for the Navy with Kyle Creed and Paul Sutphin near Norfolk, Virginia. In 1959, after living many years in and around Galax, Fred and Eva moved to Low Gap, N.C., close to the Round Peak community.

After double cataract surgery in 1960 and a period of musical inactivity, Cockerham joined the Camp Creek Boys in 1963. The other members of the band were Kyle Creed, Ernest East, Paul Sutphin, Verlen Clifton and Ronald Collins. As the group's fiddler, Cockerham led the band to a pair of first-place finishes (1971, 1973) at the Old Fiddlers' Convention in Galax, Virginia. After the Camp Creek Boys broke up, Cockerham played with Mac Snow, Gilmer Woodruff, Ambrose Lowe, Clyde Isaacs and "Knuckles" Nestor in the Virginia-Carolina Ramblers.

Fred Cockerham died four months short of his 75th birthday, on July 8, 1980. His wife, the former Eva Galyean, died just over a year later. They left four surviving children, 20 grandchildren and 29 great-grandchildren.

Discography

Clawhammer Banjo (County 701; released 1965; Cockerham performs "John Brown's Dream," "Little Maggie" and "Long Steel Rail," and, with Kyle Creed, "Big Eyed Rabbit, "John Henry" and "Step-Back Cindy")

The Camp Creek Boys (County 709; recorded and released ca. 1967 by Charlie Faurot; liner notes by Dave Freeman; "Fortune," "Cider Mills," "Let Me Fall" and "Fall on My Knees" are old-time instrumentals particularly associated with the Mount Airy–Galax region; rereleased 1997 on County CD 2719 as *Old-Time String Band*, with two bonus tracks)

Down to the Cider Mill (County 713; released 1968; recorded by Charles Faurot and Richard Nevins; produced by Charles Faurot; jacket notes by Richard Nevins; with Oscar Jenkins, Tommy Jarrell and Shag Stanley)

More Clawhammer Banjo Songs & Tunes from the Mountains (County 717; released 1969; collected and recorded by Charles Faurot and Richard Nevins in Virginia and North Carolina; produced by Faurot; liner notes by Faurot; Cockerham is featured on "Roustabout")

George Pegram (Rounder 0001; released 1970; recorded in N.C. in 1967; produced by Ken Irwin and Bill Nowlin; liner notes by Anne Gilbert; Cockerham is the featured fiddler [joining "guest" musicians Clyde Isaacs and Jack Bryant])

Back Home in the Blue Ridge (County 723; released 1971; recorded by Charles Faurot and Richard Nevins; produced by Richard Nevins; four-page insert brochure by Richard Nevins; with Jarrell and Jenkins, with Shag Stanley and Mac Snow; includes brochure)

Blue Ridge Style Square Dance Time (Mountain 301; released ca. 1972)

The Original Camp Creek Boys Through the Years (Mountain 312; released ca. 1973; consists of 12 tracks)

38th Annual Galax Old Fiddlers Convention, 1973 (Gazette 38; released 1973; the Camp Creek Boys perform "Mississippi Sawyer")

Stay All Night and Don't Go Home (County 741; released 1973; collected and recorded by Charles Faurot and Rich Nevins; produced by Rich Nevins; liner notes by Ray Alden; with Jarrell and Jenkins, accompanied by Shag Stanley)

High Atmosphere (Rounder 0028; released 1974; collected and recorded by John Cohen in Virginia and North Carolina in 1965; produced by Mark Wilson and John Cohen; nine-page booklet by Cohen and Wilson; Cockerham plays "Fortune")

1st Annual Brandywine Mountain Music Convention (Heritage VI; released in 1975; Cockerham is featured on "Deford Blues," "Let Me Fall" and "Little Satchel")

Music from Round Peak (Heritage X; released 1976; recorded by Bobby Patterson and Ray Alden; jacket notes by Lisa Ornstein; also features Tommy Jarrell on fiddle and vocals, Paul Sutphin on guitar, Mac Snow on guitar and vocals, and Ray Alden on banjo; notes by Lisa Ornstein)

Southern Clawhammer (Kicking Mule KM 213; released 1978; Cockerham performs "Breaking Up Christmas," "Buffalo Gal," "John Henry," "Pretty Polly" and "Train 45")

Visits (Heritage XXXIII; released 1981; collected, recorded and edited by Ray Alden; gatefold jacket notes by Ray Alden; Cockerham performs "Back Step Cindy" [with Tommy Jarrell] and "Little Maggie" [with Lawrence Lowe, Ernest East and Mac Snow])

Tribute to Fred Cockerham (Heritage HRC-079; released in 1989; recorded by Bobby Patterson in spring 1989; liner notes by Ray Alden; features Greg Hooven on fiddle and vocals, Riley Baugus on guitar and vocals, Ray Chatfield on banjo, Barbara Poole on bass, Marvin Cockram on bass and Verlen Clifton on mandolin)

Best Fiddle and Banjo Duets (County 2702; released 1994; recorded by Ray Alden, Charles Faurot, Richard Nevins and Dave Spilkia; produced by Ray Alden; liner notes by Ray Alden; the 21 tracks also feature Tommy Jarrell)

Blue Ribbon Banjo (Easydisc 7001; released 1996; compiled by Ken Irwin; Fred Cockerham plays "Fortune")

Blue Ridge Mountain Holiday: The Breaking Up Christmas Story (County 2722; released

1997; produced by Paul Brown; production coordinated by Burgess Hurd; field recordings made by Paul Brown, Bob Carlin, Terri McMurray, Ray Alden and Dave Spilkia; Cockerham is featured on "Old Bunch of Keys," "Breaking Up Christmas" [two versions], "Let Me Fall" and "Little Maggie")

The North Carolina Banjo Collection (Rounder 0439; 2-CD set released 1998; produced by Bob Carlin; Fred Cockerham performs "Roustabout")

Kyle Creed

Kyle Creed, an old-time clawhammer banjo player and fiddler from the Beulah community of Surry County, N.C., played with just about every musician in northwestern North Carolina and southwestern Virginia. Kyle was raised in a musical family: His father, Qualey Creed, did some quartet singing and fiddled with Kyle's uncle, John Lowe; and Kyle's grandfather, Bob Creed, played the fiddle. Qualey taught Kyle how to play the fiddle, and Kyle mirrored his father's old bow licks until in later years he started playing with bluegrass banjo picker Bobby Patterson of the Camp Creek Boys. Kyle's banjo playing—characterized by his precise clarity and subdued sparsity—was strongly influenced by John Lowe and Baughy Cockerham.

By the age of 16 Creed was making banjos from poplar wood and dried catskin. Over the years he was well known for his custom, handcrafted banjos, which were sold and distributed by his own label, Mountain Records, which he and Patterson formed in 1972. Creed married Callie Percy Hicks (b. March 17, 1912; d. January 18, 1999) in 1932. They had two daughters: Ida Lou (O'Neal) and Lenora (Gonyo).

Creed worked in the construction business in Colorado during the early 1960s, and he even rambled as far west as Oregon, where he ran a sawmill. When he returned to North Carolina he made a banjo for old Galax String Band mate Fred Cockerham, who was recovering from cataract surgery. Creed eventually persuaded Cockerham to join his band, the Camp Creek Boys (named after the creek that ran through Old Low Gap Road near Cockerham's home), in 1963. The Camp Creek Boys formed in the 1930s, but it wasn't until the folk revival of the 1960s that the band's influence in preserving and promoting old-time string band music was felt. In addition to Creed and Cockerham (both of whom could either fiddle or pick the banjo), the members included guitarists Paul Sutphin, G.F. Collins and Roscoe Russell, fiddler Ernest East, banjoist Bobby Patterson and mandolinist Verlen Clifton.

In later years Creed lived in the Coleman community of Carroll County, Virginia. He played at the 1974 National Folk Festival with Cockerham and guitarist Bobby Patterson, another former member of the Galax String Band and Camp Creek Boys.

The Camp Creek Boys in 1968 consisted of (bottom row, left to right) Paul Sutphin, G.F. Collins, (top row, left to right) Kyle Creed, Benton Flippen, and Verlen Clifton (courtesy Larry Clifton).

Discography

Clawhammer Banjo (County 701; released 1965; Kyle Creed is featured on "Darling Nellie Gray," "Ducks on the Millpond" and "Cluck Old Hen" [with Fred Cockerham])

The Camp Creek Boys (County 709; recorded and released ca. 1967 by Charlie Faurot;

liner notes by Dave Freeman; rereleased 1997 on County CD 2719 as *Old-Time String Band*, with two bonus tracks)

Blue Ridge Style Square Dance Time (Mountain M-301; released ca. 1972)

June Apple (Mountain M-302; released 1972; rereleased 1993 as Heritage HRC-CD-038, adding three bonus tracks; recorded by Bobby Patterson in Galax, Virginia, in December 1972; produced by Kyle Creed; liner notes by Zane Bennett; also features Kyle Creed [banjo], Audine Lineberry [string bass] and Bobby Patterson [guitar])

The Original Camp Creek Boys Through the Years (Mountain 312; released ca. 1973)

38th Annual Galax Old Fiddlers Convention, 1973 (Gazette 38; released 1973; the Camp Creek Boys perform "Mississippi Sawyer")

Mountain Ballads (Mountain M-303; recorded 1974 in Galax,

Kyle Creed was known for his clawhammer banjo picking, but he was equally adept at the fiddle, as shown here in the late 1970s (photo by/courtesy of Dale Morris).

Virginia; released 1974; brief liner notes by Creed; also features Bobby Patterson, Katie Golding, James Lindsey, Bob Flesher [banjo], Pete Lissman and Thomas Norman [vocals])

1st Annual Brandywine Mountain Music Convention (Heritage VI; released 1975; Creed performs "Step-Back Cindy" and "John Brown's Dream" [with Fred Cockerham])

Good Time Music: National Folk Festival (Philo 1028; released 1975; Creed can be heard on "Fire on the Mountain")

New River Jam: One (Mountain 308; released ca. 1975; Kyle Creed performs "Roustabout")

Liberty (Mountain 304; rereleased as Heritage XXVIII, 1977; Creed is featured on all 12 tracks)

Kyle Creed with Bobby Patterson: Virginia Reel (Leader 2053)

39th National Folk Festival (NCTA 77; released 1977; Kyle Creed is featured on "Roustabout")

Blue Ridge Mountain Holiday: The Breaking Up Christmas Story (County 2722; released 1997; produced by Paul Brown; production coordinated by Burgess Hurd; field recordings made by Paul Brown, Bob Carlin, Terri McMurray, Ray Alden and Dave Spilkia; Creed is featured on "Cluck Old Hen," "Breaking Up Christmas" [three versions], and "Let Me Fall")

The North Carolina Banjo Collection (Rounder 0439; 2-CD set released 1998; produced by Bob Carlin; Kyle Creed performs "Lost Indian")

Da Costa Woltz's Southern Broadcasters

In 1927 Da Costa Woltz—a natural-born promoter, musician and mayor of Galax, Virginia—persuaded friends Frank Jenkins and Ben Jarrell to join him and travel to Richmond, Indiana, to record for the Gennett label, taking advantage of the booming interest the major phonograph companies had in recording old time music. Twelve-year-old Price Goodson went with the trio, partly as a promotional gimmick.

Woltz, who was raised in Mount Airy, N.C., was a shrewd businessman who had sold a patent medicine formula to the Vicks Company. He named the band the Southern Broadcasters, even though they never did any broadcasting, southern or otherwise. The group cut 18 sides during their Gennett session, which turned out to be their only one.

The Southern Broadcasters employed a unique arrangement of fiddle (Ben Jarrell) and two banjos (Da Costa Woltz and Frank Jenkins); in fact they were one of the last bands to use this configuration. Ben Jarrell and Price Goodson (who played on only three selections) handled the vocal duties. (Goodson turned out to be one of the best Galax-area fiddle players. He practiced law until his untimely death at the age of 33.)

Discography

Mountain Sacred Songs (County 508; released 1965; edited by David Freeman; liner notes by Archie Green; consists of 12 commercial 78 rpm recordings made in the 1920s and 1930s; Da Costa Woltz's Southern Broadcasters perform "Are You Washed in the Blood of the Lamb")

Traditional Country Classics, 1927-1929 (Historical HLP 8003; released ca. 1968; edited by Joe Bussard, Jr.; liner notes by Richard Nevins; contains 14 commercial 78 rpm recorded from 1927 to 1929; Da Costa Woltz's Southern Broadcasters are featured on "Take Me Back to the Sweet Sunny South" and "Yellow Rose of Texas")

Da Costa Woltz's Southern Broadcasters (County 524; released 1972; edited by David Freeman; includes 12 of the 18 tracks the band recorded in Richmond, Indiana, in 1927; three rare songs not included in this collection—"Roving Cowboy," "Jack of Diamonds" and "Baptist Shout"—were also from that 1927 session and released on 78 rpm records; jacket notes by Richard Nevins)

Going Down the Valley: Vocal and Instrumental Styles in Folk Music from the South (New World Records NW 236; released 1977; edited by Norm Cohen; six-page sewn-in notes by Norm Cohen; consists of 18 studio recordings made from 1926 to 1938; Ben Jarrell and Da Costa Woltz's Southern Broadcasters perform "Old Joe Clark")

Blue Ridge Mountain Holiday: The Breaking Up Christmas Story (County 2722; released 1997; produced by Paul Brown; production coordinated by Burgess Hurd; field recordings made by Paul Brown, Bob Carlin, Terri McMurray, Ray Alden and

Dave Spilkia; Da Costa Woltz's Southern Broadcasters play "John Brown's Dream")

Complete Recorded Works in Chronological Order (1927–1929) (Document DOCD-8023; released 1998; contains 24 tracks)

Luther Davis

Old time fiddler Luther Franklin Davis was born on September 11, 1888, in the Meadow Creek area of Grayson County, Virginia, to Uriah Franklin, a farmer and singer, and Matilda McKnight Davis, a midwife. Luther's first bought instrument was a harmonica, but he decided he wanted a banjo after hearing Spottwood Blevins and his son Jim play fiddle and banjo on the last day of school. Davis played the banjo until learning to play the fiddle at age 15; his first fiddle was previously owned by a neighbor who had died of consumption.

Davis often played music at school breakings with Isom and Fielden Rector, or with Jim Blevins and Fred Wilson. From about August 1902 to 1935, Davis, Blevins and Wilson were an active band, playing primarily around Carroll, Grayson and Alleghany (N.C.) counties. They performed at schools, political rallies, dances and anywhere else there was a call.

In 1910 Davis married Verd Cox of Ashe County, N.C. He soon bought his own farm, later working in a furniture factory and then developing a career as an auctioneer, selling land, personal property and livestock. In 1935 Luther became deputy sheriff, a position he held until 1949. He rarely played music from 1935 until the early 1970s, when many of his songs were collected and recorded by Tom Carter and Blanton Owen for the Library of Congress's Archive of Folk Culture and the two-volume *Old Originals* series for Rounder Records (1976). Davis died in September 1986.

Discography

Old Originals, Vol. 2 (Rounder 0058; released 1978; Luther Davis performs "Piney Woods Gal" and "Evening Star Waltz")

The Old Time Way (Heritage 070; released 1986; produced by Andy Cahan and Alice Gerrard; photos by Alice Gerrard; graphics and cover design by Andy Cahan; Luther Davis is featured on Side One's 16 tracks; Roscoe [fiddle, banjo] and Leone Parish [vocals, guitar] perform 16 tracks on Side Two)

Alec (Uncle Eck) Dunford

Alec "Uncle Eck" Dunford, a fiddle player, guitarist, comedian and amateur photographer, was born in 1878 in Carroll County, Virginia. After receiving an above average education, he married Callie Frost in 1908. His wife died in 1921, though, leaving him to live alone in a little cabin on Ballard Branch, about one mile from the town of Galax, Virginia, and the home of Ernest Stoneman.

Dunford played fiddle for Ernest Stoneman during the mid to late 1920s, in the groups the Dixie Mountaineers, the Blue Ridge Cornshuckers and the Stoneman Family. He also recorded a few solo songs and several humorous monologues and skits about mountain life for Victor, marking him as one of the first country music comedians.

After Stoneman left Galax in 1932, Dunford began a musical association with the Ward family. With the Wards and as a member of the Ballard Branch Bogtrotters, Dunford recorded for the Library of Congress. In 1940 the Bogtrotters even played on network radio. From 1935 on, Dunford was a frequent performer at the Galax Fiddlers' Convention. He died in July 1953.

Discography

Anthology of American Folk Music, Vol. 1: Ballads (Folkways FA 2951; released 1952; reissued on CD as Smithsonian/Folkways SFW 40090, 1997; edited by Harry Smith; Uncle Eck Dunford is featured on "Old Shoes and Leggins")

Folk Music in America, Vol. 2: Songs of Love, Courtship... (Library of Congress LBC-02; released 1978; Dunford is featured on "Lily Monroe")

Round the Heart of Old Galax, Vol. 1 (County 533; released 1980; edited by David Freeman; liner notes by Wayne Martin; consists of 14 commercial 78 rpm recordings made in the 1920s and 1930s; Eck Dunford is featured on "Barney McCoy," "There's a Light Up in Galilee" and "Too Late")

Round the Heart of Old Galax, Vol. 2 (County 534; released 1980; edited and liner notes by Wayne Martin; consists of 14 songs, some commercial 78 rpm recordings made in the 1920s and 1930s, others from Library of Congress field recordings made by John Lomax; Dunford, Stoneman and Edwards perform "Ain't That Trouble in Mind" and "Skip to My Lou")

The Bristol Sessions: Historic Recordings from Bristol, Tennessee, Vol. 1 (Country Music Foundation CMF 011-L [2-LP set]; released 1987; edited by Bob Pinson; gatefold jacket notes by Charles K. Wolfe; consists of studio recordings made in Bristol, Tennessee, in 1927; Dunford plays "Skip to Ma Lou, My Darling"; Dunford, Ernest V. Stoneman and Miss I. Frost are featured on "Midnight on the Stormy Deep" and "The Mountaineer's Courtship")

Rural String Bands of Virginia (County CD-3502; released 1994; notes by Kinney Rorrer; remastered by Dave Glasser; Uncle Eck Dunford and Hattie Stoneman perform "What Will I Do, for My Money Is All Gone")

AS ERNEST V. STONEMAN AND HIS DIXIE MOUNTAINEERS

"The Dying Girl's Farewell"/"Tell Mother I Will Meet Her" (Victor 21129; recorded in Bristol, Tennessee, on July 25, 1927)

"The Mountaineer's Courtship" (Victor 20880; recorded in Bristol, Tennessee, on July 25, 1927)

"Sweeping Through the Gates"/"Are You Washed in the Blood?" (Victor 20844; Montgomery Ward 8136; recorded in Bristol, Tennessee, on July 25, 1927)

"I Know My Name Is There"/"No More Goodbyes" (Victor 21186; recorded in Bristol, Tennessee, on July 25, 1927)

"The Resurrection"/"I Am Resolved" (Victor 21071; recorded in Bristol, Tennessee, on July 25, 1927)

"Goodbye Dear Old Stepstone"/"All I've Got's Gone" (Edison 52489; recorded in New York City on November 21, 1928)

"Fallen by the Wayside"/"The Prisoner's Lament" (Edison 52461; also Edison 5686/5673; recorded in New York City on November 21, 1928)

"Midnight on the Stormy Deep" (Edison 5536; recorded in New York City on November 22, 1928)

"I Remember Calvary"/"He Is Coming After Me" (Edison 52479; also Edison 5676, N-20004; recorded in New York City on November 22, 1928)

"Down to Jordan and Be Saved"/"There's a Light Up in Galilee" (Victor 40078; recorded in Bristol, Tennessee, on October 31, 1928)

AS UNCLE ECK DUNFORD

"The Whip-poor-will Song" (Victor 20880; recorded in Bristol, Tennessee, on July 27, 1927)

"What Will I Do, for My Money's All Gone" (Victor 21578; recorded in Bristol, Tennessee, on July 27, 1927)

"Skip to My Lou, My Darling"/"Barney McCoy" (Victor 20938; recorded in Bristol, Tennessee, on July 27, 1927)

"Sleeping Late" (Victor 21224; recorded in Atlanta, Georgia, on October 22, 1927)

"My First Bicycle Ride"/"The Savingest Man on Earth" (Victor 21131; recorded in Atlanta, Georgia, on October 22, 1927)

"The Taffy Pulling Party" (Victor 21244; recorded in Atlanta, Georgia, on October 22, 1927)

"Old Shoes and Leggins" (Victor 40060; recorded in Bristol, Tennessee, on October 31, 1928)

AS ERNEST V. STONEMAN AND HIS BLUE RIDGE CORN SHUCKERS

"Old Time Corn Shuckin' Part 1"/"Old Time Corn Shuckin' Part 2" (Victor 20835; recorded in Bristol, Tennessee, on July 27, 1927)

"Possum Trot School Exhibition, Part 1"/"Possum Trot School Exhibition, Part 2" (Victor 21264; recorded in Atlanta, Georgia, on February 22, 1928)

"A Serenade in the Mountains" (Victor 21518; recorded in Atlanta, Georgia, on February 22, 1928)

"The Two Little Orphans"/"The Raging Sea, How It Roars" (Victor 21264; recorded in Atlanta, Georgia, on February 22, 1928)

"Sweet Summer Has Gone Away" (Victor 21578; recorded in Atlanta, Georgia, on February 22, 1928)

AS THE STONEMAN FAMILY
"The Broken-Hearted Lover" (Victor 40030; recorded in Bristol, Tennessee, on October 30, 1928)
"Angeline the Baker" (Victor 40060; recorded in Bristol, Tennessee, on October 30, 1928)
"We Parted by the Riverside" (Victor 40030; recorded in Bristol, Tennessee, on October 31, 1928)
"Going Up the Mountain After Liquor Part 1"/"Going Up the Mountain After Liquor Part 2" (Victor 40116; recorded in Bristol, Tennessee, on October 31, 1928)
"The Spanish Merchant's Daughter"/"Too Late" (Victor 40206; recorded in Bristol, Tennessee, on October 31 and November 1, 1928)

The Easter Brothers

The Mount Airy–based Easter Brothers play traditional gospel music with overtones of country and bluegrass instrumentation. The Easters—made up of brothers Russell, James and Edd—have appeared on radio and television and have toured and recorded quite extensively.

Russell was born April 22, 1930, in Mount Airy and was the first brother to take up music. In 1947 he formed a band with fiddler Wayburn Johnson. Russell married and moved to Danville, Virginia, in 1950 and formed the Green Valley Quartet in 1955 (with his brothers-in-law John and Troy Brummett and Jack Phillips). As Edd and James (born April 24, 1932) began to play they moved to Danville in 1956 and 1957, respectively, and thus was formed the Easter Brothers and the Green Valley Quartet. At one point they added another member—bass player and singer Ronald Thomas, a Mohawk Indian born near the U.S.–Canadian border who married Russell's sister-in-law. The group featured, primarily, Russell on banjo, James on guitar, and Edd on mandolin.

The Green Valley Quartet got their own radio program over WBTM in Danville, around 1956. They soon developed quite a following and recorded a number of records on their own Green Valley label. In the late 1950s and early 1960s the group worked quite a few radio shows with Don Reno and Red Smiley. The Easter Brothers made their first recordings in April 1960, in a Virginia studio owned by their manager, Carlton Haney. A second session was held at the King Records studios in Cincinnati, Ohio, on February 27, 1961. Six of those eleven recorded sides were released by King under the name "The Easter Brothers and the Green Valley Quartet" (so as to avoid confusion with the Nashville-based group the Green Valley Boys). The sides that were not released were subsequently put out on Haney's Commandment label. (All sides were later released on the 1983 Rebel album *Early Sessions*.)

The Easters recorded several more albums for Commandment in the

The Easter Brothers lineup in the late 1990s included (from left) Josh Easter, Russell Easter, Edd Easter and James Easter (courtesy Joe Hallford and Russell Easter).

1960s. Several of these tracks feature electric steel guitar and other instruments not often associated with bluegrass gospel. In 1968 the Easter Brothers recorded a standout album on County Records that features Wayburn Johnson on fiddle, Johnny Taylor of McGrady, N.C., on banjo, and Russell Easter, Jr., on banjo and Dobro.

At times the Easter Brothers had two programs over two stations in Danville, Virginia, and at WPAQ in Mount Airy. By the end of the 1960s the Easter Brothers had become familiar figures in gospel music circles from northern Georgia to southern Pennsylvania. They also made many television appearances, most notably for the Rev. Leonard Repass, who had a television ministry based in Bluefield, West Virginia. Additionally, the brothers have performed on *PTL*, *Sing Out America*, *Huff Cook* and *Camp Meeting U.S.A.* (a worldwide broadcast).

Throughout the 1970s and 1980s the Easter Brothers recorded bluegrass and gospel tunes for Old Homestead, Rebel, Benson Corporation's Life Line, and Eddie Crook's Morningstar. In 1979 they gave up their day jobs and became full-time musicians for the first time. In the mid to late 1980s the group toured over much of the eastern United States and in such states as Texas, Oklahoma, Missouri and Arkansas.

Family tradition has played a key role in the success of the Easters. Russell Easter, Jr. (born 1951), took up the Dobro at age 10 and has proven to be a most capable multi-instrumentalist. Russell Jr. now plays in the Easter Family band with wife Barbara, daughter Marti, and sons Jacob and Jared. Russell Sr.'s other son, Roger (born 1955), plays the bass fiddle. Edd's son Bobby played banjo with the band. James' son Jeff (born March 18, 1960) worked as the group's harmonica and bass player. He married Sheri Williamson of the Lewis Family and played with that band before he and Sheri set out on their own successful musical career. In 1997 Jeff and Sheri Easter were named Christian Country Group of the Year.

Among non-family members, Jimmy Edmonds of Galax, Virginia, played fiddle and banjo on many of their albums. Other "outside" musicians have included banjoist Joel Martin and bassist Allen Mills (later of Lost & Found).

Several of the Easter Brothers' songs, including "They're Holding Up the Ladder," have been recorded by numerous other gospel groups. The Easters gained their all-time biggest commercial success with the song "Thank You Lord for Your Blessings on Me."

Discography

Let Me Stand Lord (Commandment; released 1965)
Lord, I Will (Commandment C-1864; released 1966)
Country Hymn Time (Commandment; released 1967)
The Easter Brothers and Their Green Valley Quartet (County 716; released 1968; recorded in Mount Airy, N.C., in August 1968 by Charles Faurot; produced by David Freeman; consists of 12 tracks)
From Earth to Gloryland (Commandment; released 1969)
Hold On (Old Homestead 70008; released 1976)
I Feel Like Traveling On (Rebel 1595; released 1981; rereleased in 1997)
Almost Home (Rebel 1605; released 1981)
He's the Rock I'm Leaning On (Morningstar; released 1981)
Early Sessions [1960-1961] (Rebel 1615; released 1983)
The Easter Brothers (Life Line C-1332; released 1983)
Hereafter (Life Line C-1331; released 1984)
Tribute to Reno & Smiley (Rebel 1635; released 1985; Don Reno assisted on the Easter Brothers' King sessions in 1961)
The Sun's Still Shining in the Valley (Life Line 412696; released 1996)
Favorites (Life Line 495698; released 1998)
If I Could Order Christmas (Commandment-5052)
Happy Are the Days (8910)
Just Another Hill
Little Grain of Sand (Life Line LL-5050)
Songs About Mama (Life Line LL-4090)
Songs of the Inspirational Louvin Brothers (TSR 0034)
The Troops Are Coming Home (Life Line LL-1015)

We're Gonna Make It (Life Line LL-0456)
We're Going Home (Commandment-14)
Wore Out (Commandment-1733)
Snow Covered Mound (Commandment CS-1615)
Mountains and Memories (Commandment CS-1635)
Goin' Round This World (Commandment CS-1605)

Ernest East and the Pine Ridge Boys

This old-time string band from Round Peak (near Mount Airy) in Surry County was led by fiddler Ernest East, who was born on July 8, 1917. He

came from a family of nine, and two of his older brothers played the guitar. Almost every Saturday, from the age of 9, Ernest would go to Charlie Lowe's house, where he learned to frail the banjo and saw the fiddle. When Ernest was 16 he played with the Round Peak Band, which at that time included Kyle Creed, Fred Cockerham, Paul Sutphin, Lawrence Lowe (Charlie's son) and Ernest's two older brothers.

For many years East cut grain and raised tobacco and corn; he later did factory work. Upon forming the Pine Ridge Boys in 1966 he recruited the services of banjoist Gilmer Woodruff (b. 1924; d. June 1997), guitar player Mac Snow (b. 1931 in Lambsburg, Virginia) and vocalist-guitarist Scotty East (Ernest's son, born in 1952). Scotty's wife, Patsy, later joined the group.

The band adhered to the traditional sounds of old-time country music, and they displayed a tight, cohesive musicianship. The

Ernest East (top right, with fiddle) and the Pine Ridge Boys with the trophy they won for best band at Union Grove, N.C. Pictured are (bottom row, left to right) Gilmer Woodruff, Scotty East, (top row, left to right) Mac Snow, unknown bass player and Ernest East (courtesy Ernest East).

inflection, melody and tempo of their music are all flavored by the members' rural mountain heritage and lives that centered around home and church. Ernest East patterned his fiddling after local musician Tommy Jarrell, and Woodruff's picking was influenced by fellow clawhammer banjoists Fred Cockerham and Charlie Lowe.

Over the years the Pine Ridge Boys won countless trophies and prize ribbons at fiddlers' conventions, including the famous ones at Galax, Va., and Union Grove, N.C. They also performed at the Smithsonian Institution's Festival of American Folklife and the National Folk Festival.

In 1988 Ernest East was presented the Brown-Hudson Folklore Award by the North Carolina Folklore Society for "in special ways contributing to the appreciation, continuation, or study of North Carolina folk traditions." In addition, in 1990 he was the recipient of a North Carolina Folk Heritage Award.

Two months following the passing of his wife Fanny, Ernest East died on January 8, 2000.

Discography

Old-Time Mountain Music (County 718; released 1969; recorded and produced by Charles Faurot and Richard Nevins; liner notes by Nevins; 12 traditional songs, including "Sally Ann," "Richmond," "Fortune," "Mississippi Sawyer," "Suzanna Gal" and "June Apple"; "Hell Among the Round Peakers" is a tongue-in-cheek renaming of the fiddle tune "Hell Amongst the Yearlings"; "Greenback Dollar" and "Pig in a Pen" were based on performances by Fiddlin' Arthur Smith on the Grand Ole Opry)

Music from Round Peak (Heritage X; released 1976; recorded by Bobby Patterson and Ray Alden; jacket notes by Lisa Ornstein; features Fred Cockerham on fiddle and banjo; Tommy Jarrell on fiddle and vocals, Paul Sutphin on guitar, Mac Snow on guitar and vocals, and Ray Alden on banjo; notes by Lisa Ornstein)

Stringband Music from Mt. Airy: The Pine Ridge Boys and Patsy (Heritage XXIX; released 1981; also features Andy Cahan on banjo and Patsy East on bass and harmony vocals; tracks include "Sugar Hill" and "Ain't Gonna Work Tomorrow")

Visits (Heritage XXXIII; released 1981; collected, recorded and edited by Ray Alden; gatefold jacket notes by Ray Alden; Ernest East and the Pine Ridge Boys perform "Lost Indian"; Ernest East and Mac Snow play on "Little Maggie" [with Fred Cockerham and Lawrence Lowe]; East and Snow [along with Tommy Jarrell, Bobby Patterson, Al Tharp, Scott Ainslie, Ray Alden and Patsy East] perform "Visits")

Norman Edmonds *see* J.P.
Nestor and Norman Edmonds

Benton Flippen

Old-time fiddler James Benton Flippen was born in 1920, one of eight children who grew up on Sam and Luticia F. Boles Flippen's tobacco farm in northern Surry County. His father picked the banjo, and an uncle who lived in Thomasville taught him many traditional tunes. Benton started playing the banjo when he was 15, but soon followed the lead of his two brothers when he switched to the fiddle at age 18. Flippen's musical mentor was Esker Hutchins, a highly respected local fiddler and banjo picker with whom he played for several years on radio and at fiddlers' conventions.

After developing his unique styles of two-finger banjo picking and finger sliding on the neck of the fiddle, Flippen eventually joined Glen McPeak's Green Valley Boys, with whom he had a daily radio show on WPAQ in Mount Airy. Flippen was one of the first musicians to broadcast over WPAQ after it went on the air in February of 1948, playing his banjo with Hutchins and guitarist Leak Caudle.

Flippen joined the stellar group the Camp Creek Boys in 1967 after Fred Cockerham stopped playing with the band. When Kyle Creed left the Boys in 1969 and took the band's name with him, Flippen was recruited by Paul Sutphin to join the highly acclaimed Smokey Valley Boys band, which he did in 1971. Flippen played with the Smokey Valley Boys until they disbanded (but only temporarily) in 1985. From then until 1994, Flippen performed with the Dryhill Draggers.

Over the years Flippen— who worked for 37 years in a hosiery mill—won over 70 trophies at local fiddlers' conventions, including seven first-place wins at Galax alone. He traveled around the country, from Washington state to upstate New York, to play in festivals (such as Newport) and teach students how to fiddle. In 1990, Flippen

North Carolina Folk Heritage Award winner Benton Flippen rocks the bow at the 1999 Mount Airy Fiddler's Convention (photo by the author).

received the North Carolina Folk Heritage Award. Benton's son, Larry, started playing the guitar when he was about 12 years old.

Discography

Blue Ridge Barn Dance (County 746; released 1974; Benton Flippen performs "Benton's Dream" and "Pretty Little Girl")

Old Time, New Times (Rounder 0326; released 1994; recorded in various locales between 1949 and 1993; produced by Paul Brown and Ken Irwin; liner notes by Paul Brown; contains 27 tracks performed by Benton Flippen, the Smokey Valley Boys, the Green Valley Boys, the Dryhill Draggers and the Camp Creek Boys)

Blue Ridge Mountain Holiday: The Breaking Up Christmas Story (County 2722; released 1997; produced by Paul Brown; production coordinated by Burgess Hurd; field recordings made by Paul Brown, Bob Carlin, Terri McMurray, Ray Alden and Dave Spilkia; Benton Flippen performs "Breaking Up Christmas" with Larry Flippen)

WITH THE SMOKEY VALLEY BOYS

The 38th Annual Galax Old Fiddlers Convention (Gazette 38; released 1973; the Smokey Valley Boys play "Richmond Cotillion")

The Smokey Valley Boys (Rounder 0029; released 1974; recorded August 1973 in Pine Ridge, Surry County; produced by the Rounder Collective; back cover notes and interview by Bill Hicks; 14 traditional songs, mostly instrumental, including "Lost Indian," "Whoa Mule," Sally Ann," and "June Apple")

The 50th Annual Old Time Fiddlers Convention at Union Grove (Union Grove SS-9; released 1974; the Smokey Valley Boys are featured on "Pole Cat Blues")

Visits (Heritage XXXIII; released 1981; collected, recorded and edited by Ray Alden; gatefold jacket notes by Ray Alden; the Smokey Valley Boys perform "Polecat Blues")

Appalachia—The Old Traditions—Vol. 2 (Home-Made Music LP002; released 1983; collected, recorded and edited by Mike Yates in Virginia and North Carolina, 1979-80 and 1983; three-page booklet by Mike Yates; Benton Flippen and the Smokey Valley Boys play "Cotton-Eyed Joe" and "Gary Dawson's Tune")

Brandywine '83: The 10th Anniversary Celebration of the Brandywine Mountain Music Convention (Heritage 054; released 1984; the Smokey Valley Boys perform "June Apple" and "Pole Cat Blues")

The Green Glass Cloggers: Through the Ears (Rounder 0228; released 1985; recorded in Asheville, N.C., by Steven Heller; the Smokey Valley Boys accompany the Green Glass Cloggers on "Bile Them Cabbage Down" and "Nobody's Business")

Old Time Music on the Air, Vol. 1 (Rounder 0331; released 1994; produced by Old Time Music on the Radio; Benton Flippen and the Smokey Valley Boys perform "Benton's Dream")

The Foot Hill Boys

The Foot Hill Boys was a bluegrass and old-time band whose members lived in the Galax–Mount Airy region. Fiddler Wayburn Johnson was born in 1928 in Logan, West Virginia, but moved to Mount Airy as a preschooler. Before joining the Foot Hill Boys Johnson played with Woody Woody & the Woodchoppers, Art Johnson & the Southern Melodiers, Al Hawks & the Melody Makers, Charlie Monroe, Jim Eanes, Mac Wiseman, Rudy Lyle, the Johnson Brothers, Oscar Sullivan and Larry Richardson. Johnson collected numerous trophies for his fiddling, including several state championships and the Union Grove Grand Championship in 1971.

Cullen Galyean, the group's banjoist, was born in 1939. He played fiddle and banjo for the Mountain Ramblers, who were featured on a series of albums for Atlantic in 1959, and recorded three singles with Ed Vogler on M-K-B in the mid–1960s. Galyean played guitar and sang lead with the Border Mountain Boys on Homestead Records, and he played mandolin with Ralph Stanley briefly in 1969. In the 1970s and early 1980s Galyean did some picking for Glen Neaves and the Virginia Mountain Boys.

Bobby Harrison, guitarist and tenor singer, was born in Galax in 1934. He played a rare Martin 00-21 guitar. The group's mandolinist and baritone singer, Ivor Melton, was born in 1927 near Galax. He played with Harrison and Galyean for more than 20 years, a good many of which as the Virginia Mountain Boys. Bass player Johnny Vipperman was born in Mount Airy in 1929, and played with such well-known groups as Wilma Lee and Stoney Cooper.

After Johnson's untimely death on September 8, 1971, the Foot Hill Boys released a posthumous album on the County label.

Discography

Bluegrass in the Carolina Mountains (County 731; released 1972; recorded in Mount Airy, N.C., by Charles Faurot; produced by David Freeman; jacket notes by Nick Barr; 7 of the 12 songs featured are original compositions by the band members)

Grayson and Whitter

Gilliam Banmon Grayson was born November 11, 1888, at Grayson, in Ashe County, N.C. When he was six weeks old Grayson suffered serious corneal damage, which left him almost blind. He made a living as a young man by "busking" through mountain towns, playing on street corners by day and parties, shows and church concerts by night. He eventually settled down

Blind fiddler G.B. Grayson (left) and Henry Whitter recorded about 40 songs in the late 1920s, and their influence on old time music is still felt today (Southern Historical Collection, Wilson Library, The University of North Carolina at Chapel Hill).

in Laurel Bloomery, near the Tennessee–North Carolina line. Grayson played the fiddle in an unorthodox manner, holding it not under his chin but down on his shoulder, rocking it back and forth to facilitate bowing.

Grayson knew and toured with area musicians such as Clarence (Tom) Ashley and Dock Walsh, but did not meet Henry Whitter (born April 6, 1892, in Fries, Virginia) until they both played at the Johnson City, Tennessee, fiddlers' convention in the summer of 1927. Whitter was the area's first musician to record when the textile worker traveled uninvited to New York in March 1923 to record "The Wreck on the Southern Old 97" and "Lonesome Road Blues" for the General Phonograph Corporation, owners of OKeh Records. The company released his sides (some of the very earliest in the commercial hillbilly field) only in late November 1923, after the unexpected success of Fiddlin' John Carson.

Whitter was considered by many to be a below average singer; in fact, legend has it that Ernest Stoneman was prompted to begin his recording career in Bristol, Tennessee, after hearing Whitter and knowing that he could do better. Nevertheless, Whitter aggressively promoted old-time music and had hit recordings with "The Wreck on the Southern Old 97" and "Fox Chase," a harmonica solo that he recorded for Ralph Peer on August 2, 1927, during Peer's field trip to Bristol. Most of his recordings during the 1920s were solo efforts, though in 1924 he recorded with a string band, Whitter's Virginia Breakdowners, that included banjoist John Rector and fiddler James Sutphin. Whitter also helped jumpstart fellow mill worker Kelly Harrell's recording career in 1925.

In October 1927, Grayson and Whitter cut eight songs for the Gennett label. Two weeks later they recorded six more sides for Victor. During this session they made their career record, the double-sided hit of "Train 45" and "Handsome Molly" that sold over 50,000 copies and stayed in print until 1934. None of their subsequent Victor records sold as well, but "Lee Highway Blues (Going Down the Lee Highway)," recorded in 1929, sold nearly 1,400 copies and remains a fiddle standard. The pair was also the first, in 1929, to record the famed murder ballad "Tom Dooley." Other Grayson and Whitter tunes such as "Banks of the Ohio" (which they called "I'll Never Be Yours"), "Little Maggie," "Rosa Conley," "Nobody's Darling" and "Cluck Old Hen" have been covered by artists that include Bob Dylan, Mike Seeger, the Stanley Brothers, Doc Watson, Charlie Monroe, Grandpa Jones and J.E. Mainer. Despite recording together for just three years and producing only about 40 songs, Grayson and Whitter left a vast and supreme influence on early country music.

Grayson and Whitter recorded their final session, for Victor, on September 30 and October 1, 1929, in Memphis, Tennessee. On August 16, 1930, Grayson, while hitch-hiking to his brother's home in Virginia, was killed instantly when thrown from the running board of a car after it struck a log truck head on near Abingdon, Virginia. Whitter did little recording after Grayson's death. He died of diabetes in Morganton, North Carolina, on November 10, 1941.

In 1996 G.B. Grayson was posthumously given the International Bluegrass Music Association's Award of Merit for making "significant contributions to the field of bluegrass music and its development."

Discography

"Nobody's Darling"/"Handsome Molly" (Gennett 6304; recorded in New York City in early October 1927)

"You Never Miss Your Mother Until She's Gone"/"Train No. 45" (Gennett 6320; recorded in New York City in early October 1927)

"I'll Never Be Yours"/"Shout Lula" (Gennett 6373; recorded in New York City in early October 1927)

"Handsome Molly" (Champion 15629; recorded in New York City in early October 1927)

"Handsome Molly"/"Train 45" (Victor 21189; recorded in Atlanta, Georgia, on October 18, 1927)

"He Is Coming to Us Dead"/"Don't Go Out Tonight, My Darling" (Victor 21139; recorded in Atlanta, Georgia, on October 18, 1927)

"Rose Conley"/"Ommie Wise" (Victor 21625; recorded in Atlanta, Georgia, on October 18, 1927)

"Train 45" (Bluebird 5498; recorded in Atlanta, Georgia, on October 18, 1927)

"Sally Gooden" (Gennett 6733; recorded in New York City on February 21, 1928)

"She's Mine, All Mine"/"Cluck Old Hen" (Gennett 6656; recorded in New York City on February 21, 1928)

"Sweet Rosie O'Grady"/"Red or Green" (Gennett 6418; recorded in New York City on February 21, 1928)

"Cluck Old Hen" (Champion 15629; recorded in New York City on February 21, 1928)

"The Red and Green Signal Lights"/"A Dark Road Is a Hard Road to Travel" (Victor 40063; recorded in New York City on July 31, 1928)

"Joking Henry"/"Barnyard Serenade" (Victor 40038; recorded in New York City on July 31 and August 1, 1928)

"The Nine-Pound Hammer"/"Short Life of Trouble" (Victor 40105; recorded in New York City on July 31, 1928)

"I've Always Been a Rambler"/"I Saw a Man at the Close of Day" (Victor 40324; recorded in New York City on July 31, 1928, and Memphis, Tennessee, on October 1, 1929)

"Where Are You Going, Alice?"/"Little Maggie with a Dram Glass in Her Hand" (Victor 40135; recorded in New York City on July 31 and August 1, 1928)

"On the Banks of Old Tennessee"/"Tom Dooley" (Victor 40235; recorded in Memphis, Tennessee, on September 30, 1929)

"Never as Fast as I Have Been"/"Going Down the Lee Highway" (Victor 23565; recorded in Memphis, Tennessee, on September 30, 1929)

"I Have Lost You Darling, True Love"/"What You Gonna Do with the Baby" (Victor 40268; recorded in Memphis, Tennessee, on September 30 and October 1, 1929)

"On the Banks of Old Tennessee" (Bluebird 7072; Zonophone 4329 [reverse by Bill Simmons]; recorded in Memphis, Tennessee, on September 30, 1929)

"Going Down the Lee Highway" (Bluebird 5498; recorded in Memphis, Tennessee, on September 30, 1929)

"Fox Chase No. 2"/"Train Blues" (Victor 40292; recorded in Memphis, Tennessee, on October 1, 1929)

"Fox Chase No. 2" (Elektradisk 2139; Montgomery Ward 4909; recorded in Memphis, Tennessee, on October 1, 1929)

Anthology of American Folk Music, Vol. 1: Ballads (Folkways FA 2951; released 1952; reissued on CD as Smithsonian/Folkways SFW 40090 in 1997; edited by Harry Smith; G.B. Grayson performs "Omie Wise")

The String Bands, Vol. 1 (Old Timey 100; released 1962; edited by Chris Strachwitz; annotations by Strachwitz; consists of 15 commercial 78 rpm recordings made in the 1920s and 1930s; Grayson and Whitter perform "Train 45")

A Collection of Mountain Ballads (County 502; released 1964; edited by David Freeman; consists of commercial 78 rpm recordings made from 1926 to 1930; Grayson and Whitter perform "I've Always Been a Rambler")

A Collection of Mountain Fiddle Music, Vol. 2 (County 503; released 1965; edited by David Freeman; consists of commercial 78 rpm recordings made from 1927 to 1930; Grayson and Whitter perform "Going Down the Lee Highway")

Ballads and Songs (Old Timey 102; released 1965; edited by Chris Strachwitz; liner notes by Toni Brown; consists of 16 commercial 78 rpm recordings made from 1925 to 1939; Grayson and Whitter perform "Handsome Molly," "Little Maggie" and "Rose Conley")

The Railroad in Folksong (RCA Victor LPV 532; released 1966; edited by Archie Green; liner notes by Archie Green; consists of 16 studio recordings made from 1926 to

1940; G.B. Grayson and Henry Whitter are featured on "The Red and Green Signal Lights")

Grayson and Whitter (County 513; released 1968; edited by David Freeman; liner notes [on 2nd printing] by Joe Wilson; consists of 12 commercial 78 rpm recordings made from 1928 to 1930)

Traditional Country Classics, 1927–1929 (Historical HLP 8003; released ca. 1968; edited by Joe Bussard, Jr.; liner notes by Richard Nevins; contains 14 commercial 78 rpm recorded from 1927 to 1929; Grayson and Whitter are featured on "What You Gonna Do with the Baby")

Old Time Ballads from the Southern Mountains (County 522; released 1972; consists of 12 commercial 78 rpm recordings made from 1927 to 1931; Grayson and Whitter are credited on "The Banks of the Ohio")

A Fiddlers' Convention in Mountain City, Tennessee (County 525; released 1972; three-page insert booklet by Joe Wilson; consists of 12 commercial 78 rpm recordings made from 1925 to 1930; G.B. Grayson and Henry Whitter perform "Never Be as Fast as I Have Been")

Going Down Lee Highway (Davis Unlimited DU 33033; released 1977; liner notes by Frank Mare and Joe Wilson; consists of 14 commercial 78 rpm recordings made from 1927 to 1929)

G.B. Grayson & Henry Whitter: Early Classics, Vol. I (Old Homestead OHCS-157; released 1984; liner notes by Charles Wolfe; consists of 12 commercial 78 rpm recordings made from 1927 to 1929)

G.B. Grayson & Henry Whitter: Early Classics, Vol. II (Old Homestead OHCS-164; released 1984; liner notes by Charles Wolfe; consists of 13 commercial 78 rpm recordings made from 1927 to 1929)

Johnny's Gone to War: Old-Time War Songs Recorded in the Golden Age (Marimac 9109 [cassette]; released 1984; edited by Pat Conte; consists of 20 commercial 78 rpm recordings made in the 1920s and 1930s; Grayson and Whitter are credited with "He Is Coming to Us Dead")

Old-Time Mountain Ballads (County 3504; released 1996; annotated by Charles Wolfe; Grayson and Whitter perform "Rose Conley" and "I'll Never Be Yours")

Rural String Bands of Tennessee (County 3511; released 1997; notes by Charles K. Wolfe; remastered by Richard Nevins; Grayson and Whitter are featured on "Going Down the Lee Highway")

Music from the Lost Provinces (Old Hat CD-1001; released 1997; produced, booklet notes and graphic design by Marshall Wyatt; Grayson & Whitter play "Train 45," "Short Life of Trouble," "I've Always Been a Rambler" and "Handsome Molly")

Train 45: Railroad Songs from the Early 1900s (Rounder 1143; released 1998; produced by Norm Cohen and Dick Spottswood; G.B. Grayson & Henry Whitter play "Red and Green Signal Lights")

The Recordings of Grayson & Whitter (County 3517; released 1999; liner notes by Joe Wilson; consists of 15 songs recorded between 1928 and 1930)

AS NORMAN GAYLE

"I'll Never Be Yours"/"Train No. 45" (Champion 15447; recorded in New York City in early October 1927)

"Shout Lula"/"Sally Gooden" (Champion 15501; recorded in New York City in early October 1927 and February 21, 1928)

"She's Mine, All Mine"/"Red or Green" (Champion 15465; recorded in New York City on February 21, 1928)

AS DILLARD SANDERS
"I'll Never Be Yours"/"You Never Miss Your Mother Until She's Gone" (Silvertone 8160; Supertone 9247; recorded in New York City in early October 1927)

AS DAVID FOLEY
"I'll Never Be Yours" (Challenge 393; reverse by Marion Underwood and Sam Harris; recorded in New York City in early October 1927)
"You Never Miss Your Mother Until She's Gone" (Challenge 394; recorded in New York City in early October 1927)
"Train No. 45"/"Red or Green" (Challenge 397; recorded in New York City, early October 1927 and February 21, 1928)

AS GREYSON THOMAS AND WILL LOTTY
"Nobody's Darling"/"You Never Miss Your Mother Until She's Gone" (Champion 15395; recorded in New York City in early October 1927)

Clarence Greene

Old time fiddler Clarence Horton Greene was born June 26, 1894, in Cranberry Gap, Mitchell County, an area now part of Avery County, N.C. Clarence learned to play the guitar at an early age and took up the five-string banjo at age 12. He was married on November 19, 1918, to Cordie M. Coffey of Foscoe, N.C. Soon after taking up the fiddle in the early 1920s, he started winning numerous prizes at various fiddlers' conventions.

After an unsuccessful audition for OKeh Records in Atlanta and an unreleased recording session for Edison, Greene was recorded by Columbia on November 5, 1927, in Atlanta, Georgia. Two singles—"On the Banks of the Ohio" and "Fond Affection"—were issued under Greene's name, although Will Abernathy accompanied Greene's vocals and guitar work with his harmonica and autoharp. Greene and Abernathy recorded two additional sides with two singers from Brevard, N.C., as the Blue Ridge Singers. (Abernathy in fact had to take Columbia to court to recoup the group's traveling expenses.)

In October of 1928 Greene and Avery County's Wise Brothers (Omer Sr. and Bee) recorded for Columbia in Johnson City, Tennessee, and Greene did some solo work for Victor in Bristol, Tennessee. In 1929 Greene teamed up with Byrd Moore and Clarence (Tom) Ashley and recorded four sides (for which they were paid $900) in Johnson City on October 23, 1929, under the name Byrd Moore and His Hot Shots. In February 1930 Greene cut four sides (two of which were not issued) with Byrd Moore in Richmond, Indiana, for the Starr Piano Company. Greene's final recording session occurred during

(Left to right) Byrd Moore, Clarence Greene and Tom Ashley display their instruments and records (as Byrd Moore's Hot Shots) in Ashe County, N.C., 1929 (Southern Historical Collection, Wilson Library, The University of North Carolina at Chapel Hill).

the final months of 1931 with the Blue Ridge Mountain Entertainers, a group that consisted of Greene, Tom Ashley, Gwen Foster, Will Abernathy and Walter Davis. This band cut 20 sides for the American Record Corporation in New York City; the sides were released on different ARC labels under different names.

After turning down an offer to play on WLS in Chicago with Lulu Belle and Scotty, Greene formed the Toe River Valley Boys in the late 1930s. Other original band members included guitarists Homer Pitman and Ray Young, banjoist Mack Crow and Dobroist Gus Washburn. This band remained active in the 1990s, led by fiddler Oscar (Red) Wilson of Bakersville.

Greene, who now lived in Penland, N.C., formed the Mount Mitchell Ramblers in the 1940s, with Walter Davis on banjo and Jay McCool on guitar. The Ramblers broadcast on WBRM Radio at Marion. Greene continued playing with the Toe River Valley Boys, who found success at local fiddlers' conventions in the late 1940s and early 1950s. In early November 1953 the Farmers Federation of Asheville sponsored a trip to New York City by a string band that included Greene and Steve Ledford on fiddles, Gaither Robinson on banjo, Herman Jones on guitar and "Panhandle Pete" Nash on bass.

Clarence's son (resulting from a second marriage, to Hazel Willis, whom he wed on December 29, 1930), Clarence Howard Greene (born April 29, 1945), started playing guitar with him by the summer of 1961. They, along with Gus Washburn and Donald McKinney, provided music for the popular outdoor drama *Horn in the West* in Boone. Clarence Howard Greene is a mandolinist and guitarist who has played with the Toe River Valley Boys, the Lincoln County Partners, Cedar Creek, and the Maple Ridge Band. He is also a prolific writer and historian of old time music.

Clarence Horton Greene died unexpectedly on October 22, 1961, at Spruce Pine, N.C.

Discography

"On the Banks of the Ohio"/"Fond Affection" (Columbia 15311-D; recorded in Atlanta, Georgia, on November 5, 1927; also features Will Abernathy)

"Johnson City Blues"/"Ninety-Nine Years in Jail" (Columbia 15461-D; recorded in Johnson City, Tennessee, on October 15, 1928; also features the Wise Brothers)

"Goodnight, Darling"/"Little Bunch of Roses" (Victor V-40141; recorded in Bristol, Tennessee, on October 30, 1928)

AS THE BLUE RIDGE SINGERS

"I Want to Go There Don't You"/"Glory Is Now Rising in My Soul" (Columbia 15228-D; recorded in Atlanta, Georgia, on November 5, 1927)

AS CLARENCE GREENE AND THE WISE BROTHERS

"Pride of the Ball"/"Kitty Waltz" (Columbia 15680-D; recorded in Johnson City, Tennessee, on October 15, 1928)

AS BYRD MOORE AND HIS HOT SHOTS

"Frankie Silvers"/"The Hills of Tennessee" (Columbia 15536; recorded in Johnson City, Tennessee, on October 23, 1929)

"Careless Love"/"Three Men Went A-Hunting" (Columbia 15496; recorded in Johnson City, Tennessee, on October 23, 1929)

AS MOORE AND GREENE

"Cincinnati Rag"/"Pig Apple" (Champion 16357; Superior 2838; recorded in Richmond, Indiana, on February 13, 1930)

WITH THE BLUE RIDGE MOUNTAIN ENTERTAINERS

"Cincinnati Breakdown"/"Honeysuckle Rag" (Banner 32432; Romeo 5134; Oriole 8134; Perfect 12805; recorded in New York City on December 1, 1931)

"Washington and Lee Swing"/"Goodnight Waltz" (Banner 32356; Romeo 5116; Oriole 8116; Perfect 12782; Conqueror 7942; recorded in New York City on December 1, 1931)

AS TOM ASHLEY AND CLARENCE GREENE

"Penitentiary Bound"/"Short Life of Trouble" (Conqueror 8149; recorded in New York City on November 30, 1931)

"Short Life of Trouble"/"Corrine Corrina" (Banner 32427; Romeo 5129; Oriole 8129; Perfect 12800; New World 236 ["Corrine..." only]; recorded in New York City on November 30 and December 2, 1931)

AS TOM ASHLEY AND GWEN FOSTER
"Baby All Night Long"/"My Sweet Farm Girl" (Vocalion 02780; recorded in New York City on November 30 and December 1, 1931; Greene plays only on "Baby...")

AS TOM ASHLEY AND GWEN FOSTER/BLUE RIDGE MOUNTAIN ENTER-
TAINERS
"I Have No Loving Mother Now"/"Bring Me a Leaf from the Sea" (Banner 32478; Romeo 5152; Oriole 8152; Perfect 12822; Melotone 12425; recorded in New York City on December 1 and 2, 1931; Greene plays only on "I Have...")

AS TOM ASHLEY
"Over at Tom's House"/"The Fiddler's Contest" (Conqueror 8103; recorded in New York City on December 1, 1931)
A Collection of Mountain Songs (County 504; released 1965; edited by David Freeman; consists of commercial 78 rpm recordings made from 1927 to 1930; Byrd Moore and His Hot Shots perform "Careless Love")
The String Bands, Vol. 2 (Old Timey 101; released 1965; edited by Chris Strachwitz; liner notes by Strachwitz; consists of 16 commercial 78 rpm recordings made from 1922 to the 1950s; Byrd Moore and His Hot Shots are featured on "Three Men Went A-Hunting")
Ballads and Songs (Old Timey 102; released 1965; edited by Chris Strachwitz; liner notes by Toni Brown; consists of 16 commercial 78 rpm recordings made from 1925 to 1939; Byrd Moore and His Hot Shots perform "Frankie Silvers")
Mountain Blues (County 511; released ca. 1966; edited by David Freeman; consists of 12 commercial 78 rpm recordings made in the 1920s and 1930s; Clarence Greene performs "Johnson City Blues")
Roots 'n' Blues: The Retrospective (1925–50) (Columbia Legacy 47911/47912-15; released 1992; brochure notes by Pete Welding and Lawrence Cohn; Clarence Greene plays "Johnson City Blues")
Old-Time Mountain Ballads (County 3504; released 1996; annotated by Charles Wolfe; Clarence Greene performs "Frankie Silvers")

Albert Hash

Old-time fiddler and musical instrument craftsman Albert Hash was born June 27, 1917, on Cabin Creek in Whitetop, Virginia, to Abraham Lincoln Hash and Della May (Long) Hash. His uncle, Emmett Long, was a clawhammer banjo player, and Albert was influenced by the fiddling of his great uncle George Finlay. A primary inspiration for Albert was Corbitt Stamper, whom he first heard fiddle in the mid–1920s. At about the age of 10 Albert made his first fiddle from some boards and a cheese crate.

Albert Hash (left) and the Whitetop Mountain Band (from left, Emily Spencer, Flurry Dowe, Thornton Spencer) in a casual pose from the late 1970s (photo by Mark V. Sanderford/courtesy Dale Morris).

Growing up, Hash took a keen interest in local musicians such as John Stringer, Howard Wyatt and Black Charlie Miller. The annual Whitetop Mountain Fiddlers' Convention provided Hash with additional exposure to old-time music. As a teenage Hash's musical hero was fiddler G.B. Grayson. After Grayson's tragic death in 1930, Henry Whitter asked Hash—who had memorized most of Grayson and Whitter's tunes—to play with him at schools and theaters across the mountains of North Carolina and Virginia. They played together for about a year.

In the 1940s Hash played in a number of bands, the most outstanding of which was the original White Top Mountain Band: Dent Blevins (mandolin), Frank Blevins (guitar), Henry Blevins (guitar), Archie Finlay (guitar) and Hash (fiddle). Hash then played with John Yates and the Spice Bottom Boys out of Taylor's Valley, Virginia. In the 1950s Hash played on and off with the Carolina Troubadours, a group that included Dean Hart (bass), Gerald Little (drums), Bob Powers (electric guitar), Jim Poe (guitar), Elmer Powers (electric guitar), Clay Wilson (lead singer) and Brian Adams (electric steel guitar).

During World War II Hash worked as a tool and die maker at Uncle Sam's Navy, a torpedo factory in Alexandria, Virginia. He attended some

Albert Hash (left) teaching the tricks of the trade to a young Brian Grim (who later formed the Konnarock Critters) in Willard Gayheart's "Lesson for Brian" (courtesy Willard Gayheart).

fiddlers' conventions in that region before returning to Grayson County after the war ended. Hash then gained employment as a machinist at Sprague Electric Company in Lansing, Ashe County, N.C. He then worked as a model maker for five years or so at Brunswick Powder Works in Sugar Grove, Virginia. Hash still played music, but only intermittently.

In the mid–1960s, when there was renewed interest in old-time mountain music, Hash taught the art of instrument making and repair to Wayne Henderson, a young guitar picker and luthier from nearby Rugby, Virginia. Henderson in turn helped persuade Hash to again return to fiddling. The duo formed a band called the Virginia-Carolina Boys, and for eight years they played on WKSK in West Jefferson, N.C.

About three years after the demise of the Virginia-Carolina Boys, Hash formed the Whitetop Mountain Band, which has recorded for the Heritage and Mountain labels. Other band members have included Hash's brother-in-law, fiddler Thornton Spencer (born 1935) of Whitetop; Thornton's wife, vocalist-guitar player Emily Paxton Spencer (raised in Arlington, Virginia);

bass fiddler Tom Barr of Galax, Virginia; guitarist-singer Becky Haga Barr of Galax; banjoist Flurry Dowe (born 1960; originally from Montgomery, Alabama) of Grayson County, Virginia; and guitarist Fred Taylor of Jefferson, N.C. Also playing with the band at various times have been Estil Ball, Paul Spencer, Ted Trivette, Kenneth Blevins, Spence Pennington (of Warrensville, N.C.) and Leon Hill.

Albert and his wife Ethel had two daughters, Rosemary Joyce (born ca. 1945) and Audrey Hash Ham (born ca. 1949, she now lives in Mouth of Wilson, Virginia), both of whom are multi-instrumentalists and luthiers. Albert Hash died from a heart attack on January 28, 1983, but his memory lives on in the annual Albert Hash Memorial Festival.

The Whitetop Mountain Band, which was split up in 1992 when the Spencers and Barrs went their separate ways, was reconstituted in the late 1990s with Thornton Spencer on fiddle, Emily Spencer on clawhammer banjo and handling vocals, Johnny Gentry on guitar and Nancy Gentry on bass. The Gentrys are from the Mountain Park community in Surry County, N.C.

Discography

Old Originals, Vol. 2 (Rounder 0058; released 1978; Albert Hash performs "Nancy Blevins" and "Cripple Creek")

Two original members of the Whitetop Mountain Band, Emily and Thornton Spencer, perform at the 1999 Wayne C. Henderson Festival at the Grayson Highlands State Park in Virginia (photo by the author).

WITH THE WHITETOP MOUNTAIN BAND
39th National Folk Festival (NCTA 77; released 1977; Albert Hash and the Whitetop Mountain Band perform "I'll Fly Away" and "Single Girl")
Whitetop (Mountain M-311; rereleased as Heritage 041 ca. 1981; consists of 12 cuts)
Cacklin' Hen (Mountain M-313; rereleased as Heritage XXVII in 1977)
Albert Hash and the Whitetop Mountain Band (Heritage XXV; released 1979; produced
by Fred Williams; recorded and jacket design by Bobby Patterson; photography
by Mark V. Sanderford; notes by Emily Spencer and Patterson; consists of 14
tracks)
Winebarger's Mill (Heritage 046C; released 1983; recorded in Galax, Virginia, in 1979
and 1983, and [two tracks] for the Conservation Foundation/National Forest
Film in September 1977; produced by Fred Williams; jacket notes by Andy
Cahan)
My Old Home's in Whitetop Mountain (released 1991)
Swing Your Partner and Promenade! (Heritage HRC-C-126; released 1998; recorded
and mixed by Bobby Patterson; photography by Jerry Bryant; notes by Thorn-
ton & Emily Spencer and Johnny & Nancy Gentry; also features the calls of
Bryan Dolinger and Dean Carr and the flatfoot dancing of C.T. Janney and
Jackie Martin)

Wayne Henderson

Wayne C. Henderson, a superb guitar picker and nationally renowned
craftsman of musical instruments, lives in Rugby, Virginia, and is a native of
Ashe County, where he was born on May 3, 1947. Wayne's father Walter
Henderson was an old-time fiddler and a member (along with E.C. Ball and
Wade Reedy) of the Rugby Gully Jumpers string band from about 1936 to
1940.

Wayne received a plastic toy guitar from his grandfather when he was 3
years old and started playing a real guitar—his brother Max's Gibson Recording King—when he was 5. He tried to build one when he was 10, using a
cardboard box with a whittled-down two-by-four for a neck. He used fishing
line for the strings. He was a little more successful with his next attempt, using
veneer and weatherstripping glue, but the glue soon melted and the guitar
came apart. Eventually Wayne's father introduced him to Albert Hash, a
fiddler and luthier who took Henderson under his wing and taught him the
tricks of the trade. Hash gave Henderson some mahogany plywood from
which Henderson made a guitar that became his first sale, around 1964.

Henderson learned about music from his family and neighbors such as
Kathryn Reedy, who taught him Carter Family tunes. He was also strongly
influenced by guitarist E.C. Ball, who also hailed from Rugby and ran a country store where Henderson learned to pick.

Henderson's first job as a player came in 1964, on a Saturday morning

Performing as the High County Ramblers are (left to right) Larry Pennington, Johnny Miller, Herb Key, Carol Henderson and Wayne Henderson (courtesy Herb Key).

radio show on WKSK in West Jefferson, N.C. Wayne's brother Max, Albert Hash, Rector Haire and Boyd Stewart were also members of the Virginia-Carolina Boys, who played together for eight years. Jim Brooks (born 1932) and J.C. King were banjo players from Jefferson who played rather frequently with the group. (Brooks, who in the early 1950s had played with Alex and Ola Belle Campbell and the New River Boys and Girls, would later play in the Tarheel Travelers with Rector Haire, Gene Owens, Carroll Haire, Ralph Pennington and his brother Harold.)

From 1968 until 1973 Henderson worked part-time for George Gruhn and Randy Wood making and repairing vintage instruments in Nashville, Tennessee. Henderson next played in a band with his wife Carol (violin), brother Max (mandolin), Gerald Anderson (bass), Harry Jones (rhythm guitar) and Carson Cooper (banjo). This group stayed together until around 1985, at which time Henderson joined the High County Ramblers. He played with the Ramblers for a few years before beginning the practice—still followed today—of playing with a varied, fluid cast of musicians whom are referred to as his "pickin' buddies."

Performing on a live radio show on December 12, 1998, out of WKSK in West Jefferson, N.C., are (left to right) Tim Lewis, Wayne Henderson, Max Henderson and Herb Key (courtesy Herb Key).

Henderson's unique picking method has been called "pinch picking" because he plays exclusively with fingerpicks and appears to be "pinching" the strings when playing. Rather than using a flatpick, though, Henderson alternates his thumb and forefinger to play the single-note lines of fiddle tunes and old-time songs.

Over the years Henderson has built more than 200 guitars, more than 75 mandolins, more than 20 banjos, and a few fiddles, dulcimers and Dobros. He builds his guitars from walnut, maple and spruce, and no two Henderson guitars are exactly alike.

Henderson has built guitars for, among others, Doc Watson, Norman Blake, Peter Rowan, Mick Maloney and Eric Clapton, who came across a Henderson guitar in a recording studio in New York and put in an order after playing it. He has also built a mandolin for Ricky Skaggs.

Wayne has played in Taiwan, Hong Kong, Thailand, South Korea, Indonesia, the Philippines, Oman, Pakistan and Sri Lanka, participating in a National Council for the Traditional Arts tour of Southeast Asia in 1982. In 1990 he joined Jerry Douglas, John Cephas, Ledward Kaapana, Albert Lee and Tal Farlow on the first "Masters of the Steel-String Guitar" tour sponsored by the N.C.T.A. In late 1999 he made another such tour, along with Eddie Pennington, Cephas, Phil Wiggins and Johnny Bellard.

Henderson has played at Carnegie Hall—using a guitar he built—and frequently picks with Doc Watson and many of his musical friends. He received a National Heritage Fellowship Award from the National Endowment for the Arts in 1995, and a guitar and mandolin he built were displayed in the Smithsonian Institution.

In 1995 the first Wayne C. Henderson Music Festival and Guitar Competition was held in Grayson Highlands State Park, which is close to Henderson's home. Proceeds from the event went toward a couple of music camp scholarships. Henderson also teaches at guitar camps including the Augusta Heritage Workshop, Mars Hill College Blue Ridge Old-Time Music Week, and Puget Sound Guitar Workshop. A frequent winner at festivals, Henderson took first prize in guitar at the 1997 and 1998 Galax Old Fiddlers' Conventions, and in 1998 he was also named the best all-around performer.

Discography

36th Annual Galax Old Fiddlers Convention (Gazette 36; released 1971; Wayne Henderson performs "Little Rosewood Casket")

37th Annual Galax Old Fiddlers Convention (Gazette 37; released 1972; Wayne Henderson performs "Cannon Ball Blues")

38th Annual Galax Old Fiddlers Convention (Gazette 38; released 1973; Wayne Henderson performs "Rose Wood Casket")

Wayne Henderson and Ray Cline Guitar Pickin' with Herb Key (Heritage IX; released 1977; recorded by Bobby Patterson in January of 1976; produced by Fred Williams; cover artwork by Willard Gayheart; jacket notes by Dale Allen; Cline accompanies Henderson on guitar, while Key strums the upright bass)

45th Annual Galax Old Fiddlers Convention (Gazette 45; released 1980; Wayne Henderson performs "Grey Eagle")

The High County Ramblers (Heritage XIII; released 1986; liner notes by Dale Morris; consists of 14 field and studio recordings; musicians include Larry Pennington on banjo, Raymond Pennington on mandolin, Paul Gentle on rhythm guitar, Herb Key on bass, Wayne Henderson on lead guitar and Johnny Miller on fiddle)

Wayne Henderson and Robin Kesinger: Contest Favorites (Flyin' Cloud 010; released 1989)

Rugby Guitar (Flying Fish 542/70542; released 1990; engineered by Pete Reiniger; liner notes by Joe Wilson; also featured are Randy Greer on mandolin, Emily Spencer on banjo and fiddle, Thornton Spencer on fiddle and guitar, Gerald Anderson on guitar and Scott Freeman on fiddle)

Folk Masters: Great Performances Recorded Live... (Smithsonian/Folkways 40047; released 1993; Wayne Henderson performs "Gray Eagle" accompanied by Randy Greer on mandolin and Tony Testerman on bass)

W.C. Henderson & Company (Hay Holler 107; released 1994; produced by Dale Allen, Wayne Henderson and Joseph C. Robins; engineered by Allen Conner; mixed by Butch Robins, Wayne Henderson and Allen Conner; also features Doc Watson, Jeff Little, Butch Robins, David Holt, Carson Cooper, Gerald Anderson, Randy Greer, Tony Testerman, Katy Taylor, Herb Key, Helen White, Tim Lewis and Kevin Jackson)

Wayne Henderson and Steve Kaufman: Not Much Work for Saturday (Hay Holler 109; released 1996; Kaufman is a three-time national guitar champion)

The American Fogies, Vol. 1 (Rounder 0379; released 1996; produced by Ray Alden; Wayne Henderson performs "Chow Time")
Blue Ridge Mountain Holiday: The Breaking Up Christmas Story (County 2722; released 1997; produced by Paul Brown; production coordinated by Burgess Hurd; field recordings made by Paul Brown, Bob Carlin, Terri McMurray, Ray Alden and Dave Spilkia; Henderson performs "Cherokee Shuffle" with Jim Lloyd and Gerald Anderson)
60th Annual [Galax] Old Fiddlers' Convention (Heritage HRC-C-712; released 1997; Wayne Henderson picks "Done Gone")

The Highlanders

A Galax-based bluegrass band, the Highlanders were formed in 1970 and recorded numerous albums on the Princess and Heritage labels. The central figures in this still-active band have been singer-guitarist Willard Gayheart, banjoist Jimmy Zeh and guitarist-banjoist Bobby Patterson.

Gayheart was born and raised in Lotts Creek, which is near Hazard, Kentucky. As a young boy he listened to the Blue Sky Boys and the Monroe Brothers, and taught himself how to play the guitar. He left home to attend Berea College in 1949, and in 1962 he moved to Galax. Around 1963 an early version of the Highlanders, called the Mountain County Boys, was formed with Gayheart on guitar, Junior Wooten on fiddle, Gus Ingo of Wytheville on mandolin and Bobby Patterson of Galax on banjo. After Ingo left the band to play with the McPeak Brothers, Warren Casto was brought in on mandolin.

Zeh—a native of Rocky Mount, Virginia, and now a resident of Galax—started playing with the group in 1966, a musical reunion of sorts for him and Gayheart, for both had played for a time with the famed Mountain Ramblers. Over the years the members of the Highlanders have included bassist Marvin Cockram of Meadows of Dan, Virginia, and Roy Bourne of Elk Creek, Virginia, on Dobro. Mike Sizemore later replaced Casto on mandolin. Patterson, a former Camp Creek Boy, has played multiple instruments for the band and also produced their work on Heritage, his own label.

In addition to his musical and songwriting talents, Gayheart is recognized as one of the preeminent portrait artists in the Southeast. He specializes in drawing local mountain musicians, using pencil, charcoal and watercolors.

Gayheart formed another band, Skeeter and the Skidmarks, in the early 1990s. This progressive old-time band made two recordings on the Hay Holler label. An equally talented songwriter, Gayheart penned Ric-O-Chet's "My Last Run," which stayed on the bluegrass charts for several weeks in 1996. In the late 1990s Gayheart joined the five-piece acoustic band Alternate Roots. The Highlanders continued to play at festivals and other gatherings well into the late 1990s. Bobby Patterson and Marvin Cockram are still in the band, playing with banjoist Tim Lineberry, fiddler Johnny Jackson of Woodlawn, Virginia, lead singer and guitarist Johnny Joyce of Stuart, Virginia, and harmony singer Helen Cockram (Marvin's wife). Jackson has performed and recorded with bands that include Alex Campbell and Ola Belle Reed, Ted Lundy and the Southern Mountain Boys, the Virginia Mountain Boys and the Christian Quartet.

Discography

This, That & More (Princess)
Appalachian Hills (Princess)
Get on Board (Princess)
Doin' Things Our Way (Heritage I; released 1974)
Buddy Pendleton and the Highlanders: Live (Blue Ridge Records [no number]; released ca. 1978; recorded by Fred Williams and Bobby Patterson; cover artwork and jacket notes by Willard Gayheart; Pendleton is a multi-winner of the "world champion" fiddlers' contest at Union Grove, N.C.)
Gus Ingo's Mandolin Album (Heritage XX; released 1979; recorded, cover and jacket notes by Bobby Patterson; Ingo is backed up by the Highlanders [Gayheart, Zeh and Cockram], as well as Buddy Pendleton on fiddle and Wayne Henderson on lead guitar)
The Highlanders with Tim Lineberry: From There to Here (Heritage HRC-C 618)
The Highlanders with John Jackson & Tim Lineberry: Four Days in August (Heritage HRC-CD 121; released 1996)

The Hill Billies

The Hill Billies, an early old-time string band, radio and vaudeville act, was organized in Galax, Virginia, in the mid–1920s. The band's original members were fiddler Alonzo Elvis "Tony" Alderman of Carroll County, Virginia, pianist-vocalist Al Hopkins, who lived in Gap Creek, N.C., in southern Ashe County, Al's brother Joe Hopkins on ukulele, Tennessee fiddler Charlie Bowman, and banjoist John Rector, a Galax general store operator who arranged the band's initial recording session. Rector had recorded in 1924 with Henry Whitter's Virginia Breakdowners but was dissatisfied with the results and wanted to put together another band.

The Hopkins-Alderman-Rector Band (as they were originally called) recorded six titles for the OKeh Recording Company on January 15, 1925, in New York City. On that day Al Hopkins referred to his band as a group of North Carolina hillbillies, which in turn inspired OKeh talent scout Ralph S. Peer to list the six selections on company ledger sheets as performed by the "Hillbillies." The term "hillbilly" had been in general usage in America

The Hill Billies, an early old time string band, radio and vaudeville act, toured up and down the East Coast in the late 1920s and early 1930s (Southern Historical Collection, Wilson Library, The University of North Carolina at Chapel Hill).

since the turn of the twentieth century, but this was the first time the word was used in reference to early country or rural Southern folk music. "Hillbilly" distinguished white, Southern, rural mountain music from black or "race" music.

The Hill Billies' music—unique in that it prominently featured Hopkins' portable piano—was first released in February 1925 and broadcast in March on WRC out of Washington, D.C. A series of extensive tours took them from the Deep South to the Northeast. In 1927 they played in New York City and broadcast over WJZ.

The following year they performed in vaudeville shows and theaters in New York, New Jersey and Pennsylvania. In 1928 they also made the 15-minute short *The Hill Billies*, the first film featuring country music for Vitaphone (Warner Bros.). Washington, D.C., became their home base, and there they were invited to play for President Calvin Coolidge.

Most of the Hill Billies' recordings (for Victor [never issued], OKeh, Vocalion and Brunswick—as the Buckle Busters) featured twin fiddlers

Alderman and Bowman. Banjo duties were performed at various times by Rector, Jack Reedy and Walter Bowman. The group's guitarists included Elbert Bowman, Joe Hopkins, Walter "Sparkplug" Hughes, and Frank Wilson on slide. Uncle "Am" Stuart, a pioneer of country music recording, held down the fiddle chores along with Fred Roe, "Dad" Williams and Ed Belcher. The band also employed the string bass of Henry Roe and the often hilarious harmonica and ukulele playing of Elmer and John Hopkins.

The Hill Billies had disbanded by 1933 following the death of Al Hopkins—the band's spiritual and professional leader—in a 1932 automobile accident.

Discography

"Old Joe Clark"/"Whoa! Mule" (OKeh 40376; recorded in New York City ca. January 1925)

"Silly Bill"/"Old Time Cinda" (OKeh 40294; recorded in New York City ca. January 1925)

"Cripple Creek"/"Sally Ann" (OKeh 40336; recorded in New York City ca. January 1925)

John Rector (left), the founding member of the Hill Billies, takes part in a 1984 jam session with Frank Bode (guitar) and Dale Morris (banjo) while Whit Sizemore (hat) and Chester McMillian look on (photo by Alice Gerrard/courtesy Dale Morris).

"Mountaineers Love Song"/"Cripple Creek" (Vocalion 15367 and Vocalion 5115; recorded in New York City ca. April 1926)

"Old Joe Clark"/"Silly Bill" (Vocalion 15369 and Vocalion 5117; recorded in New York City ca. April 1926)

"Mississippi Sawyers"/"Long Eared Mule" (Vocalion 15368 and Vocalion 5116; recorded in New York City ca. April 1926)

"Fisher's Hornpipe"/"Blue-Eyed Girl" (Vocalion 5017; recorded in New York City on October 21 and 22, 1926)

"Cackling Hen"/"Donkey on the Railroad Track" (Vocalion 5020; recorded in New York City on October 21 and 23, 1926)

"East Tennessee Blues"/"Governor Alf Taylor's Fox Chase" (Vocalion 5016; recorded in New York City on October 21, 1926)

"Walking in the Parlor"/"Cumberland Gap" (Vocalion 5024; recorded in New York City on October 22, 1926)

"Cinda"/"Round-Town Girls" (Vocalion 5025; recorded in New York City on October 22, 1926)

"Bristol, Tennessee Blues"/"Buck-Eyed Rabbits" (Vocalion 5023; recorded in New York City on October 22, 1926)

"Sourwood Mountain"/"Ragged Annie" (Vocalion 5022; recorded in New York City on October 22, 1926)

"Texas Gals"/"Going Down the Road Feeling Bad" (Vocalion 5021; recorded in New York City on October 22 and 23, 1926)

"Sally Ann"/"Kitty Waltz" (Vocalion 5019; recorded in New York City on October 23, 1926)

"Betsy Brown"/"Kitty Wells" (Vocalion 5018; recorded in New York City on October 23, 1926)

"Sweet Bunch of Daisies"/"Daisies Won't Tell" (Vocalion 5178 and Brunswick 174; recorded in New York City on May 13, 1927)

"Sleep, Baby, Sleep"/"Darling Nellie Gray" (Vocalion 5186 and Brunswick 185; recorded in New York City on May 13 and 16, 1927)

"Black-Eyed Susie"/"Cluck Old Hen" (Vocalion 5179 and Brunswick 175; recorded in New York City on May 13, 1927)

"Hear Dem Bells" (Vocalion 5173; recorded in New York City on May 16, 1927)

"Georgia Buck"/"Baby Your Time Ain't Long" (Vocalion 5182 and Brunswick 183; recorded in New York City on May 16 and 17, 1927)

"She'll Be Coming 'Round the Mountain" (Vocalion 5240 and Brunswick 181; recorded in New York City on May 16, 1927)

"Oh Where Is My Little Dog Gone" (Vocalion 5183 and Brunswick 187; recorded in New York City on May 17, 1927)

A Collection of Mountain Fiddle Music (County 501; released 1963; edited by David Freeman; consists of commercial 78 rpm recordings made from 1927 to 1930; the Hill Billies perform "Cluck Old Hen")

A Fiddlers' Convention in Mountain City, Tennessee (County 525; released 1972; three-page insert booklet by Joe Wilson; consists of 12 commercial 78 rpm recordings made from 1925 to 1930; the Hill Billies are featured on "Blue-Eyed Girl," "Boatin' Up Sandy" and "Buck Eyed Rabbits")

The Hill-Billies (County 405; released 1974; edited by David Freeman; liner notes and four-page brochure by Joe Wilson; consists of 12 commercial 78 rpm recordings made from 1925 to 1932)

Tennessee Strings (Rounder 1033; released 1979; edited by Charles Wolfe; liner notes by Charles Wolfe; consists of 16 commercial 78 rpm recordings made in the

1920s and 1930s; Charlie Bowman with the Hill Billies perform "The Hickman Rag")

Complete Recordings, Volume 1, 1925–1926 (Document DOCD-8039-CD; released 1998; consists of 23 songs)

Complete Recordings, Volume 2, 1926–1927 (Document DOCD-8040-CD; released 1998; consists of 23 songs)

Complete Recordings, Volume 3, 1927–1928 (Document DOCD-8041-CD; released 1998; consists of 24 songs)

AS AL HOPKINS AND HIS BUCKLE BUSTERS

"East Tennessee Blues"/"Round-Town Girls" (Brunswick 103; recorded in New York City on October 21 and 22, 1926)

"Bristol, Tennessee Blues"/"Buck-Eyed Rabbits" (Brunswick 104; recorded in New York City on October 22, 1926)

"Cinda"/"Sally Ann" (Brunswick 105; recorded in New York City on October 22 and 23, 1926)

"Governor Alf Taylor's Fox Chase"/"Kitty Waltz" (Brunswick 106; recorded in New York City on October 21 and 23, 1926)

"Sweet Bunch of Daisies"/"Daisies Won't Tell" (Brunswick 174; recorded in New York City on May 13, 1927)

"Black-Eyed Susie"/"Cluck Old Hen" (Brunswick 175; recorded in New York City on May 13, 1927)

"Nine Pound Hammer"/"C.C. & O. No. 558" (Brunswick 177; recorded in New York City on May 13 and 16, 1927)

"Whoa! Mule"/"Johnson Boys" (Brunswick 179; recorded in New York City on May 13 and 14, 1927)

"Blue Ridge Mountain Blues"/"Echoes of the Chimes" (Brunswick 180; recorded in New York City on May 12 and 14, 1927)

"She'll Be Coming 'Round the Mountain" (Brunswick 181; recorded in New York City on May 16, 1927)

"Boatin' Up the Sandy"/"Bug in the Taters" (Brunswick 182; recorded in New York City on May 14 and 17, 1927)

"Georgia Buck"/"Baby Your Time Ain't Long" (Brunswick 183; recorded in New York City on May 16 and 17, 1927)

"Down to the Club"/"The Feller That Looked Like Me" (Brunswick 184; recorded in New York City on May 13 and 16, 1927)

"Sleep, Baby, Sleep"/"Darling Nellie Gray" (Brunswick 185; recorded in New York City on May 13 and 16, 1927)

"Ride That Mule"/"Roll on the Ground" (Brunswick 186; recorded in New York City on May 16 and 17, 1927)

"Oh Where Is My Little Dog Gone"/"Wasn't She Dandy" (Brunswick 187; recorded in New York City on May 17, 1927)

"Gideon's Band"/"Old Dan Tucker" (Brunswick 295; recorded in New York City on December 20, 1928)

"Old Uncle Ned"/"Blue Bell" (Brunswick 300; recorded in New York City on December 20, 1928)

"West Virginia Gals"/"Carolina Moonshiner" (Brunswick 318; recorded in New York City on December 20, 1928)

"Polka Medley (Intro: Rocky Road to Dublin/Jenny Lind)"/"Marsovia Waltz" (Brunswick 321; recorded in New York City on December 20, 1928)

"Wild Hoss"/"Medley of Old Time Dance Tunes (Soldier's Joy/Turkey Buzzard/

When You Go A-courting)" (Brunswick 335; recorded in New York City on December 20, 1928)

Mountain Frolic (Brunswick 59000; released 1947 [78 rpm format]; reissued in Japan on Coral MH 174; edited by Alan Lomax; 18-page booklet by Lomax; consists of studio recordings made from 1927 to 1931; Al Hopkins and His Buckle Busters perform "Black Eyed Susie" and "Cluck, Old Hen")

Songs of the Railroad Recorded 1924–1934 (Vetco 103; released ca. 1971; liner notes by Bob Hyland; consists of 16 commercial 78 rpm recordings made from 1924 to 1934; Al Hopkins and His Buckle Busters perform "C.C. and O. Number 558" and "The Nine Pound Hammer")

The Cold-Water Pledge, Vol. 1: Songs of Moonshine and Temperance Recorded in the Golden Age (Marimac 9104 [cassette]; released 1984; edited by Pat Conte; contains brief insert leaflet; booklet by W.K. McNeil sold separately; Al Hopkins and His Buckle Busters are featured on "Carolina Moonshiner")

AS CHARLIE BOWMAN
"The Hickman Rag"/"Possum Up a Gum Stump, Cooney in the Hollow" (Vocalion 15337 and Vocalion 5118; recorded in New York City ca. April 1926)

AS CHARLIE BOWMAN AND HIS BROTHERS
"Roll On Buddy"/"Gonna Raise a Ruckus Tonight" (Columbia 15357; recorded in Johnson City, Tennessee, on October 16, 1928)

"Polly Ann"/"Katy-did Waltz" (Columbia 15372; recorded in New York City on February 20, 1929)

"Forky Deer"/"Moonshiner and His Money" (Columbia 15387; recorded in New York City on February 20, 1929)

Hill Brothers and Simmons

Brothers Bill and Dewey (born April 8, 1906) Hill grew up in Surry County, on a farm about 12 miles south of Mount Airy. Like their other siblings, Bill and Dewey were musically inclined: Bill picked the autoharp and fiddle, while Dewey played the guitar and harmonica. Willie Simmons, a neighbor, sang with the brothers, who learned to sing out of the seven-shape-note books taught at the local singing schools.

In April 1930, Dewey and his brother Sam traveled with Earl R. Nance and his family to New York City to record sacred and secular songs for ARC. (Bill, only 15 at the time, was considered too young for the trip.) In 1932, with the Depression ruining the local farm economy, Bill moved to Stanley-town, Virginia, to work for the Stanley Furniture Company. For a short time Dewey joined him, but by 1935 he had returned to Surry County. While in Henry County Bill and Dewey played with local musicians and performed in a string band called the Henry County Revelers over WBTM in Danville, Virginia. Other band members were Guy Norton (fiddle), Lancaster Turner (banjo), their brother Sam Hill (autoharp) and Curtis Turner (guitar).

(From left) Bill Hill, Willie Simmons and Dewey Hill in Henry County, Virginia, around 1935 (Blue Ridge Heritage Archive).

The Hill Brothers and Simmons passed a personal audition for the RCA Victor Company in Charlotte, North Carolina, in August 1937. They cut six tracks—four religious and two secular numbers—during their session on August 6 which were released on the Bluebird and Montgomery Ward labels.

Within a year of this session the Hill brothers started their own families, and subsequently the trio performed together only on occasion. Willie Simmons died on April 10, 1964. Dewey Hill remained in Ararat, had regular radio programs on WBOB in Galax, Virginia, and WPAQ in Mount Airy between 1948 and the late 1960s, and sometimes worked with shape-note singing schools. He performed right up to his death on September 23, 1975. Bill Hill retired in 1980 but later fronted a band, Bill Hill and the Sounds of Country, that played in a four-county area (including his home county of Henry) surrounding Martinsville, Virginia.

Discography

"Just Over in the Glory Land"/"I Am on My Way to Heaven" (Bluebird 7223; recorded in Charlotte, North Carolina, on August 6, 1937)

"I'm Glad I Counted the Cost"/"Just Over in the Glory Land" (Montgomery Ward 7372; recorded in Charlotte, North Carolina, on August 6, 1937)
"Looking to My Prayers"/"I Am on My Way to Heaven" (Montgomery Ward 7373; recorded in Charlotte, North Carolina, on August 6, 1937)
"Sweetheart, I Have Grown So Lonely"/"In the Hills of Old Virginia" (Montgomery Ward 7374; recorded in Charlotte, North Carolina, on August 6, 1937)

Abe Horton

Abe Horton, a clawhammer banjoist and fiddler from Fancy Gap, Virginia, was born on April 11, 1917. His father, Denny A. Horton, played the banjo and fiddled, and Abe took up the fiddle at age 11. Horton's clawhammer style was influenced by his wife's grandfather, Frill Webb (1874–1952), a resident of the Crooked Oak community of Carroll County who played banjo frequently with Abe's father. Abe adopted Webb's method of "double noting" with his left hand. Horton also developed a two-finger style called "secon."

Horton was partially disabled following a tour of duty in World War II and did not play music for 23 years. He organized the Pine River Boys string band around 1970. Other band members included guitarists and vocalists Maybelle Harris and Foy James (Jake) Lewis and fiddlers Walter Morris and Richard Bowman. The Pine River Boys performed at the 1977 National Folk Festival. Horton recorded three albums with the Pine River Boys and two others with blind fiddler and frailer Harold Hausenfluck of Richmond, Virginia, whom he first met in 1972 at the fiddlers' convention in Saltville, Virginia.

Discography

The Pine River Boys Old Time String Band: Hoedown Time (Mountain 305; released 1973)

The Pine River Boys with Maybelle: Out Back (Heritage III; released 1974)

39th National Folk Festival (NCTA 77; released 1977; Abe Horton performs "House Carpenter")

The Pine River Boys with Maybelle: Wild Hog in the Woods (Heritage [no number]; released 1978; recorded and cover by Bobby Patterson; jacket notes by Hal McMullen; also features Maybelle Harris on guitar, Jake Lewis on guitar and Richard Bowman on fiddle)

Abe Horton: Old-Time Music from Fancy Gap (Heritage XIX; released 1978; recorded by Bobby Patterson; album photo by Lincoln Fajardo)

Harold & Abe: Cornbread, Molasses, and Sassafras Tea (Heritage XXIII; released 1978; recorded and cover by Bobby Patterson; jacket notes by Hal McMullen; photography by Lincoln Fajardo)

Abe Horton performs in 1977 as part of the State of Virginia's "Music in the Schools" program (Blue Ridge Heritage Archive).

Abe Horton & Harold Hausenfluck: Sweet Sunny South (Heritage 043; released 1984; recorded by Bobby Patterson in July 1983; produced by Abe & Harold; photography by Clayton Robinson; art direction and design by Ginger M. Kuykendall; jacket notes by Dale Morris)

Ben Jarrell

Benjamin Franklin Jarrell was born in May 1880 in the Round Peak area of Surry County. As early as 1910 he was exposed to vaudeville and parlor music on an old cylinder phonograph. Growing up, Jarrell played frequently with Charlie Lowe (1878–1964), a highly regarded clawhammer banjo player. In 1918 Jarrell left his wife Susan and large family to ramble through the far northwest of Oregon and Washington for three years (spending 18 months in jail for making whiskey) before setting down as a Mount Airy storekeeper in 1921.

Jarrell soon developed considerable skills on the fiddle. In 1927 he traveled to Richmond, Indiana, to record as a member of Da Costa Woltz's Southern Broadcasters string band. Ben fiddled in the old style, called "rocking the bow," which he passed along to his son Tommy, an accomplished old-time fiddler and banjo picker in his own right. Ben Jarrell died in December of 1946.

Discography

"Merry Girl" (Gennett 6143; Jarrell is accompanied by Da Costa Woltz's Southern Broadcasters)

"I Know My Name Is Written There" (Gennett 6164; with Da Costa Woltz's Southern Broadcasters)

"When You Ask a Girl to Leave Her Happy Home" (Gennett 6176; with Da Costa Woltz's Southern Broadcasters)

Going Down the Valley: Vocal and Instrumental Styles in Folk Music from the South (New World Records NW 236; released 1977; edited by Norm Cohen; six-page sewn-in notes by Norm Cohen; consists of 18 studio recordings made from 1926 to 1938; Ben Jarrell and Da Costa Woltz's Southern Broadcasters perform "Old Joe Clark")

Tommy Jarrell

Old-time fiddler and banjoist Thomas Jefferson (Tommy) Jarrell was born March 1, 1901, to Benjamin (Ben) Franklin Jarrell and Susan (Susie) Letisha Amburn Jarrell, a farm family living on Old Low Gap Road, at the foot of Fisher Peak, in the Round Peak section of Surry County. His father Ben was a popular fiddler and member of Da Costa Woltz's Southern Broadcasters string band, which made several records in the 1920s.

Tommy was around 7 when he learned his first tune on the banjo from farmhand Baugie Cockerham. About a year later, Tommy's father bought him his first banjo. At the age of 13, Tommy began to fiddle on his dad's fiddle;

about a year later, he bought his own for $10 from Huston Moore. Jarrell always kept this fiddle, which is now part of the Smithsonian Institution collection in Washington, D.C.

Like his father, Tommy played the old-style fiddle, referred to as "rocking the bow." Tommy was also influenced by the fiddling of his Uncle Charley Jarrell, who married the aunt of fellow Beulah old-time country musician Fred Cockerham. But the single greatest influence on Tommy's playing was Charlie Lowe. Lowe was born in 1878 in the Round Peak area and was the region's preeminent drop thumb clawhammer banjoist. By the time Tommy was 15 he was fiddling at local dances with Lowe.

Tommy's "frailing" style of banjo playing made heavy use of hammering ons, pulling off, slides and drop-thumbing. Comfortable with either fretted or fretless banjos, Jarrell added characteristic nuances to his renditions that influenced many later generations of musicians.

When his father Ben left for Oregon in 1918 to make whiskey, Tommy himself was forced to start making homemade liquor in 1920 to make ends meet. Tommy's family moved to Mount Airy in 1922, and on December 23, 1923, he married Nina Frances Lowe. In 1925 Jarrell stopped making whiskey and playing poker, and in April began working for the N.C. Department of Transportation, a job he retired from in 1966.

Jarrell was little known outside the local area, however, until the mid–1960s when his son B.F. (Benny) Jarrell, a disc jockey in North Carolina, encouraged Alan Jabbour, then a member of the Hollow Rock String Band and later the director of the Library of Congress' American Folklife Division, to visit the Jarrell home and record his father. (Benny [1933–1987] was a member of Jim Eanes' Shenandoah Valley Boys, and he recorded a fiddle album for Heritage Records [*Lady of the Lake*] in the mid–1970s.) The release of this authentic music inspired many urban traditional music enthusiasts to make pilgrimages to Mount Airy to meet Jarrell.

In addition to his extensive recording career, Jarrell played at many colleges and universities around the country. He played at the Smithsonian Institution in Washington, D.C., and in 1982 was selected as one of the 15 master folk artists in the first National Heritage Fellowships of the National Endowment for the Arts. The year before Jarrell was presented the Brown-Hudson Folklore Award by the North Carolina Folklore Society for "in special ways contributing to the appreciation, continuation, or study of North Carolina folk traditions."

In addition to his music Jarrell was featured in several video documentaries, including *Sprout Wings and Fly* (produced by Les Blank, Cece Conway and Alice Gerrard), *My Old Fiddle* (produced by Les Blank) and *Legends of Old Timey Music*. After many years of only occasional musical activity, Jarrell soon returned to his music and acted as teacher for those banjo and fiddle players who sought his instruction. He died on January 8, 1985.

Artist Willard Gayheart's rendition of "Jammin' with Uncle Tommy," featuring legendary old time fiddler Tommy Jarrell (courtesy Willard Gayheart).

Discography

Clawhammer Banjo (County 701; released 1965; also features Kyle Creed and Fred Cockerham)

Down to the Cider Mill (County 713; released 1968; recorded by Charles Faurot and Richard Nevins; produced by Charles Faurot; jacket notes by Richard Nevins; with Fred Cockerham, Oscar Jenkins and Shag Stanley)

More Clawhammer Banjo Songs & Tunes from the Mountains (County 717; released 1969; collected and recorded by Charles Faurot and Richard Nevins in Virginia and North Carolina; produced by Faurot; liner notes by Faurot; Jarrell plays "Cripple Creek" and "John Brown's Dream")

Back Home in the Blue Ridge (County 723; released 1971; recorded by Charles Faurot and Richard Nevins; produced by Richard Nevins; four-page insert brochure by Richard Nevins; with Cockerham and Jenkins, with Shag Stanley and Mac Snow; includes brochure)

June Apple (Mountain M-302; released 1972; rereleased 1993 as Heritage HRC-CD-038, adding three bonus tracks; recorded by Bobby Patterson in Galax, Virginia, in December 1972; produced by Kyle Creed; liner notes by Zane Bennett; also features Kyle Creed [banjo], Audine Lineberry [string bass] and Bobby Patterson [guitar])

Stay All Night and Don't Go Home (County 741; released 1973; collected and recorded by Charles Faurot and Rich Nevins; produced by Rich Nevins; liner notes by Ray Alden; with Cockerham and Jenkins, accompanied by Shag Stanley; Jarrell's fiddle and vocal are featured on 8 of the 14 tracks, including 5 ballads)

The 50th Annual Old Time Fiddlers Convention at Union Grove (Union Grove SS-9; released 1974; Jarrell performs "Jack of Diamonds")

Come Go with Me: Tommy Jarrell's Banjo Album (County 748; released 1974; collected and recorded by Charles Faurot and Rich Nevins; produced by Rich Nevins; liner notes by Charles Faurot)

Joke on the Puppy (Mountain M-310; released 1976; rereleased as Heritage HRC-C-044 in 1992; also features Chester McMillian on guitar and Steve Roberts on banjo)

Music from Round Peak (Heritage X; released 1976; recorded by Bobby Patterson and Ray Alden; jacket notes by Lisa Ornstein; also features Fred Cockerham on fiddle, banjo and vocals, Paul Sutphin on guitar, Mac Snow on guitar and vocals, and Ray Alden on banjo)

Sail Away Ladies (County 756; released 1976; collected and recorded by Bobby Patterson; edited by Barry Poss and Charles Ellertson; annotations by Barry Poss)

Pickin' on Tommy's Porch (County 778; released ca. 1978; collected and recorded in Galax, Virginia, by Bobby Patterson; edited by Rich Nevins; liner notes by Mike Seeger; also features Chester McMillian and Andy Cahan)

Clawhammer Banjo, Vol. 3 (County 757; released 1978; most recordings by Charlie Faurot and Richard Nevins, made in North Carolina, Virginia and West Virginia; edited by Faurot; liner notes by Blanton Owen; Jarrell is featured on "As Time Draws Near")

Folk Music in America, Vol. 14: Solo & Display Music (Library of Congress LBC-14; released 1978; Jarrell performs "Drunken Hiccups")

Visits (Heritage XXXIII; released 1981; collected, recorded and edited by Ray Alden; gatefold jacket notes by Ray Alden; Jarrell performs "Holly Ding" [with Fred Cockerham] and "Visits" [with Mac Snow, Scotty East, Bobby Patterson, Al Tharp, Scott Ainslie, Ray Alden and Patsy East])

Appalachia—The Old Traditions—Vol. 2 (Home-Made Music LP002; released 1983; collected, recorded and edited by Mike Yates in Virginia and North Carolina, 1979-80 and 1983; booklet by Yates; Jarrell performs "Roundtown Gals" and "Train on the Island")

Brandywine '83: The 10th Anniversary Celebration of the Brandywine Mountain Music Convention (Heritage 054; released 1984; Jarrell is featured on "Groundhog" and "Today Has Been a Lonesome Day")

Been Riding with Old Mosby (Folkways FTS 31109; released 1986; recorded in Toast, N.C., in September 1984 by Eric Davidson and Ellen Victoria; annotated by Ellen Victoria and Eric Davidson; Frank Bode (guitar, vocals) with Jarrell (fiddle) and Paul Brown (banjo); the title of the album comes from a line in "My Home's Across the Blue Ridge Mountains" that refers to General John Singleton Mosby, the "Grey Ghost of the Confederacy," a guerrilla cavalry leader in the Shenandoah Valley)

Rainbow Sign (County 791; released 1986; collected and recorded in Galax, Virginia, in 1984 by Andy Cahan; liner notes by Andy Cahan; Jarrell is accompanied by Verlen Clifton [mandolin], Alice Gerrard [guitar] and Andy Cahan [banjo])

Galax International (Heritage 067; released 1988; Jarrell, with Paul Brown and Mike Fenton, performs "Rochester Schottische")

Third Annual Farewell Reunion (Rounder 0313; released 1994; Tommy Jarrell and Paul Brown play "Old Time Sally Ann")

Best Fiddle and Banjo Duets (County 2702; released 1994; recorded by Ray Alden, Charles Faurot, Richard Nevins and Dave Spilkia; produced by Ray Alden; liner notes by Ray Alden; the 21 tracks also feature Fred Cockerham)

Young Fogies (Rounder 0319; released 1994; Tommy Jarrell performs "Visits" with Scotty and Patsy East)

Blue Ridge Mountain Holiday: The Breaking Up Christmas Story (County 2722; released 1997; produced by Paul Brown; production coordinated by Burgess Hurd; field recordings by Brown, Bob Carlin, Terri McMurray, Ray Alden and Dave Spilkia; Jarrell is featured on "Old Bunch of Keys," "Breaking Up Christmas" and "Cluck Old Hen")

The North Carolina Banjo Collection (Rounder 0439; 2-CD set released 1998; produced by Bob Carlin; Tommy Jarrell performs "John Henry")

The Legacy of Tommy Jarrell: Volume 1: Sail Away Ladies (County 2724; released 1999; produced by Barry Poss; recorded by Bobby Patterson; edited by Poss and Charles Ellertson; liner notes by Richard Nevins; consists of 15 fiddle solos)

Frank Jenkins

Frank Jenkins was born in Dobson, N.C., in 1888. For most of his life Jenkins worked in sawmills and on tobacco farms, passing the nighttime "curing" hours with fiddle and banjo playing. During slack farming seasons he traveled around with medicine-type shows. Jenkins also formed a family band that put on shows in nearby communities and dominated many of the fiddling conventions in the area (his "show" pieces were "Home Sweet Home" on banjo and "Sunny Home in Dixie" on fiddle).

Jenkins, noted for his three-finger style of fiddling, was a member of Da Costa Woltz's Southern Broadcasters in the 1920s. He then formed his own group, the Pilot Mountaineers, which included Ernest V. "Pop" Stoneman on guitar. Jenkins mastered a three-fingered, classically derived banjo approach that bore many similarities to that popularized by Earl Scruggs. Jenkins died in 1945.

Discography

"Home Sweet Home" (Gennett 6165; Silvertone 8181; Supertone 9167; ?5080; recorded in Richmond, Indiana, April–May 20, 1927)

"Baptist Shout" (Gennett 6187; recorded in Richmond, Indiana, April–May 20, 1927)

Old Time Fiddle Classics (County 507; released 1965; edited by David Freeman; consists of commercial 78 rpm recordings made in the 1920s and 1930s; Frank and Oscar Jenkins perform "Sunny Home in Dixie" with Ernest Stoneman)

Oscar Jenkins (banjo), Frank Jenkins (fiddle) and Ernest V. Stoneman recorded for Gennett in the late 1920s (Blue Ridge Heritage Archive).

Mountain Banjo Songs and Tunes (County 515; released 1968; liner notes by John Burke; consists of 12 commercial 78 rpm recordings made from 1925 to 1933; Frank Jenkins performs "Home Sweet Home")

Old Time Ballads from the Southern Mountains (County 522; released 1972; consists of 12 commercial 78 rpm recordings made from 1927 to 1931; Frank Jenkins' Pilot Mountaineers are featured on "Burial of Wild Bill")

The North Carolina Banjo Collection (Rounder 0439; 2-CD set released 1998; produced by Bob Carlin; Frank Jenkins performs "Baptist Shout")

AS FRANK JENKINS' PILOT MOUNTAINEERS
"The Railroad Flagman's Sweetheart"/"A Message from Home Sweet Home" (Conqueror 7269; recorded in Richmond, Indiana, on September 12, 1929)
"When the Snowflakes Fall Again"/"The Burial of Wild Bill" (Conqueror 7269; recorded in Richmond, Indiana, on September 12, 1929)
"Sunny Home in Dixie"/"Old Dad" (Gennett 7034; Supertone 9677; recorded in Richmond, Indiana, on September 12, 1929)
Old-Time Mountain Ballads (County 3504; released 1996; annotated by Charles Wolfe; Frank Jenkins' Pilot Mountaineers perform "The Burial of Wild Bill")
When I Was a Cowboy, Vol. 2 (Yazoo 2022; released 1997; Frank Jenkins & His Pilot Mountaineers are featured on "The Burial of Wild Bill")

Oscar Jenkins

Oscar Jenkins, the son of banjo-fiddle legend Frank Jenkins, was born on February 10, 1909, and grew up in Dobson, Surry County. He developed a unique fiddling style of noting with just two fingers. Jenkins' banjo style was just as unique—he actually took off the fifth string of his Gibson Mastertone when he found he rarely used it. When he was 19 years old Jenkins played the banjo in his father's Pilot Mountaineers band.

Jenkins frequently played with old friends Fred Cockerham, Kyle Creed and Tommy Jarrell. Jenkins, Jarrell and Cockerham released three joint albums of traditional mountain music. Jenkins recorded on banjo with his Mountaineers and with Ernest V. "Pop" Stoneman. Oscar Jenkins died in April 1982.

Discography

AS OSCAR JENKINS' MOUNTAINEERS
"Burial of Wild Bill"/"The Railway Flagman's Sweetheart" (Paramount 3240; Brunswick 8249; recorded in Chicago, Illinois, in August 1929)
Old Time Fiddle Classics (County 507; released 1965; edited by David Freeman; consists of commercial 78 rpm recordings made in the 1920s and 1930s; Frank and Oscar Jenkins perform "Sunny Home in Dixie" with Ernest Stoneman)
Down to the Cider Mill (County 713; released 1968; recorded by Charles Faurot and Richard Nevins; produced by Charles Faurot; jacket notes by Richard Nevins; with Fred Cockerham, Tommy Jarrell and Shag Stanley)
Back Home in the Blue Ridge (County 723; released 1971; recorded by Charles Faurot and Richard Nevins; produced by Richard Nevins; four-page insert brochure by Richard Nevins; with Cockerham and Jarrell, with Shag Stanley and Mac Snow; includes brochure)
Stay All Night and Don't Go Home (County 741; released 1973; collected and recorded by Charles Faurot and Rich Nevins; produced by Rich Nevins; liner notes by Ray Alden; with Cockerham and Jarrell, accompanied by Shag Stanley)

David Johnson

Talented multi-instrumentalist David Ray Johnson was born in Millers Creek (Wilkes County), N.C., on February 11, 1954, to Billie Ray and Elizabeth Caudill Johnson. David was the latest in a line of gifted musicians: His grandfather, Bill Johnson (August 10, 1910–August 28, 1996) was a clawhammer banjoist and a maker of guitars, banjos and fiddles. Bill's son and David's father, Billie Ray (born August 28, 1930), played guitar with the Foggy River Boys on WKBC Radio in North Wilkesboro and later joined the Rocky Road Boys. David's mother, Elizabeth (Betty), also plays the guitar.

David Johnson first began playing his father's Gibson guitar when he was 4, and two years later in 1960 received a Kay acoustic guitar as a gift from his father. Just as Bill had taught Billie Ray, David learned from his father how to build and repair musical instruments. By age 10 David was playing in his father's square dance band, the Country Ramblers. He soon added the banjo and fiddle to his repertoire, and later picked up the steel guitar to play in Marshall Craven's local band, the Country Cousins, in 1969. Johnson played with the Country Cousins for 12 years.

On January 1, 1981, Johnson formed his own popular local group called Dixie Dawn, which served as the house band at Shadrack's in Boone (Watauga County, N.C.) and Jubilee Junction in Wilkesboro. Dixie Dawn has recorded

Talented multi-instrumentalist David Johnson performs on the Watson Stage at the 1999 MerleFest (photo by the author).

about half a dozen records and still plays its blend of country, bluegrass and acoustic music at least twice weekly.

Johnson began recording at the age of 15, in the spring of 1969 for the soundtrack of a nationally distributed film about Holly Farms Foods (now Tyson Foods) in North Wilkesboro that was produced by Les Blank. Other musicians who played on the soundtrack included Marshall Craven, Drake Walsh, and David's father, Billie Ray. David has devoted much of his time to the studio, functioning as a session musician and also recording his own material.

David Johnson now works as a session musician (having sat in with Ralph Stanley, Tony Rice and Randy Travis, among others, and been named National Gospel Studio Musician of the Year) and programmer for Horizon Music, a gospel music company in Nashville. He plays virtually all the string instruments and the harmonica. Johnson has had a number of his recordings released on the Mountain Home label, including *Wooden Offerings* (1996) and

Praises, Promises & Prayers (1997). In addition to his duties at Horizon, Johnson also does overdub work with Marshall Craven at the Star Recording Company in Millers Creek.

Discography

Scottish & English Early Ballads (Folkways Records FW 8779; also features vocalist Shanna Beth McGee)
Bluegrass (Folkways Records FTS 31056; released 1983; produced by John R. Craig; also features Billie Ray Johnson)
Clawhammer Banjo (Folkways FTS 31094; released 1983; produced by John R. Craig)
Old Time North Carolina Mountain Music (with Bill, Billie Ray & David Johnson) (Folkways Records FTS 31105; released 1985; recorded at Star Recording Company in Millers Creek, N.C.; produced by John R. Craig; annotated by John R. Craig and David Johnson)
Wooden Offerings (Mountain Home 66; released 1996; produced by David Johnson; engineered and mixed by Van Atkins; liner notes by David Johnson and Tony Rice; also features Tim Surrett on acoustic bass)
Praises, Promises & Prayers (Mountain Home 610; released 1997; arranged and produced by David Johnson; engineered by Van Atkins)

Herb Key

Herb Key, born October 25, 1936, in Wilkesboro, N.C., is an accomplished folksinger, guitarist and bass player. Key was a longtime member of the High County Ramblers along with Wayne Henderson, alongside whom he now works in repairing musical instruments. The duo frequently play gigs with shopmate/mandolinist Gerald Anderson.

Key learned to play the guitar at any early age; both of his parents played, and he learned on an old guitar of his mother's. In high school one of Key's teachers, Bill Amburn, helped him form an acoustic band that also included Otis Campbell. After school Key played with fiddler Tiny Pruitt in the Green Valley Boys, which had a live Saturday show on WKBC Radio in North Wilkesboro. The other members of the band were David Triplett, banjoist Cecil Johnson and Campbell. The Green Valley Boys did well in local contests, winning a couple of ribbons at the Union Grove Fiddlers' Convention.

Key played with Ralph Pennington before joining the High County Ramblers in 1970s. The principal members of the band were rhythm guitarist Paul Gentle, banjoist Larry Pennington (now with the Big Country Bluegrass band) and mandolinist Raymond Pennington. Also playing with the band were Wayne Henderson on lead guitar and Johnny Miller on fiddle. The Ramblers won a pair of first prizes at the Galax fiddlers' convention and recorded for the Heritage label.

(From left) Otis Campbell, Tommy Johnson, Bill Caudill and Herb Key of the
Green Valley Boys Gospel Quartet in 1962 (courtesy Herb Key).

After his association with the High County Ramblers, Key went through a period of musical inactivity. He started playing again, though, with Wayne Henderson in the mid to late 1980s. In addition to helping out at Henderson's luthier shop in Rugby, Virginia, Key does repair work one or two nights a week at his home shop in Wilkesboro.

Discography

Wayne Henderson and Ray Cline Guitar Pickin' with Herb Key (Heritage IX; released 1977; recorded by Bobby Patterson in January of 1976; produced by Fred Williams; cover artwork by Willard Gayheart; jacket notes by Dale Allen; Key plays the upright bass, while Cline [from Traphill, N.C.] and Henderson [from Rugby, Va.] pick guitars)

The High County Ramblers (Heritage XIII; released 1986; liner notes by Dale Morris; consists of 14 field and studio recordings; musicians include Larry Pennington on banjo, Raymond Pennington on mandolin, Paul Gentle on rhythm guitar, Herb Key on bass, Wayne Henderson on lead guitar and Johnny Miller on fiddle)

Steve Kilby

James Stephen Kilby was born November 26, 1954, in North Wilkesboro, N.C., into a musical family: His grandfather, Cranor Kilby, was a fine old-time fiddler and banjoist, and his father, Clifford (Curly) Kilby, was a guitarist and tenor singer who played with the Carolina Playboys and L.W. Lambert and the Carolina Neighbors but died at the age of 25 in February 1956. Steve began playing the guitar at age 12 and was taught his first chords by his grandmother and his first tunes and songs by his grandfather.

In the late 1960s Kilby played guitar with the Green Valley Boys, who also consisted of guitarist Harvey Baity, banjoist Morris Beshears and bass fiddler James Kerley. A subsequent band called Bluegrass Times featured Kilby and Baity on guitars, Eric Ellis on banjo, Don Phillips on fiddle and Kerley on bass.

After trying his hand at five-string banjo for a few years, in 1975 Kilby joined the bluegrass band Hoyt Herbert and the Strings of Five. Led by the banjo-playing Herbert, the band recorded the album *Just Pickin'* in 1978 for the Atteiram label out of Georgia. Kilby left the Strings of Five that same year.

In the early 1980s Kilby played with Blue Ridge Grass, the Sullivan Brothers and the Clarence Greene–John Hartley Band. From November 1985 to late 1991 Kilby picked the guitar in Garland Shuping's band, Wild Country. Shuping was a former banjoist with Jim and Jesse and a mandolinist for Jimmy Martin.

Kilby has won many awards for his guitar playing, including the North Carolina state championship at Cool Springs School and first place at the 1979 and 1980 Galax Old Fiddlers' Conventions. He was also the "best all-around performer" at Galax in 1980. Kilby, later a resident of Piney Creek, N.C., can also play the mandolin, mandola and banjo.

In the late 1990s Kilby played in the Wilkes County–based bluegrass band Kingsberry Run, which also consisted of mandolinist John Akin, banjoist Ramona Taylor, fiddler Nathan Leath and bassist Bill Williams. Kilby also worked as a weekend recording engineer with Heritage Records in Galax, Virginia.

Award-winning guitarist Steve Kilby picks out a tune at the 1999 Mount Airy Bluegrass and Old Time Fiddlers' Convention (photo by the author).

Discography

Steve Kilby, 11-26-54 (Heritage HRC-074; released 1988; recorded by Bobby Patterson; mixed by Jimmy Edmonds; cover design by Fred Carlson; jacket notes by Harold Mitchell; photography by Gary Osborne; also features Eric Ellis on banjo, Clarence Greene on mandolin, Butch Barker on bass, Jim Scancarelli on fiddle, Helen White on banjo and mandolin, and Susan Francis on autoharp)

Sunday Night (Heritage HRC-C-099; released 1992; recorded by Bobby Patterson and Steve Kilby; photography by Gary Osborne; all 14 songs written by Kilby; also features Donnie Scott on Dobro, Bill Williams on bass, David Johnson on fiddle and viola, Jim Scancarelli on fiddle and Butch Barker on bowed bass)

James King

Bluegrass singer James King was born on September 9, 1958, in Martinsville, Virginia. His family soon moved to Cana, Virginia, where James was raised. His father Jim played guitar and sang tenor in several local bands, and his late uncle Joe Edd King was an accomplished fiddler. James, Jim and Joe Edd played in a local band called the Country Cousins for many years.

Joe Edd, who was 10 years James' senior, was a great influence on James' musical upbringing, as were the Stanley Brothers. James, in fact, worked with his hero Ralph Stanley as a guest vocalist in the late 1980s, before which he worked regularly with Bobby and T.J. Lundy, brothers of the late Ted Lundy.

James King made his solo debut in 1993 on Rounder's *These Old Pictures*, recorded with members of the Johnson Mountain Boys. That was followed by subsequent solo efforts on Rounder in 1995 and 1998, for which King and his band were named the 1997 "Emerging Artists of the Year" by the International Bluegrass Music Association. In 1997 he teamed with Dudley Connell, Glen Duncan, Joe Mullins, Don Rigsby and Marshall Wilborn and recorded as the "supergroup" Longview. This band won honors as the 1998 IBMA's "Event of the Year" and "Song of the Year" (for "Lonesome Old Home").

James King picks one of his hard-core bluegrass numbers at the 1999 Merle-Fest in Wilkesboro, N.C. (photo by the author).

Discography

These Old Pictures (Rounder 0305; released 1993; produced by Ken Irwin; features King on vocals, Dudley Connell on guitar and harmony vocals, David McLaughlin on mandolin and lead guitar, Tim Smith on fiddle, Tom Adams on banjo and Marshall Wilborn on bass)

Lonesome and Then Some (Rounder 0350; released 1995; produced by Ken Irwin; liner notes by Jon Hartley; features King on lead vocals, Dudley Connell on guitar and tenor vocals, Tom Adams on banjo, Tim Smith on fiddle, Mike Compton on mandolin, David McLaughlin on crosspick guitar and baritone vocals and Marshall Wilborn on bass)

Bluegrass Greats (Easydisc 7007; released 1996; Longview performs "There's a Brighter Mansion Over There"; James King plays "Indecision")

Bed by the Window (Rounder 0425; released 1998; produced by Ken Irwin; liner notes by Charles Wolfe; features King on guitar and vocals, Kevin Prater on mandolin, vocals and lead guitar, Jason Moore on bass, Adam Poindexter on banjo and guitar, Bobby Hicks on fiddle and Owen Saunders on fiddle)

Bluegrass Spirit (Easydisc 7021; released ca. 1998; King performs "Message for Peace")

WITH LONGVIEW

Longview (Rounder 0386; released 1997; produced by Ken Irwin and Longview; liner notes by Bill Evans; features King on vocals, Dudley Connell on guitar and vocals, Glen Duncan on fiddle, Joe Mullins on banjo and vocals, Don Rigsby on mandolin and vocals and Marshall Wilborn on bass)

High Lonesome (Rounder 0434; released 1999; produced by Ken Irwin, Ronnie Freeland and Longview; features King on vocals, Dudley Connell on guitar and vocals, Glen Duncan on fiddle and vocals, Joe Mullins on banjo and vocals, Don Rigsby on mandolin and vocals and Marshall Wilborn on bass)

Joe Edd King

Fiddler Joe Edd King (born ca. 1948) grew up in Cana, Virginia, and started teaching himself to play his brother's fiddle when he was 6 years old. As a teenager Joe Edd played and toured with the Country Cousins, along with his brother Jim and nephew James. In the summer of 1965, while touring in Wilmington, Delaware, Joe Edd got a job offer from Ted Lundy, whom he had met the previous summer in Galax and whom was co-leader of the Southern Mountain Boys with Bob Paisley. King took Lundy up on his offer and played with the Southern Mountain Boys for two years.

King left Delaware in 1968 to serve two years in the Navy, but upon returning from service played with Wayne Golding, Wesley Golding and Jimmy Arnold in the Virginia Cut-Ups and recorded an album for Latco Records in 1971. King began fiddling for the Country Boys in 1972, joining guitarist Donald Clifton, mandolinist Ronnie Lyons, banjoist David Hiatt and bassist Wayne Creed. A disciple of Kenny Baker, King won first place in fiddling at the 1973 Galax Fiddlers' Convention. King died in an automobile accident on July 13, 1975.

Discography

38th Annual Galax Old Fiddlers' Convention (Gazette 38; released 1973; Joe Edd King performs "Texas Quickstep")

Joe Edd King with the Country Boys (Heritage XI; released 1976; recorded by Bobby Patterson; cover artwork by Willard Gayheart; notes by Ginger Correll and Ted Lundy)

The Konnarock Critters

Old time string band the Konnarock Critters was formed in 1986 by fiddler Brian Grim and his sister Debbie Grim, who plays the banjo (in addition to, outside of the band, guitar, clawhammer banjo, bass, fiddle and piano). Brian, who lives in Elk Creek, learned at age 8 to play the fiddle from Albert Hash of Whitetop, Virginia. When Debbie was 7 she started taking music lessons from Thornton and Emily Spencer at the Mount Rogers Fire Hall on Whitetop Mountain. Brian was 11 and Debbie was 10 they began playing in a local dance group called the Whitetoppers. Their mother, who played the guitar and encouraged her children's interest in music, was also in the band, which played every night for two and a half years at the Troutdale Fire Hall.

Guitarist Jim Lloyd of Rural Retreat, Virginia, has been with the band since 1989. A fourth generation musician and storyteller, Lloyd also plays the banjo, autoharp, fiddle and bass fiddle. Lloyd previously played with the Willow River String Band and Mountain Fling, and in 1994 and 1995 he hosted a popular live music performance program on WBRF in Galax, Virginia, called "Blue Ridge Back Roads." He is now the coordinator of the "Living Traditions" series of the William King Regional Arts Center in Abingdon.

Bassist Al Firth of Charlottesville, Virginia, joined the Critters in 1994. Firth began playing the washtub bass—left-handed—with a bluegrass band

Members of the Konnarock Critters are (left to right) Brian Grim, Debbie Grim, Al Firth and Jim Lloyd (courtesy Brian Grim).

while at the University of Connecticut in 1973. He later played with such popular old-time string bands as the Red Hots, Swamp Root String Band (which played for the Green Glass Cloggers), the Rambler Classics and the Falls City Ramblers. Firth also plays jazz, blues, swing, rock 'n' roll and even Cajun music.

Other band members over the years have included guitarist Sam Payne of Fries, Virginia, and bassists Terry Semones of Hillsville, Virginia, and Butch Barker and Dale Morris of Galax, Virginia.

The Critters have provided music for square dancers, flatfooters and cloggers, including an old time square dance team from Whitetop called the Grayson Whitetoppers. In the summer of 1990 they had a weekend engagement at Dollywood in Pigeon Forge, Tennessee, and in April 1997 played at the Footloose Festival in Derbyshire, England.

The Critters have also played at various fundraisers, fiddlers' conventions and festivals up and down the East Coast, winning top awards in both band and individual competitions. Debbie Grim, a resident of Konnarock, won first prize in clawhammer banjo at the 1997 Galax Old Fiddlers' Convention.

Discography

Old Favorites (Heritage HRC-C-113; released 1994; notes by Bobby Patterson; consists of 13 tracks; also features Wayne Henderson on bass and Blanche Nichols on guitar and vocals on "Lonesome Road Blues")
Cornbread and Sweetpeas (Marimac 9068D; released 1997; consists of 17 tracks)
Rattletrap (Marimac 9070; released 1999; consists of 17 songs and tunes)

L.W. Lambert

Banjo picker Luin Wilford Lambert, Jr., was born on April 18, 1926, in the Summers community of Wilkes County. His father, L.W. Sr., and mother, Grace Luella Gregory Lambert, both played the banjo. In 1938 a family band called the Carolina Neighbors was formed, with L.W. Sr. on the banjo, L.W. Jr. on the guitar and his sister LaVaughn on the mandolin. They played at local social events in a ten-mile radius of their home.

In his late teens, L.W. heard Earl Scruggs on the radio and sought to emulate his three-finger style, which was the chief influence on his playing. A year or two after marrying Edith Lucille Pardue in January of 1947, L.W. reformed the Carolina Neighbors. He played a Gibson RB-100 banjo; the other members were his sister LaVaughn on guitar, her husband Harold Tomlin on mandolin, Zeb Speece on guitar and Pee Wee Yokeley on fiddle. This group's first radio work was a Saturday morning show on WKBC Radio in

North Wilkesboro. They also joined the cast of Dwight Barker's WSIC Saturday Nite Jamboree in Statesville.

The Carolina Neighbors did their first recording around 1952, cutting a 78 rpm record for the Blue Ridge label. LaVaughn Tomlin and Zeb Speece left the band around 1955 and were replaced by Curly Kilby on guitar and Ralph Pennington—formerly with the Stanley Brothers—on bass.

L.W. then moved to WPAQ in Mount Airy and added fiddler Cub McGee and bassist Elmer Bowers to his lineup. Following the death of Kilby at age 25, Lambert began playing with Johnny Compton at WPAQ and did a few shows with Charlie Monroe.

Around 1955 the Murphy brothers—Dewey, Fred and John—reorganized their band the Blue River Boys and added Lambert on the banjo. This ensemble stayed together for about six years, finally disintegrating after Dewey and Fred joined the ministry and Pee Wee Yokeley died at the age of 34.

After several years of freelancing and doing radio and television work, Lambert joined the Border Mountain Boys in 1968. The other members of the band were fiddler Tommy Malbouef, guitarist Cullen Galyean (who was later replaced by Winford Hunt), bassist Buck Arrington and mandolinist Jim Holder. The group recorded on the Homestead label just before illness forced Lambert to leave the band in 1970.

In 1972 L.W. Lambert reorganized the Blue River Boys to include his cousin Herb Lambert on mandolin, Ray Cline on lead guitar, Tommy (Red) Malboeuf on fiddle, Joe Greene on bass and Elbert Arrington on guitar. The rejuvenated band won 31 of the 34 fiddlers' conventions it entered that year and took home more than $15,800 in prize money.

Over the years the lineup of the Blue River Boys was juggled to include bassist Danny Campbell, guitarists Harold Murphy and Herb Green, and fiddlers Terry Baucom, Tim Smith (born May 29, 1955), Roger Ledford and Robin Warren. On May 17, 1980, L.W. Lambert and the Blue River Boys played at the Lincoln Center in New York City on the same bill with Emmylou Harris, Norman Blake and the Whites. The group eventually disbanded around 1985.

L.W. Lambert lives today on a 160-acre farm in Olin, N.C., and remains active in music.

Discography

AS L.W. AND HAROLD AND THE CAROLINA NEIGHBORS
"The Battle in Korea"/"I Won't Write Another Letter to You Darling" (Blue Ridge 204; released ca. 1952)

AS THE BORDER MOUNTAIN BOYS
Bluegrass on the Mountain (Homestead)

AS L.W. LAMBERT AND THE BLUE RIVER BOYS
Natural Grass (United U-0039; released 1973)
"Sweet Georgia on My Mind"/"Ridin' Dusty" (Blue River Records)
The Old, Old Man (Anvil RSR 373; released 1976)
Bluegrass Gospel (Anvil/New Dimension; released 1978)

AS A FEATURED MUSICIAN
Fiddlin' Art Wooten: A Living Legend (Homestead 104; released 1976)
Fiddlin' Art Wooten: A Living Bluegrass Legend (Dominion Records A-116; Wooten, who has played with Bill Monroe and the Stanley Brothers, among others, is from Sparta, N.C.)
Tim Smith, 1978 World Champion Fiddler (Anvil RSR 802; Smith, from Sparta, N.C., can also be heard on Heritage's *Favorite Pastimes* [1986])
Jim Shumate: Bluegrass Fiddle Supreme (Country Road RSR-1152)
Authentic Bluegrass (Anvil; released 1982)
The Redeemed Quartet: Climbing Higher (Reflection Sound Studios)
The Redeemed Quartet: Visions of Heaven (New Dimension)

Last Run
(formerly Ric-O-Chet)

Last Run, one of the top bluegrass bands of the Central Blue Ridge in the 1990s, was formed under the name Ric-O-Chet on January 13, 1989, by Jimmy Trivette, Eric Ellis, David Pendley and Steve Lewis. (An earlier version of Last Run was the very first band to play at the first Eddy Merle Watson Memorial Festival [MerleFest] on April 30, 1988.) The band took its original name, Ric-O-Chet, from the instrumental "Ricochet" recorded by David Grisman and Tony Rice, the latter of whom would incidentally produce the band's second album on the Rebel label, with which they signed in March of 1994.

Bassist and tenor singer James William (Jimmy) Trivette was born in Boone (Watauga County), N.C., on January 8, 1949. His father played clawhammer banjo and his mother played guitar, mandolin and some banjo. Jimmy was exposed to bluegrass music at an early age and received his first guitar when he was 10. After a decade of musical inactivity he joined the Blue Ridge Gospel Review as the group's mandolinist. His bandmate at this juncture was a young guitarist named Steve Lewis, who would later be a founding member of Ric-O-Chet.

In the early 1990s Trivette played with a Fender long-scale Bullet electric bass, but he now strums a 1950s model Kay upright bass fiddle. In 1992 he was a member (along with Laurie Lewis and Dudley Connell) of the backup band for a National Council for the Traditional Arts–sponsored

Bluegrass band Last Run—(left to right) Steve Lewis, Randy Greer, Jimmy Trivette, Tim Lewis—on stage at the 1998 Todd Days Festival (in Todd, N.C.) (photo by the author).

nationwide Masters of the Banjo tour that included J.D. Crowe and Ralph Stanley.

The band's original banjoist, Eric Wayne Ellis, was born in North Wilkesboro, N.C., on August 12, 1958. He won the North Carolina banjo championship in 1976 and 1978, and the prestigious Galax, Virginia, contest in 1981. Ellis played with the band from January 1989 to October 1992. He made two recordings with the band at Star Studios and helped them showcase at the 1990 IBMA Trade Show in Owensboro, Kentucky.

Before his stint with Ric-O-Chet, Ellis played with Bluegrass Times (alongside Steve Kilby), the Grass Valley Boys (a band headed by fiddler Tiny Pruitt), Southern Express (with Eddie and David Pendley), Heritage, Wells Fargo and Sure Fire (which had two releases on the Heritage label, *River of Teardrops* and *The First Flower of Spring*). Since his stay with Ric-O-Chet Ellis has picked with the Lincoln County Partners, Cedar Creek and Wyatt Rice. For nearly a decade Ellis worked with fiddler Jim Shumate (a North Carolina Folk Heritage Award winner in 1995) and recorded with him on a couple of Heritage releases.

Ric-O-Chet's original mandolinist, David Keith Pendley of Morganton, N.C., was born on June 22, 1959. He played bass at age 15 in 1974 for Southern Express, which was headed by his father, guitarist Eddie Pendley. In January 1978 he became bassist for the Country Bluegrass Boys with mandolinist Clarence Greene, banjoist John Hartley and guitarist Jim Smith. Prior to joining Ric-O-Chet, Pendley also played with R.C. Harris's Blue Denim and the Prospectors, and made some recordings in 1984 with Clarence Greene and John Hartley.

Banjoist-guitarist Steve Douglas Lewis was born June 20, 1964, in Boone and now resides in Todd (Ashe County), N.C. Lewis started playing the guitar when he was 9 or 10 and was strongly influenced by the work of Doc Watson and Tony Rice. When Lewis was 13 he ended up in a group called the Daniel Boone Bluegrass Express, which accompanied the then–world champion Daniel Boone Cloggers. He then played in the Blue Ridge Gospel Review with Jimmy Trivette, followed by short stints with Sweetwater, Tommy Faile's band and Vintage Blend.

Around 1978 Lewis switched from guitar to banjo and played that instrument for the next eight years. In 1986 he won first prize in the banjo competition at the Galax Old Fiddlers' Convention. Upon Ellis' departure in late 1992, Lewis took over banjo chores for Ric-O-Chet, and Randy Greer of West Jefferson became the band's guitarist.

Greer (born July 31, 1964) handles both rhythm and lead guitar chores with equal skill and ease. Also a noted mandolin player, Greer had previously had a stint with Appalachian Trail, the SPBGMA's 1994 national band champion. He has played at the world-renowned Carnegie Hall in New York City with Wayne Henderson.

Ric-O-Chet went through another reorganization when David Pendley and Jimmy Trivette (temporarily) went their separate ways in 1996. Randy Greer switched over to mandolin, Steve Lewis went back to playing primarily guitar, and Tim Lewis (no relation to Steve), came on board to pick the banjo. Les Deaton of Mooresville, N.C.—born March 19, 1951, and formerly a member of the Carolina Bluegrass Band and the Bluegrass Cardinals— joined the band as acoustic bassist. Trivette soon rejoined the band and made his solo recording debut in 1998. In 1999 the group disbanded after a decade of playing acclaimed, hard-driving bluegrass.

Discography

Ric-O-Chet (Rebel CD-1716; released 1994; produced by Tim Stafford; special guests include Rob Ickes on Dobro and Stuart Duncan on fiddle)

Carolina Memories (Rebel CD-1722; released 1995; produced by Tony Rice; special guests include David Johnson on fiddle and Rob Ickes on Dobro)

AS JIMMY TRIVETTE

By Request (Jamsu 4951; released 1998; produced and mixed by David Pendley and Wesley Easter; musicians and vocalists include Jimmy Trivette, Steve Lewis, Tony Testerman, Randy Greer, Charles Welch, Scott Freeman, David Pendley, Tim Lewis and Sue Trivette)

The Laurel Fork Travelers

The Laurel Fork Travelers old-time string band was formed in 1993 by fiddler Arnold Spangler and banjoist Marvin Felts, both natives of Carroll County, Virginia. Arnold and his younger sister Clara Spangler Sutphin, a guitarist, came from a family of 18. Some of Arnold's sisters played the pump organ and sang, but he was the only boy to take up music and dancing. Arnold was most active in the 1940s and 1950s, playing radio programs and local shows with Uncle Don Dean's band, the Lonesome Road Boys, and Little Joe and the Virginia Playboys.

Before teaming up with Spangler, Marvin Felts and his wife Dea played for many years in the Blue Sky Ramblers and were regular performers at fiddlers' conventions and on WPAQ Radio's "Merry-Go-Round" program out of Mount Airy, N.C. Marvin plays the banjo, fiddle and mandolin, while Dea plays the bass and fiddle. Guitarist Charlie Bowman joined the group in the mid–1990s.

Since they were organized the Laurel Fork Travelers have played at Mabry Mill on the Blue Ridge Parkway, at local country stores, the Blue Ridge Music Association, the Rex Theater, the "Merry-Go-Round" program and the Ferrum College Folklife Festival. They have also recorded a pair of albums for Heritage Records.

Discography

Picking and Singing Old-Time (Heritage HRC-C-114; released 1995; recorded by Bobby Patterson; notes by Dea Felts; consists of 16 tracks; guest musicians include guitarists Adam Marshall and Bobby Patterson and harmonica player Paul Hiatt)
Bound to Ride (Heritage HRC-C-117; released 1996; recorded by Bobby Patterson; notes by Dea Felts; consists of 16 tracks)

Lonesome Pine Fiddlers *see* Larry Richardson

Lulu Belle and Scotty

Radio, record and motion pictures stars Lulu Belle and Scotty were the nation's leading husband-and-wife country team of the 1930s, 1940s and 1950s. For some 20 years they starred on the *National Barn Dance* from WLS Chicago and for three years (1938–1940) were also featured on *Boone County Jamboree* over WLW Cincinnati.

Lulu (or Lula) Belle's given name was Myrtle Eleanor Cooper. She was born December 24, 1913, in Boone (Watauga County), North Carolina, to John Reed Cooper and Sidney Olive Marie Knupp Cooper. At age 16 she moved with her parents to Evanston, Illinois, and by 1932, after a couple of tryouts, landed a job at WLS in Chicago, a powerful 50,000-watt radio station that reached all parts of the Midwest and much of the South. Station manager John Lair teamed her up with Ramblin' Red Foley of Berea, Kentucky, as the song-comedy duo of Lulu Belle and Burrhead, and in November 1932 put her on the nation's most prestigious country music radio program, *National Barn Dance*. When this didn't work out, Lair decided to team Lulu Belle and Skyland Scotty, a lanky banjo picker and songwriter who was also from the mountains of North Carolina.

Scott Greene Wiseman was born November 8, 1909, in Ingalls, Alleghany County. An uncle, "Honey" Waits, taught him to frail on the banjo. When he was 7 years old, Scott sold a pig for $4.95 and brought a mail order guitar, and by the time he was in his teens was a serious collector of Southern folk songs and a regular performer on the guitar and harmonica at local square dances.

Wiseman attended Duke University (Durham, North Carolina) and

Popular husband-and-wife singing team Lulu Belle and Scotty made their mark in radio, recordings and film (photo by K. Smith/Southern Historical Collection, Wilson Library, The University of North Carolina at Chapel Hill).

Fairmont (West Virginia) State Teacher's College. At Fairmont he was an announcer, program director and singer of mountain ballads at WMMN radio and picked up the nickname "Skyland Scotty." Wiseman made his professional singing debut on WRVA in Richmond, Virginia, in 1927. After graduation in 1932, Wiseman successfully auditioned for a spot at WLS in the spring of 1933, boosted by a recommendation from Bradley Kincaid.

Lulu Belle and Scotty hit it off both professionally on *National Barn Dance* and romantically—the two were married in Naperville, Illinois, on December 13, 1934. In 1936 Lulu Belle was the most popular female on radio, according to the readers of *Radio Guide* magazine. By 1943 Lulu Belle and Scotty were in constant demand for public appearances, for which they commanded $500 a day and transportation. Around this time it was reported that Lulu Belle and Scotty held more box office records at theaters, parks and fairs than any other acts in the Midwest. *Billboard* magazine named them one of the six "greatest moneymakers" in the country music business in 1943. The team remained top radio stars until they retired from active performing in 1958.

Lulu Belle and Scotty appeared in seven motion pictures, beginning in 1938 with Roy Rogers in *Shine On, Harvest Moon* and continuing through 1945's *Under Western Skies*.

On the recording front, in December 1933 Wiseman cut four solo efforts for Bluebird, and a session in the spring of 1934 resulted in ten releases on the Conqueror label. Lulu Belle and Burrhead, in 1934, made four for Conquerer. In 1935 Lulu Belle and Scotty recorded a number of old-time and novelty songs for the American Record Corporation, the label for which Lulu Belle had made her first recordings with Red Foley in the early 1930s. Scotty's partly recomposed version of Bascom Lamar Lunsford's "Good Old Mountain Dew," recorded for Vocalion in 1939, became the standard used by all subsequent artists who covered the song. Two of their original love songs— "Remember Me" (Vocalion, 1939) and their most famous, "Have I Told You Lately That I Love You?" (Vogue, 1945)—would become country standards.

After World War II Lulu Belle and Scotty recorded for such labels as Emerald, London, Ka-Hill, Trutone and Mercury. In the early 1950s they made a series of popular radio transcriptions titled *Breakfast in the Blue Ridge*.

The "Hayloft Sweethearts" retired from the *National Barn Dance* to their mountain home in Spruce Pine, N.C., in 1958. Scott took his master's degree from Northwestern in 1958 and taught school, farmed, and served as a bank director. Lulu Belle served two terms in the North Carolina legislature from 1975 to 1978, representing the counties of Avery, Burke and Mitchell. She was the first Democrat to serve her district since 1922 and the first woman ever to fill the position.

Lulu Belle and Scotty recorded periodically during this time, cutting three albums for Starday in the 1960s and a final one for Old Homestead in 1974. They also made albums for Birch and Speer and played a few rare concert dates in the 1970s.

Scotty died as the result of a massive heart attack on February 1, 1981, in Gainesville, Florida, while returning to the mountains from a Florida vacation. *Wiseman's View: The Autobiography of Skyland Scotty Wiseman* was posthumously published by the North Carolina Folklore Society (as Volume 33 of the *North Carolina Folklore Journal*) in 1986. Lulu Belle remarried in 1983, to Ernest Stamey, a retired lawyer and longtime family friend. Lulu Belle recorded a solo album titled *Snickers and Tender Memories with Lulu Belle* for Old Homestead in 1986.

Lulu Belle and Scotty were nominated for the Country Music Hall of Fame in 1979 and 1980, and Wiseman was inducted into the Nashville Songwriters Association's Hall of Fame in 1971.

Lulu Belle Wiseman Stamey died on February 8, 1999.

Discography

Lulabelle and Scotty (Super SR-6201; released 1963)
The Sweethearts of Country Music (Pine Mountain PMR-312; released 1963; recorded in Charlotte, N.C.; rereleased as Starday SCD 206)
Down Memory Lane (Starday 285; released 1964; recorded in Charlotte, N.C.)

Lulu Belle & Scotty (Starday 351; released 1965)

Just a Closer Walk with Thee (Birch BRS 1948; released 1974)

Have I Told You Lately That I Love You? (Old Homestead OHS 90037; released 1974)

Sweethearts Still (Starday SLP 351; released 1975; jacket notes by Terry Tomlin; features Jerry Shook and Pete Wade on guitars, Billy Linneman on bass and Roy Wiggins on steel guitar; rereleased in 1994 as Hollywood 260, and in 1996 as King 351)

Lulu Belle and Scotty (Castle Germany; released 1980)

Early and Great—Volume I (Old Homestead 168; released 1985; jacket notes by John W. Morris)

Snickers and Tender Memories with Lulu Belle (Old Homestead 90175; released 1986)

Tender Memories Recalled (Mar-Lu 8901; released 1989; jacket notes by Marshall Dial)

Tender Memories Recalled, Volume 2 (Mar-Lu 8902; released 1989; jacket notes by William E. Lightfoot; consists of 12 radio broadcasts from 1961)

The North Carolina Banjo Collection (Rounder 0439; 2-CD set released 1998; produced by Bob Carlin; Scotty Wiseman performs "Sugar Babe")

Filmography

Shine On, Harvest Moon (Republic; 57 minutes; released 1938; directed by Joseph Kane; associate produced by Charles E. Ford; screenplay by Jack Natteford; starring Roy Rogers, Mary Hart, Stanley Andrews and William Farnum)

Village Barn Dance (Republic; 74 minutes; released 1940; directed by Frank McDonald; associate produced by Armand Schaefer; screenplay by Dorrell McGowan and Stuart McGowan; starring Richard Cromwell, Doris Day, George Barbier and Esther Dale)

Country Fair (Republic; 74 minutes; released 1941; directed by Frank McDonald; associate produced by Armand Schaefer; screenplay by Dorrell McGowan and Stuart McGowan; story by Jack Townley; starring Eddie Foy, Jr., June Clyde, Guinn "Big Boy" Williams and William Demarest)

Hi, Neighbor! (Republic; 72 minutes; released 1942; directed by Charles Lamont; associate produced by Armand Schaefer; screenplay by Dorrell McGowan and Stuart McGowan; starring Jean Parker, John Archer, Janet Beecher and Marilyn Hare)

Swing Your Partner (Republic; 72 minutes; released 1941; directed by Frank McDonald; associate produced by Armand Schaefer; screenplay by Dorrell McGowan and Stuart McGowan; starring Roger Clark, Esther Dale, Judy Clark and Charles Judels)

Sing, Neighbor, Sing (Republic; 70 minutes; released 1944; directed by Frank McDonald; associate produced by Donald H. Brown; screenplay by Dorrell McGowan and Stuart McGowan; starring Brad Taylor, Ruth Terry, Virginia Brissac and Beverly Lloyd)

National Barn Dance (Paramount; 76 minutes; released 1944; directed by Hugh Bennett; produced by Walter MacEwen; screenplay by Lee Loeb and Hal Fimberg; starring Jean Heather, Charles Quigley, Robert Benchley and Mabel Paige; Lulu Belle and Scotty perform "When Pa Was Courtin' Ma")

Under Western Skies (Universal; 57 minutes; released 1945; directed by Jean Yarbrough; produced by Warren Wilson; screenplay by Stanley Roberts and Clyde Bruckman; story by Stanley Roberts; starring Martha O'Driscoll, Noah Beery, Jr., Leon Errol and Leo Carrillo)

Emmett Lundy

Emmett W. Lundy of Delhart was reputed to be one of the finest old-time fiddlers from the Galax, Virginia, area. Born during the Civil War, Lundy acquired much of his older repertoire from an elderly, reclusive fiddler named Green Leonard, whose playing is legendary, even today, in Grayson County. Lundy also greatly influenced younger men, such as Crockett Ward, Eck Dunford, Charlie Higgins, Kahle Brewer and Da Costa Woltz, who played in string bands. Ward and Dunford, in fact, spent days at a time at Lundy's home, and Brewer and Higgins credited Lundy with teaching them much of their music.

Lundy made only two commercial recordings, both in 1925 for OKeh when he accompanied his second cousin Ernest Stoneman to New York for a May recording session: "Long Eared Mule" and "Piney Woods Gal" were fiddle-harmonica duets with Stoneman. Reportedly not pleased with the fidelity of these recordings, Lundy did not record again until 16 years later, this time for the Library of Congress. He recorded over 30 pieces for the LOC, accompanied by his sons Kelly on guitar and Geedy on banjo.

Stuart Lundy, the twelfth of 15 children born to Emmett and Nancy Jennings Lundy, recorded an album with Kelly (the youngest of the 15 siblings) in 1990 called *Last Time Together* (Heritage HRC-086). Stuart, a fiddler, was born on April 7, 1908, and died on March 15, 1978. Kelly, born in 1914, also worked with banjoist Larry Richardson and fiddler Otis Burris and was a frequent winner at the Galax Old Fiddlers' Convention in the 1930s, 1940s and 1950s.

Kelly Lundy, along with sister Katy Lundy Golding and nephews Jerry, T.J. and Bobby Lundy, recorded as the Lundy Family and were featured on *Back in Galax Again* (Heritage HRC-C-105; released in 1992). T.J. was also a member of the Hotmud Family, which recorded *Meat and Potatoes and Stuff Like That* on Flying Fish (FF 251).

Legendary old-time fiddler Emmett Lundy is pictured here with wife Alice Joines (courtesy Blue Ridge Heritage Archive/Andy Cahan and Pauline Sharp).

Discography

WITH E.V. STONEMAN

"Piney Woods Gal"/"Long Eared Mule" (OKeh 40405; recorded in New York City on May 27, 1925)

Fiddle Tunes from Grayson County (String/Topic 802; recorded in 1941 by the Library of Congress; released 1977; consists of 20 tracks; features Kelly Lundy on guitar)

Round the Heart of Old Galax, Vol. 3 (County 535; released 1980; liner notes by Wayne Martin; consists of 14 songs, some commercial 78 rpm recordings made in the 1920s and 1930s, others from Library of Congress field recordings of 1941; Emmett Lundy is featured on "Ducks in the Millpond" and "Mississippi Sawyer" [both with Kelly Lundy and Geedy Lundy], "Piney Woods Gal" [with E.V. Stoneman, recorded in 1925 for OKeh] and "Waves on the Ocean" [with Kelly Lundy])

Ted Lundy

Teddy Joe Lundy, who had a long musical association with Alex Campbell and Ola Belle (Campbell) Reed, was born January 26, 1937, in Galax, Virginia, to banjo player Charles Edgar and guitarist Rena (Edwards) Lundy. Emmett Lundy, the legendary old-time fiddler, was Ted's great uncle. Ted started picking a guitar at 8 and took up the banjo at age 14. Ted preferred the newer three-finger Scruggs style over the clawhammer playing that his father used.

At 15 Ted started playing with Glen Neaves of Galax and Estil Ball of Rugby on Galax radio station WBOB. Two years later, Lundy went to Bluefield, West Virginia, with Udell McPeak and became banjoist for Jimmy Williams and the Shady Valley Boys on WHIS. The band later moved to WCYB in Bristol, Tennessee. Lundy stayed with them for about a year, earning about $40 a week by touring schools, theaters and halls.

In 1956 Lundy moved to Wilmington, Delaware, where an older brother lived. His first musical experience there was playing banjo (replacing John Miller, who switched to fiddle) with Rome Jackson and the Tennessee Pals. In 1959 Lundy and Fred Hannah put together a band called the Southern Mountain Boys, with Hannah on mandolin, Sonny Miller on fiddle, Donald Baer on bass, and Lew Childers on guitar. The group played over local radio stations WILM in Wilmington and WCOJ in Coatesville, Pennsylvania.

The Southern Mountain Boys played together for about four years before agreeing to play with the well-known Alex Campbell and Ola Belle Reed (both Ashe County natives) and the New River Boys each Sunday at Sunset Park in West Grove, Pennsylvania, during 1963 and 1964. They also broadcast live each Saturday night over WWVA after the Jamboree.

The Mountain Boys continued to work as a separate entity even while playing with Alex and Ola Belle. While working at the Eagle club in Oxford,

Galax native Ted Lundy was featured in renowned artist Willard Gayheart's "Blue Ridge Masters" collectors' series (courtesy Willard Gayheart).

Pennsylvania, Lundy met guitarist Bob Paisley, also an Ashe County native. Lundy then persuaded a 17-year-old fiddler from Cana, Virginia, Joe Edd King, to join his group. In 1967 Ted's second cousin and Emmett's grandson, Jerry Lundy (born ca. 1942), replaced King as the band's fiddler.

The Southern Mountain Boys returned to Lundy's hometown and won the Best Band award at the 1971 and 1972 Galax Old Time Fiddlers' Conventions. The group did not record another album until 1972, when they recorded for Gerd Hadeler's German firm, the GHP Recording Company. New band members at this point included five-string bass player Wes Rineer (born ca. 1939) from Lancaster, Pennsylvania, and mandolinist John Haftl, a former rock musician from Philadelphia whom Lundy met in January 1972. The group then recorded albums for Rounder in 1973, 1976 and 1978.

By 1976 Paisley was coleader of the band. Hannah left the band after the GHP session; subsequent mandolinists included Don Eldreth and Ted's older son, T.J. In addition to Rineer, Don Baer and Bill Graybeal played bass with the group at various times. Paisley left to start his own band in 1979. Ted Lundy committed suicide by leaping off the Delaware Memorial Bridge on June 23, 1980.

Discography

Virginia Breakdown (County 705; released 1967; Sonny Miller and the Southern Mountain Boys perform "Blackberry Blossom," "Grey Eagle [Hornpipe]," "Katy Did" and "Sally Goodin")

Ted Lundy & the Southern Mountain Boys (GHP; released 1972)

The Old Swinging Bridge (Rounder 0020; released 1973; recorded in Bethesda, Maryland, in August 1972; produced by the Rounder Collective; jacket notes by Carl Goldstein)

38th Annual Galax Old Fiddlers Convention (Gazette 38; released 1973; Ted Lundy performs "Cluck Old Hen")

1st Annual Brandywine Mountain Music Convention (Heritage VI; released 1975; Ted Lundy and the Southern Mountain Boys perform "Bill Cheatum")

Springtime in the Mountains (County 749; released 1975; Ted Lundy and the Southern Mountain Boys are featured on "Dark Hollow," "I've Never Been So Lonesome," "Please Don't, Honey Please" and "Poor Ellen Smith")

Slipping Away (Rounder 0055; released 1976)

39th National Folk Festival (NCTA 77; released 1977; Ted Lundy plays "Sally Ann")

Lovesick and Sorrow (Rounder 0107; released 1978; consists of 12 tracks)

Rounder Bluegrass, Vol. 1 (Rounder 11511; released 1987; Ted Lundy and the Southern Mountain Boys perform "Old Swinging Bridge")

Rounder Old-Time Music (Rounder 11510; released 1988; Ted Lundy and the Southern Mountain Boys perform "It Rained a Mist")

Rounder Banjo (Rounder 296/11542; released 1988; Ted Lundy performs "Goodbye Liza Jane" with Bob Paisley)

Hand-Picked: 25 Years of Bluegrass on Rounder Records (Rounder 22123; released 1995; 2-CD collection; booklet notes by Frank Godbey; Ted Lundy performs "Old Swinging Bridge")

Spencer Moore

Guitar picker Spencer (Spence) Moore was born February 7, 1919, in Ashe County, North Carolina, one of Robert and Molly Owens Moore's 11 children. When he was young, his family moved to Konnarock, Virginia. In the 1930s Spencer and his brother Joseph toured the East Coast and were compared to the Monroe Brothers and the Blue Sky Boys.

In 1948 Moore moved to Chilhowie, Virginia, to farm tobacco. He joined the army in World War II and served in North Africa, Italy and Greece. Gen. Dwight D. Eisenhower enjoyed Moore's music so much that he gave him a Gibson guitar, which was subsequently stolen. Moore later played for presidents Jimmy Carter and Ronald Reagan at Washington's Smithsonian Institution and Lincoln Theater.

When Moore came home in 1959 he was recorded by Alan Lomax, the country's foremost folk music collector, for inclusion on an album featuring a cross-section of American singers. Moore continues singing and playing his 1952 Gibson guitar (which he bought for $185) well into the late 1990s.

Discography

Blue Ridge Mountain Music (Atlantic SD-1347; released 1960; recorded by Alan Lomax with Shirley Collins in 1959; four-page booklet by Lomax; Spence Moore performs "Jimmy Sutton")

Banjo Songs, Ballads, and Reels from the Southern Mountains: Southern Journey 4 (Prestige

Ashe County (N.C.) native Spence Moore on the porch of his Smyth County (Va.) home in 1983 (Blue Ridge Heritage Archive).

International INT 25004; released 1961; collected and recorded by Alan Lomax with Shirley Collins and Anne Lomax in 1959 and 1960; produced by Kenneth S. Goldstein; eight-page booklet by Alan Lomax; Spence Moore and Roy E. Birns perform "The Girl I Left Behind")

Bad Man Ballads: Southern Journey 9 (Prestige International INT 25009; released 1961 [reissued as Rounder 1705 *Southern Journey, Vol. 5: Bad Man Ballads—Songs of Outlaws and Desperadoes* in 1997]; collected and recorded by Alan Lomax with Shirley Collins and Anne Lomax in 1959 and 1960; produced by Kenneth S. Goldstein; 11-page booklet by Alan Lomax; Spencer Moore and Everett Blevins perform "The Lawson Murder")

The Alan Lomax Collection Sampler (Rounder CD 1700; released 1997; collected and recorded by Alan Lomax; produced and edited by Gideon D'Arcangelo; Spencer Moore is featured on "The Girl I Left Behind")

The Mountain Ramblers

In 1954 the Mountain Ramblers were formed to do a regular radio show over station WBOB in Galax, Virginia. Playing much old-time material in more of a country and western style than bluegrass (at least early on), the Ramblers were a regular feature on WBOB for 13 years.

Led by the group's founder and guitarist, James Lindsey, and fiddler Glen Neaves of Fries, the Mountain Ramblers entered the 1958 Galax Fiddlers' Convention and won the coveted first prize in the band division—quite an amazing feat considering they had never before entered a fiddle contest. The rest of the band consisted of Cullen Galyean (banjo), Ivor Melton (mandolin), Thurman Pugh (bass) and Herb Lowe (guitar). The Ramblers would go on to win two more first prizes at Galax, three "Grand Band" championships at Union Grove (1962, 1963 and 1965) and dozens of other awards at smaller conventions.

James Lindsey was born on August 14, 1921, in the Island Creek community near Hillsville, Virginia. His first band was a small country outfit in 1953 that included vocalist Frances Diamond, electric steel player Wayne Robinson and rhythm guitarist Harold Hill. Calling themselves the Mountain Ramblers, they played before packed schoolhouses and did radio and television dates over a wide area, taking in WDBJ and WSLS in Roanoke and WSJS in Winston-Salem, N.C.

The band split up in the middle of 1956, and soon after Thurman Pugh (born July 16, 1956) approached Lindsey about forming a new group, in which Pugh would play bass fiddle. They rounded up Buford Kegley, a local disk jockey, on acoustic guitar, Bill Bowls on steel guitar, and Herb Lowe on guitar and mandolin. Fiddler Fred Mulkey stayed with the band for only six months, and, after Bowls also quit, noted Galax banjoist and fiddler Cullen Galyean joined the Ramblers. The group began three-part harmony singing at this point, with Pugh singing lead, Lowe tenor and Galyean baritone. In 1957 mandolinist Ivor Melton started playing with the Ramblers.

In the spring of 1958 Charles Hawks (born October 16, 1928) brought his bluegrass banjo into the group, allowing Galyean to switch to fiddle. Later that year Alan Lomax was in the Galax area, recording music for his "Southern Folk Heritage" series for Atlantic Records. Looking for a bluegrass band, he was referred to the Mountain Ramblers. Lomax recorded them (minus Lowe, who had to be replaced at the last minute by Eldridge Montgomery) in a historic session on the night of September 1, 1958, at the homeplace of Dr. W.P. Davis in Galax.

The release of the Atlantic series brought fame and notoriety to the Mountain Ramblers. The band personnel remained constant until July of 1960, when Lowe, Galyean and Hawks went their separate ways. Mount Airy banjoist Walter Dawson played with the band until his tragic death in 1961, at the age of 27. Galax fiddler Talmadge Smith then joined the group, followed by Roy Melton on electric guitar and Hozy Montgomery and Beverly Davis (W.P.'s daughter) on bluegrass banjo.

Otis Burris came in on fiddle in 1962, bringing with him instant success for the Mountain Ramblers at Union Grove (three band championships in four years), Galax (two first places), and numerous smaller conventions all over Virginia, West Virginia and North Carolina. Burris would stay with the band for six years.

Upon Burris' departure in 1968, the band experienced another period of instability. Charles Hawks was in and out of the band, Eldridge Montgomery left after 10 years, and several Galax musicians had stints with the group, including Don Weston (banjo and fiddle), Willard Gayheart (guitar) and Jimmy Zeh (banjo).

Joe Drye, a native of Concord, N.C. whom Lindsey met while playing on WPAQ in Mount Airy, joined the band in September of 1968, the same year he won the N.C. State Fiddling Championship at Cool Springs. Other new band members in the late 1960s included banjoist Carson Cooper of Sugar Grove, Virginia, and guitarist Jim McKinnon of Marion, Virginia (who joined the group in 1966). With this lineup the Ramblers won five straight first prizes at conventions in 1968.

In 1970 McKinnon left the Ramblers, and two new guitarists were introduced: Don Blevins of Marion and Darrell Rowland of Chilhowie. In the mid–1970s Eldridge Montgomery rejoined the band, whose new faces included Larry Lindsey (James' son) on lead guitar and Wendell Cockerham on banjo.

From 1978 to 1982 the Ramblers had a Saturday night program on WBOB called "Carroll-Grayson Hoedown." A new addition to the band in the mid–1980s was Ronnie Higgins, James Lindsey's son-in-law, on guitar and sharing lead/tenor vocals. During this period the Ramblers had a monthly 45-minute radio spot on WPAQ in Mount Airy.

The Mountain Ramblers' distinctive mixture of old-time and bluegrass instrumentation made them uniquely suited to playing mountain dance music, and their exposure on the Atlantic recordings and others landed them near legendary status among mountain bluegrass bands.

Discography

Sounds of the South (Atlantic SD-1346; released 1960; rereleased 1993 as Atlantic 7-82496-2; recorded by Alan Lomax with Shirley Collins in 1959; four-page booklet by Lomax; the Mountain Ramblers perform "Jesse James"; 1993 rerelease also includes "Baptizing Down by the Creek," "Big Ball's in Boston," "Big Tilda," "Cotton-Eyed Joe," "John Henry," "Little Rosewood Casket," "Oh, Miss Liza," "Old Country Church," "Old Hickory Cane," "Old Joe Clark," "Shady Grove" and "Silly Bill")

Blue Ridge Mountain Music (Atlantic SD-1347; released 1960; recorded by Alan Lomax with Shirley Collins in 1959; four-page booklet by Lomax; the Mountain Ramblers contribute "Big Ball in Boston," "Big Tilda," "Cotton Eyed Joe," "John Henry," "Liza Jane," "The Old Hickory Cane," "Rosewood Casket," "Shady Grove" and "Silly Bill")

White Spirituals (Atlantic SD-1349; released 1960; recorded and edited by Alan Lomax in 1959; four-page booklet by Lomax; the Mountain Ramblers are credited on "Baptizing Down by the River" and "The Old Country Church")

American Folk Songs for Children (Atlantic SD-1350; released 1960; recorded and edited by Alan Lomax in 1959; four-page booklet by Lomax; the Mountain Ramblers perform "Glen's Chimes," "Johnson's Old Gray Mule," "Old Joe Clark," "Train 111" and "Whoa Mule")

Southern White Spirituals: Southern Journey 11 (Prestige International INT 25011; released 1961; rereleased as Rounder 1704 *Southern Journey, Vol. 4: Brethren, We Meet Again* in 1997; collected and recorded by Alan Lomax with Shirley Collins and Anne Lomax in 1959 and 1960; produced by Kenneth S. Goldstein; eight-page booklet by Alan Lomax; the Mountain Ramblers perform "My Lord Keeps a Record")

The 37th Old-Time Fiddlers' Convention at Union Grove, North Carolina (Folkways FA 2434; released 1962; collected and recorded by Mike Seeger and Lisa Chiera in 1961; edited by Mike Seeger and John Cohen; six-page brochure by Harper Van Hoy, Mike Seeger and John Cohen; the Mountain Ramblers perform "Sally Ann" and "Twinkle Little Star")

Union Grove 50th Anniversary Album (Union Grove SS-8; released 1962; the Mountain Ramblers perform "Silly Bill")

Old Time Fiddling at Union Grove: The 38th Old Time Fiddlers' Convention at Union Grove, North Carolina (Prestige Folklore FL14030; released 1963; the Mountain Ramblers perform "Breakdown")

Galax Va. Old Fiddlers' Convention (Folkways FA 2435; released 1964; recorded by Lisa Chiera, Michael Eisenstadt, Alice Schwebke and Brian Sinclair in Galax, Virginia, 1961–63; six-page brochure by Lisa Chiera; the Mountain Ramblers are featured on "Honeysuckle Rag")

Virginia Breakdown (County 705; released 1967; the Mountain Ramblers perform "Fortune," "Red Apple Rag," "Richmond Cotillion" and "Sail Away Ladies" with Otis Burris on fiddle)

More Goodies from the Hills (Union Grove SS-3; released 1969; the Mountain Ramblers are featured on "Gold Rush")

Mountain Dance Music from the Blue Ridge (County 720; released 1969; jacket notes by Dave Freeman; consists of 12 instrumental tracks featuring Joe Drye on fiddle)

The Mountain Ramblers (GHP 908; released in 1970; recorded May 1970; produced by Charles Faurot; consists of 12 songs)

Glen Neaves *see* The Virginia Mountain Boys

J.P. Nester and Norman Edmonds

John Preston Nester (born November 26, 1876) and Norman S. Edmonds (born February 9, 1889, in Wythe County, Virginia) were a banjo-fiddle duo that played in Carroll County, Virginia, before deciding to try out for a commercial record company. In 1927 they traveled to Bristol, Tennessee, where the Victor Company was holding auditions. Along with the Carter Family, Alfred Karnes, Jimmie Rodgers, and the Johnson Brothers, Nester and Edmonds were successful, and they cut four tracks (only two of which were issued) on August 1, 1927. (The Victor Company chose to issue the fiddle-clawhammer banjo dance numbers as "John Preston Nester" only.)

After this session Nester and Edmonds returned to Hillsville, and they declined to record again when Victor returned to Bristol in 1928. Both men remained in Carroll County and continued to play music—but never again professionally—for many years. Nester died on April 10, 1967. Norman Edmonds was the special guest at the 1970 Galax Old Fiddlers' Convention, and he fiddled on an album for Davis Unlimited several years prior to his death on November 21, 1976.

Discography

"Train on the Island"/"Black-Eyed Susan" (Victor 21707; recorded August 1, 1927, in Bristol, Tennessee)

Anthology of American Folk Music, Vol. 3: Songs (Folkways FA 2953; released in 1952; reissued as Smithsonian/Folkways SFW 40090 in 1997; edited by Harry Smith; J.P. Nester performs "Train on the Island")

Ballads and Breakdowns from the Southern Mountains: Southern Journey 3 (Prestige International INT 25003; released 1961; rereleased as Rounder 1702 *Southern Journey, Vol. 2: Ballads and Breakdowns* in 1997; collected and recorded by Alan Lomax with Shirley Collins and Anne Lomax in 1959 and 1960; produced by Kenneth S. Goldstein; annotated by Alan Lomax; Norman Edmonds, Paul Edwards and

Rufus Quesinberry perform "Breaking Up Christmas," and, only on Rounder 1702, "Bonaparte's Retreat")

The 37th Old-Time Fiddlers' Convention at Union Grove, North Carolina (Folkways FA 2434; released 1962; collected and recorded by Mike Seeger and Lisa Chiera in 1961; edited by Mike Seeger and John Cohen; six-page brochure by Harper Van Hoy, Mike Seeger and John Cohen; Norman Edmonds and the Old Timers perform "Instrumental" and "Sally Ann")

28th Annual Galax Old Fiddlers Convention (Folk Promotions 825/ Kanawha 302; released 1963; Norman Edmonds performs "Monkey on a String")

Galax Va. Old Fiddlers' Convention (Folkways FA 2435; released 1964; recorded by Lisa Chiera, Michael Eisenstadt, Alice Schwebke and Brian Sinclair in Galax, Virginia, 1961–63; six-page brochure by Lisa Chiera; Norman Edmonds is featured on "Kingdom's Come" and "Walk in the Parlor" [with the Old Timers])

Old time fiddler Norman Edmonds in the mid–1970s (photo by Mark Sanderford; Blue Ridge Heritage Archive).

Old Time Fiddling at Union Grove: The 38th Annual Old-Time Fiddlers Convention at Union Grove, North Carolina (Prestige 14039; released 1964; Norman Edmonds plays "Walking in the Parlor")

Train on the Island: Traditional Blue Ridge Mountain Fiddle Music by Norman S. Edmonds (Davis Unlimited DU 33002; released ca. 1970; consists of 14 tracks by Edmonds)

Round the Heart of Old Galax, Vol. 3 (County 535; released 1980; liner notes by Wayne Martin; consists of 14 songs, some commercial 78 rpm recordings made in the 1920s and 1930s, others from Library of Congress field recordings of 1941; J.P. Nester and Norman Edmonds are featured on "Black Eyed Susie" and "Train on the Island"—the only two issued duets they made in 1927 for Victor)

Rural String Bands of Virginia (County CD-3502; released 1994; notes by Kinney Rorrer; remastered by Dave Glasser; J.P. Nester and Norman Edmonds perform "Train on the Island")

The New Ballard's
Branch Bogtrotters

Taking their name from the famed old-time band of the 1930s and early 1940s, the New Ballard's Branch Bogtrotters took an unprecedented four straight first prizes in the old-time band competition (1993, 1994, 1995 and 1996) at the Galax Old Fiddlers' Convention and have made a handful of recordings on the Heritage label.

The founding members of the New Bogtrotters include award-winning fiddler Greg Hooven, clawhammer banjoist Peco Watson, guitarist Dennis Hall, highly decorated guitarist Mike Brown, mandolinist Dallas Hall and bassist Dale Morris.

Hooven was born in 1968 and started playing the fiddle in a two-finger style when he was about 12 years old. His fiddling was influenced by Whit Sizemore, Edgar Higgins, Thornton Spencer (who taught him, at age 14, to properly use four fingers), Kahle Brewer, Fred Cockerham and Rafe Brady. Hooven made two recordings on the Heritage label: *Tribute to Fred Cockerham* (079) and *Old Sport* (083), the latter with his band Back-Step (accompanied by Nicholas McMillian, Chester McMillian, Ray Chatfield and Marvin Cockram) in 1991. He plays with Alec (Uncle Eck) Dunford's old fiddle, which was passed down to bandmates Dennis and Dallas Hall's parents, Oscar and Laramie Hall. Hooven used the historic instrument to capture first prize in old time fiddle at the 1994 and 1996 Galax Old Fiddlers' Conventions.

Peco Watson grew up in Grayson County, Virginia, and took up the clawhammer banjo in 1974. He plays a banjo crafted by Kyle Creed, who was a great influence and teacher. Watson and Hooven have played in bands together since the mid–1980s.

Like Dennis Hall, Mike Brown has been playing guitar for nearly a quarter century, starting when he was just 12 years old. As a youngster he played with respected fiddler Jimmy Arnold of Fries, Virginia. He later picked the guitar, country-style, with Buford Kegley. Brown is a frequent winner at area fiddler conventions, including first place in guitar at the 1994, 1995 and 1996 Galax competitions.

Morris grew up in Carroll County, Virginia, and has been playing bass and guitar for more than 20 years. An authority on the Galax music scene, he has played and recorded with several local musicians, including Whit Sizemore (the Shady Mountain Ramblers), Kyle Creed, Rafe Brady, Enoch Rutherford (the Gold Hill Band) and Brian and Debbie Grim (the Konnarock Critters).

Hooven left the band in the late 1990s and formed his own group called the Galax Way. Joining up with the New Bogtrotters in the late 1990s was

The award-winning New Ballard's Branch Bogtrotters: (front row, left to right) Dale Morris, Dennis Hall, Greg Hooven, (back row, left to right) Mike Brown, Dallas Hall and Peco Watson (courtesy Dale Morris).

Greg Hooven, a two-time winner in old time fiddle at Galax, on stage at the Mount Airy Fiddlers' Convention in 1999 (photo by the author).

fiddler Kirk Sutphin of Walkertown, N.C, and bassist Bill Slys. With this new lineup the Bogtrotters took yet another first prize in the Galax old-time band category, in 1999.

Discography

Same Branch, Different Trotters (Heritage HRC-C-109)
Hot to Trot (Heritage HRC-C-115)
The Galax Way: A Collection of Old Time Mountain Tunes & Songs (Heritage HRC-CD-116; released 1995; recorded and mixed by Bobby Patterson in Galax, Virginia; contains selections from HRC 109 and 115, plus two previously unreleased tracks)
60th Annual [Galax] Old Fiddlers' Convention (Heritage HRC-C-712; released 1997; the New Ballard's Branch Bogtrotters perform "Jimmy Sutton")

North Carolina Ridge Runners

Ashe County string band the North Carolina Ridge Runners recorded a couple of sides for Columbia on April 17, 1928, accompanying Frank Blevins and His Tar Heel Rattlers and the Carolina Night Hawks to Atlanta, Georgia.

The Ridge Runners were comprised of fiddler Elmer Elliott, a schoolteacher and part-time postal worker; guitarist Gleason (Dock) Miller, a longtime friend of Elliott's; and Willie Fugate, who could play the banjo, guitar or mandolin. Elliott, who was born in 1904, learned music at an early age from his uncle Joe Elliott, who played fiddle, and cousin Will Elliott, who picked the banjo.

Unlike Blevins, the Ridge Runners had no contract with Columbia, but their audition so impressed recording director Frank Walker that he recorded two of their songs that day, "Nobody's Darling" and "Be Kind to a Man When He's Down."

Elmer Elliott moved to southeast Pennsylvania in the mid–1930s and started playing with fellow displaced Ashe Countians Arthur "Slick" Wood, Lester "Shorty" Miller, Bryan Dolinger and Ola Belle Campbell (Reed). Still called the North Carolina Ridge Runners, they gained a significant radio market over Pennsylvania, Maryland and Delaware. Popular figures at music parks such as Sunset Park in West Grove, Pennsylvania, the Ridge Runners stayed together, in various combinations, for nearly twenty years.

Discography

"Nobody's Darling"/"Be Kind to a Man When He's Down" (Columbia 15650-D; recorded on April 17, 1928, in Atlanta, Georgia)

Elmer Elliott (left) and Gleason (Dock) Miller of the North Carolina Ridge Runners in Ashe County, N.C., circa 1928 (courtesy Marshall Wyatt).

Music from the Lost Provinces (Old Hat CD-1001; released 1997; produced, booklet notes and graphic design by Marshall Wyatt; the North Carolina Ridge Runners are featured on "Nobody's Darling" and "Be Kind to a Man When He's Down")

Bob Paisley

James Robert Paisley, who played for many years in the Southern Mountain Boys and founded the Southern Grass traditional bluegrass band, was born March 14, 1931, in Ashe County, North Carolina. While Bob was an infant his family migrated to Landenberg, Pennsylvania. Paisley's parents played old-time music for their own entertainment (his father was a clawhammer banjo picker), and Bob took up harmonica and guitar while still a child. Paisley was also influenced by radio acts on the *Grand Ole Opry*, recording artists such as the Monroe Brothers and Blue Sky Boys, and regional bands such as the North Carolina Ridge Runners.

After military service in the 1950s, Paisley married Vivian O'Connor and started working as a chemist. He soon joined fiddler Ralph Jamison's country-western band in nearby Wilmington, Delaware. Around 1964, when Bob met Ted Lundy, a banjo picker transplanted from Galax, Virginia, and a veteran of Alex Campbell and Ola Belle and the New River Boys and Girls, the two joined with others to form the Southern Mountain Boys. The group cut four albums (three on Rounder) between 1973 and 1978, on which two Paisley was credited as coleader.

Paisley played with the Southern Mountain Boys for about 15 years. In 1979 he had a series of hip ailments, but after recovering he reorganized the old group as the Southern Grass, with his son Daniel on guitar and Ted's eldest son, T.J. Lundy, on mandolin. (Jerry Lundy, Ted's distant cousin, fiddled with both the Southern Mountain Boys and Southern Grass.) The band gained a following fairly quickly on the festival circuit and recorded an album for Rounder in 1981 with new band members LeRoy Mumma, Dick Staber, Randy Stewart and Earl Yager.

In the 1980s the Southern Grass cut numerous albums, made four tours of Europe, and went to Japan in 1986. The band saw many new faces, including Randall Boring, Steve Huber and Richard Underwood on banjo; Joe Allison and Bob Lundy on mandolin; Jack Leiderman on mandolin and fiddle; and Michael Paisley (Bob's son) on bass fiddle. In the 1990s the band consisted of Bob, sons Dan and Mike, Lundy, Leiderman and Underwood.

Discography

Ted Lundy & the Southern Mountain Boys (GHP; released 1972)
The Old Swinging Bridge (Rounder 0020; released in 1973; recorded Bethesda, Maryland, in August 1972; produced by the Rounder Collective; jacket notes by Carl Goldstein)
Slipping Away (Rounder 0055; released 1976)
Lovesick and Sorrow (Rounder 0107; released 1978)
Bob Paisley and Southern Grass (Rounder 0142; released 1981; consists of 12 tracks)
An Old Love Affair (Brandywine; released 1982)

Pickin' in Holland (Strictly Country; released 1983; recorded in The Netherlands on March 31, 1982)

I Still Love You Yet (Mountain Laurel; released 1985)

Rounder Bluegrass, Vol. 1 (Rounder 11511; released 1987; Ted Lundy and the Southern Mountain Boys perform "Old Swinging Bridge")

Home of Light and Love (Mountain Laurel; released 1988)

Rounder Old-Time Music (Rounder 11510; released 1988; Ted Lundy and the Southern Mountain Boys perform "It Rained a Mist")

Rounder Banjo (Rounder 296/11542; released 1988; Bob Paisley performs "Goodbye Liza Jane" with Ted Lundy)

Angels Rejoiced: Live in Holland (Strictly Country 20; released 1989; Bob Paisley and the Southern Grass perform "When My Time Has Come to Go")

No Vacancy (Brandywine; released 1992)

25 Years of Strictly Country (Strictly Country 45; released 1996; Bob Paisley and the Southern Grass are featured on "Behind These Prison Waltz of Love")

Who Will Calm the Storm (Strictly Country 26; released 1996; Bob Paisley and the Southern Grass perform "Two Little Boys" and "Fire on the Mountain")

Live in Holland (Strictly Country 25; released 1997)

Steeped in Tradition (Brandywine 1004; released 1999; consists of 12 tracks)

Roscoe and Leone Parish

Roscoe Parish and his younger sister, Leone, were traditional musicians from Carroll County who both taught at Coal Creek School. Leone (born on July 20, 1902) taught first, second and fourth grades at Coal Creek, first called Glenwood School, from 1926 to 1965, and helped her students form a rhythm band. A multi-instrumentalist, Leone played the autoharp, ukulele, piano, guitar and organ and performed at most school functions, including graduation. A major influence on her life and music was her older sister Ninnie (1890–1984), also a teacher.

Roscoe (born in 1897) played both the fiddle and banjo, and he built the instruments he played. His father, Johnny Franklin Parish (who married Mattie Lou Matthews in 1889), played the fiddle and banjo and taught him many songs; Roscoe's oldest son was named after Johnny and plays the guitar, fiddle and mandolin. Roscoe, who married Dora Arizona (Zona) Ling in 1928, frequently entertained at Coal Creek School, accompanied by his brothers Earl on banjo and Fred on guitar. Roscoe died in 1984; Leone died on November 25, 1988.

Discography

Old Time Tunes from Coal Creek (Heritage V; released 1975; recorded and liner notes by Bobby Patterson; Roscoe and Leone Parish are featured on "Miss Johnson's Hornpipe," "Tildy Moore," "Ole Buzzard," "Ain't Gonna Rain No More," "Liquor

Seller," "The Boatsman's Daughter" and "Chinquapin"; also featured are the
Pipers Gap Ramblers)

The Old Time Way (Heritage 070; released 1986; produced by Andy Cahan and Alice
Gerrard; photos by Alice Gerrard; graphics and cover design by Andy Cahan;
Roscoe [fiddle, banjo] and Leone Parish [vocals, guitar] perform 16 tracks on Side
Two; fiddler Luther Davis [1887–1986] is featured on Side One's 16 tracks)

Pipers Gap Ramblers

Two sets of brothers—Ike (1876–1945) and Haston (1874–1952) Lowe,
who played fiddle and banjo, and Josh and Walter Hanks on guitar and tam-
bourine—formed the Pipers Gap Ramblers in about 1916. They were from
the Coal Creek section of Carroll County and often played for community
dances in Pipers Gap and the surrounding area.

In September 1927 the group traveled to Winston-Salem, N.C., to try
out for OKeh Records. The Pipers Gap Ramblers had a successful audition
and then recorded six sides, of which two were released. The band members
were reportedly dissatisfied with the vocal mix, and subsequently lost interest in recording. The group continued to play music in and around Galax,
Virginia, until disbanding sometime in the 1940s.

Discography

"I Ain't Nobody's Darling"/"Yankee Doodle" (OKeh 45185; recorded September 26,
1927, in Winston-Salem, North Carolina)

Round the Heart of Old Galax, Vol. 3 (County 535; released 1980; liner notes by Wayne
Martin; consists of 14 songs, some commercial 78 rpm recordings made in the
1920s and 1930s, others from Library of Congress field recordings of 1941; the
Pipers Gap Ramblers perform "I Ain't Nobody's Darling" and "Yankee Doo-
dle"—the only issued recordings from their solo recording session in 1927 for
OKeh)

Old Time Tunes from Coal Creek (Heritage V; released 1975; recorded and liner notes
by Bobby Patterson; the Pipers Gap Ramblers are featured on "I Ain't Nobody's
Darling" and "Yankee Doodle"; also featured are Roscoe Parish, Leone Parish
and John Patterson)

Frank Proffitt

Frank Noah Proffitt was born June 1, 1913, in Laurel Bloomery, Tennessee, near the North Carolina border. His father, Wiley Proffitt—a farmer,
cooper and tinker—moved the family to the extreme western part of Watauga

County—a region once known as Pick Britches, what the locals now call "the Beaver Dams country"—when Frank was just a youngster. Wiley taught his son the art of handcrafting banjos and also handed down many songs to Frank, as did Frank's Uncle Noah and an aunt, Nancy Prather.

Over the years Frank Proffitt collected hundreds of traditional songs and stories from his friends and neighbors. He worked primarily as a farmer and carpenter, but over the years he also worked on road crews, WPA projects and TVA projects, sometimes as far away as Oak Ridge, Tennessee, and Toledo, Ohio.

Anne and Frank Warner first met Proffitt in 1938, when they made a return visit to Nathan Hicks, a dulcimer maker and Proffitt's father-in-law, in Beech Mountain. Proffitt taught the regional ballad "Tom Dooley"—based on the real-life 1866 murder of Laura Foster and the subsequent hanging of the convicted Thomas Dula in Wilkes County—to the Warners, who recorded the song in 1940. Frank Warner taught his version to Alan Lomax, who shortened it to three verses and published it in 1947 in his *Folk Song USA*. Warner recorded "Tom Dooley" for Elektra Records in 1952 but did not copyright his version. Seven years later, the Kingston Trio's 45-RPM recording of "Tom Dooley" sold over 3 million copies and won a Gold Record award. A copyright dispute over the song was settled out of court, granting royalties to Proffitt, Warner and Lomax after 1962.

Subsequent "Tom Dooley" publicity led to Proffitt's first public appearance, in 1961 at the University of Chicago's First Annual Folk Festival. Proffitt went on to play at the Old Town (Chicago) School of Folk Music in 1962, the Asheville Folk Festival in 1963, the National Folk Festival (Kentucky, 1963), the "North Carolina Day" concert at the 1964 World's Fair in New York, and the 1964 Newport Folk Festival.

Proffitt went on to record over 120 songs for the Warners and albums for Folkways Records and Folk-Legacy Records. Proffitt, a noted banjo and dulcimer craftsman (his fretless banjos were extremely popular), died on November 24, 1965. He is buried in a small cemetery near the home he built with his own hands for his family. His epitaph says: "Going across the mountain,/Oh, fare you well."

Discography

Frank Proffitt Sings Folk Songs (Folkways 2360; released 1962; collected and recorded by Sandy Paton near Reese, N.C., in 1961; 7-page annotated booklet by Anne and Frank Warner and Sandy Paton; the first recordings of Proffitt include his own composition, "Beaver Dam Road," and the satirical Civil War song "Old Abe")

Frank Proffitt (Folk-Legacy 1; recorded by Sandy Paton at Proffitt's home in January 1962; edited and annotated [22-page booklet] by Paton; released March 1962 [reissued in 1967 in England as Topic 12T162]; includes lyrics and Proffitt's version of "Tom Dooley," the first song he heard his father pick on the banjo; "Handsome Molly" was recorded by G.B. Grayson in 1927 and sung by Doc Watson on *Old Time Music at Clarence Ashley's*; Ashley and the Carolina Tar Heels recorded a similar version of "I'm Going Back to North Carolina" for Victor in 1928; features three original songs by Proffitt: "Trifling Woman," "Going Across the Mountain" and "Tom Dooley")

Traditional Music at Newport 1964, Part 2 (Vanguard VRS-9183/VSD-79183; released 1965; collected, recorded and edited by Ralph Rinzler with Jack Lothrop at Newport, Rhode Island, in 1964; liner notes and four-page brochure by Ralph Rinzler; Proffitt is featured on "My Home's Across the Blue Ridge Mountains" and "Poor Man")

Frank Proffitt Memorial Album (Folk-Legacy 36; released spring 1969; recorded in Huntington, Vermont, ca. 1963 by Sandy Paton; notes [18-page booklet] by Sandy Paton; lyrics provided; includes the last tapes Proffitt made before his death; features four original songs: "Poor Man" [based on the great drought of 1932], "Shull's Mills" [referring to a small community about 10 miles south of Proffitt's home], "Poor Soldiers" [a Civil War song learned from Nancy Prather] and "Blackberry Wine" [a sad tale told to Proffitt by a beggar in Mountain City, Tennessee])

High Atmosphere (Rounder 0028; released 1974; collected and recorded by John Cohen in Virginia and North Carolina in 1965; produced by Mark Wilson and John Cohen; nine-page booklet by Cohen and Wilson; Proffitt performs "Cumberland Gap," "Pretty Crowing Chicken" and "Satan, Your Kingdom Must Come Down")

The North Carolina Banjo Collection (Rounder 0439; 2-CD set released 1998; produced by Bob Carlin; Frank Proffitt performs "Cumberland Gap")

Holland Puckett

Holland Puckett was born July 15, 1899, on a farm in The Hollows, Patrick County, Virginia. He lived between Ararat, Virginia, and nearby Mount Airy, North Carolina. Puckett had strong ties to such important Surry County musicians as Ben Jarrell and Da Costa Woltz. In April 1927 Puckett traveled with Woltz and his band, the Southern Broadcasters, to Richmond, Indiana, to record for Gennett. Although he recorded solo, many of his records were issued under the pseudonyms Harvey Watson, Si Puckett, Riley Wilcox, and Robert Howell.

Puckett, who played the banjo, guitar and harmonica, worked as a bookkeeper for a Mount Airy tobacco warehouse. He died on July 28, 1934, allegedly from a knife wound inflicted during a fight over a poker game.

Discography

"Put on Your Old Gray Bonnett"/"Weeping Willow Tree" (Gennett 6144; Challenge 270; recorded in Richmond, Indiana, ca. April 1927)

Gennetts of Old Time Tunes

Holland Puckett

HOLLAND PUCKETT

Exclusive Gennett Artist

OUT from the mountains near The Hollow, Virginia, came this long rangy mountaineer to record for Gennett. Holland has a style all his own, singing and playing his guitar and harmonica in a most pleasing manner.

PUT ON YOUR OLD GRAY BONNETT— WEEPING WILLOW TREE — *Old Time Singin' & Playin— Guitar & Harp Acc.* — 6144 .75

A MOTHER'S ADVICE—*Old Time Singin' & Playin'— Guitar Acc.* CHARLES A. BROOKS—*Old Time Singin' & Playin— Guitar Acc.* — 6163 .75

DRUNKEN HICCOUGHS—*Old Time Singin' & Playin'— Guitar Acc.* THE BROKEN ENGAGEMENT—*Old Time Singin' & Playin' —Guitar Acc.* — 6189 .75

HE LIVES ON HIGH—*Old Time Singin' & Playin'— Guitar Acc.* I'LL REMEMBER YOU LOVE IN MY PRAYERS— *Old Time Singin' & Playin'—Guitar Acc.* — 6206 .75

THE KEY HOLE IN THE DOOR—*Old Time Singin' & Playin'—Guitar Acc.* THE DYING COWBOY—*Old Time Singin' & Playin'— Guitar Acc.* — 6271 .75

"Long rangy mountaineer" Holland Puckett was spotlighted in a 1927 Gennett catalogue (Blue Ridge Heritage Archive).

"A Mother's Advice"/"Put on Your Old Gray Bonnett" (Champion 15299; recorded in Richmond, Indiana, ca. April 1927)

"The Bright Sherman Valley"/"Put on Your Old Gray Bonnett" (Challenge 329; recorded in Richmond, Indiana, ca. April-May 1927)

"Put on Your Old Gray Bonnett" (Herwin 75554; reverse by Da Costa Woltz's Southern Broadcasters; recorded in Richmond, Indiana, ca. April 1927)

"Weeping Willow Tree" (Champion 15334; Silvertone 8158; Supertone 9243; reverse by David Miller, John McGhee; recorded in Richmond, Indiana, ca. April 1927)

"A Mother's Advice"/"Weeping Willow Tree" (Challenge 330; recorded in Richmond, Indiana, ca. April 1927)

"The Broken Engagement"/"Weeping Willow Tree" (Bell 1179; recorded in Richmond, Indiana, ca. April-May 1927)

"He Lives on High"/"I'll Remember You Love in My Prayers" (Gennett 6206; Challenge 270; recorded in Richmond, Indiana, ca. April 1927)

"He Lives on High" (Challenge 15333; Silvertone 5075; Silvertone 8176; Supertone 9263; reverse by Ben Jarrell; recorded in Richmond, Indiana, ca. April 1927)

"A Mother's Advice"/"Chas. A. Brooks" (Gennett 6163; Herwin 75556; recorded in Richmond, Indiana, ca. April 1927)

"The Dying Cowboy"/"The Keyhole in the Door" (Gennett 6271; recorded in Richmond, Indiana, ca. April-May 1927)

"The Dying Cowboy" (Champion 15428; Herwin 75557; reverse by Bradley Kincaid, David Miller; recorded in Richmond, Indiana, ca. April 1927)

"Come and Kiss Me, Baby Darling"/"The Dying Cowboy" (Silvertone 5065; Silvertone 25065; Silvertone 8152; Supertone 9253; recorded in Richmond, Indiana, ca. April-May 1927)

"Drunken Hiccoughs"/"The Broken Engagement" (Gennett 6189; recorded in Richmond, Indiana, ca. May 1927)

"Drunken Hiccoughs" (Champion 15356; reverse by John Hammond; recorded in Richmond, Indiana, ca. May 1927)

"The Keyhole in the Door"/"Drunken Hiccoughs" (Challenge 328; recorded in Richmond, Indiana, ca. May 1927)

"The Broken Engagement"/"The Bright Sherman Valley" (Herwin 75562; recorded in Richmond, Indiana, ca. May 1927)

"The Bright Sherman Valley"/"Come and Kiss Me, Baby Darling" (Gennett 6433; recorded in Richmond, Indiana, ca. May 1927)

"The Keyhole in the Door"/"The Bright Sherman Valley" (Silvertone 5064; Silvertone 25064; Silvertone 8153; Supertone 9254; recorded in Richmond, Indiana, ca. May 1927)

"I'll Remember You in My Prayers" (Herwin 75559; reverse by Ben Jarrell; recorded in Richmond, Indiana, ca. May 1927)

"Little Birdie"/"Come and Kiss Me, Baby Darling" (Herwin 75563; recorded in Richmond, Indiana, ca. May 1927)

"The Old Cottage Home"/"The Maple on the Hill" (Gennett 6532; recorded in Richmond, Indiana, ca. May 11, 1928)

"Little Bessie"/"The Old Cottage Home" (Supertone 9342; recorded in Richmond, Indiana, ca. May 11, 1928)

"The Maple on the Hill"/"Faded Bunch of Roses" (Supertone 9186; recorded in Richmond, Indiana, ca. May 11, 1928)

"Faded Bunch of Roses"/"Little Bessie" (Gennett 6720; recorded in Richmond, Indiana, ca. May 11, 1928)

The Red Fox Chasers

This old-time string band, organized in 1927, consisted of vocalist-guitarist A.P. "Fonzie" Thompson, vocalist–harmonica player Bob Cranford, banjoist Paul Miles and fiddler Guy Brooks. The four musicians met at the 1927 Union Grove Fiddler's Convention, and on April 15, 1928, they recorded eight sides for the Gennett Company of Richmond, Indiana. Miles named the group and arranged for their first recordings.

The Red Fox Chasers went on to record 40 more sides (most written by Brooks) for various companies. Several of their hits remained influential for years: "Did You Ever See a Devil, Uncle Joe?" "Stolen Love," "Goodbye Little Bonnie," "Little Darling Pal of Mine," "Honeysuckle Time," "Sweet Fern," "Wreck on the Mountain Road" and "Pretty Polly." They also recorded a number of mountain gospel favorites for Gennett. Because Gennett routinely leased many of its sides to specialty labels like those run by Sears Roebuck and Montgomery Ward, some of the Red Fox Chasers' biggest sellers came out under other names, such as the Virginia Possum Tamers and the Black Mountain Gang.

The band made its last recordings in 1929, but in January 1931 Thomp-

The Red Fox Chasers: (left to right) Guy Brooks, Bob Cranford, A.P. Thompson and Paul Miles (courtesy Marshall Wyatt).

son and Cranford recorded 12 sides as a duo. Miles recorded for the Library of Congress in the late 1930s.

Thompson and Cranford were neighbors in the Thurmond community of Wilkes County. As youngsters they learned to sing from seven-shape gospel songbooks and received vocal lessons from a traveling music teacher, who helped them perfect their harmony singing. In his teens Thompson learned to play the guitar, and Cranford took up the mouth harp (harmonica) as the duo began performing old-time regional music for local audiences.

Miles and Brooks also grew up together, in nearby Alleghany County. Miles practiced on a homemade fretless banjo crafted from a meal sifter and groundhog hide, while Brooks sawed on a fiddle he earned by gathering chestnuts. They played mostly fiddle music until they teamed up with Thompson and Cranford.

Discography

"That Sweetie of Mine" (Champion 16243)
"Otto Wood" (Champion 16261)
"Sweet Fern" (Champion 16490)
"Katy Cline" (Champion 16676)
"Two Babes in the Woods" (Champion 16768)
"Under the Double Eagle" (Gennett 6461)
"The Arkansas Traveler" (Gennett 6516)
"Weeping Willow Tree" (Gennett 6547)
"Mississippi Sawyer" (Gennett 6568)
"Stolen Love" (Gennett 6636)
"Something Wrong with My Gal" (Gennett 6672)
"The Red Fox Chasers Makin' Licker, Part 1/2" (Gennett 6886)
"Little Darling Pal of Mine" (Gennett 6901)
"The Red Fox Chasers Makin' Licker, Part 3/4" (Gennett 6912)
"Virginia Bootleggers" (Gennett 6930)
"Devilish Mary" (Gennett 6945)
"How I Love My Mabel" (Gennett 6959)
A Collection of Mountain Ballads (County 502; released 1964; edited by David Freeman; consists of commercial 78 rpm recordings made from 1926 to 1930; the Red Fox Chasers perform "Wreck on the Mountain Road")
The Red Fox Chasers (County 510; released 1967; edited by David Freeman; liner notes by Richard Nevins; consists of 12 commercial 78 rpm recordings made from 1928 to 1930)
Old-Time String Band Classics (County 531; recordings made from 1927 to 1933)
Traditional Country Classics, 1927–1929 (Historical HLP 8003; released ca. 1968; edited by Joe Bussard, Jr.; liner notes by Richard Nevins; contains 14 commercial 78 rpm recorded from 1927 to 1929; Cranford, Miles and Thompson perform "Honeysuckle Time")
The Cold-Water Pledge, Vol. 1: Songs of Moonshine and Temperance Recorded in the Golden Age (Marimac 9104 [cassette]; released 1984; edited by Pat Conte; contains brief insert leaflet; booklet by W.K. McNeil sold separately; consists of 19 commercial 78 rpm recordings made from 1925 to 1937; A.P. Cranford and Bob Thompson perform "Jim and Me")

The Cold-Water Pledge, Vol. 2: Songs of Moonshine and Temperance Recorded in the Golden Age (Marimac 9105 [cassette]; released 1984; edited by Pat Conte; contains brief insert leaflet; booklet by W.K. McNeil sold separately; consists of 19 commercial 78 rpm recordings made from 1925 to 1937; the Red Fox Chasers are featured on "Virginia Bootlegger")

Old-Time Mountain Ballads (County 3504; released 1996; annotated by Charles Wolfe; the Red Fox Chasers perform "Wreck on the Mountain Road")

AS THOMPSON, CRANFORD & MILES
"The Blind Man and His Child" (Gennett 6602)

AS THOMPSON & MILES WITH THE RED FOX CHASERS
"Put My Little Shoes Away" (Gennett 6914)
"The Girl I Loved in Sunny Tennessee" (Gennett 6930)

Ola Belle Reed *see* Alex Campbell & Ola Belle [Reed]

Jack Reedy

Banjo picker Jack Reedy did extensive touring, recording and radio work from the mid–1920s to the late 1930s. A native of Smyth County, Virginia, Reedy was associated with many Central Blue Ridge musicians, including H.M. Barnes' Blue Ridge Ramblers, the Hill Billies, and Frank and Ed Blevins.

With the Blue Ridge Ramblers Reedy toured the East Coast vaudeville circuit during the late 1920s and early 1930s. The Ramblers' lineup included fiddler Fred Roe and guitarist Henry Roe, both of Bristol, Tennessee, and whom would later join steel guitarist Frank Wilson of Charlotte, North Carolina, and guitarist Walter (Sparkplug) Hughes from Damascus, Virginia, in Reedy's Walker Mountain String Band, which recorded for Brunswick in 1928.

Reedy, later in 1928, teamed up with Bristol fiddler Jack Pierce, guitarist Malcolm Warley of Bristol and Damascus, Virginia, guitarist Carl Cruise. This band, called the Smyth County Ramblers, recorded a pair of numbers for the Victor Company on October 27, 1928.

Reedy, whose finger-picking on banjo predated the popular bluegrass style by 15 years, later played in the Southern Buccaneers band with the Blevins brothers and Corwin Matthews. This quartet played many theaters in West Virginia and between 1933 and 1936 participated in the White Top Folk Festival in Washington County, Virginia.

In the late 1930s Reedy did radio work in Bristol, Tennessee, and Bluefield, West Virginia. He tried to make a full-time living with his music, but it was never possible for him to give up working at furniture factories. Reedy was still playing music when he died of a heart attack in Bluefield, Virginia, in 1940.

Discography

WITH H.M. BARNES' BLUE RIDGE RAMBLERS

"Golden Slippers"/"Old Joe Clark" (Brunswick 313; recorded January 28, 1929, in New York City)

"Repasz Band March"/"Our Director March" (Brunswick 361; Melotone 18022; recorded January 28, 1929, in New York City)

"Lineman's Serenade"/"Goin' Down the Road Feelin' Bad" (Brunswick 327; recorded January 28, 1929, in New York City)

"Who Broke the Lock on the Hen-House Door?"/"She'll Be Comin' Round the Mountain When She Comes" (Brunswick 310; Brunswick 1027; Supertone 2052/2093; recorded January 28, 1929, in New York City)

Jack Reedy at the White Top Folk Festival in 1933 (courtesy Marshall Wyatt).

"Blue Ridge Ramblers' Rag"/"Flop Eared Mule" (Brunswick 346; Supertone 2093; recorded January 28, 1929, in New York City)

"Honolulu Stomp"/"Three O'Clock in the Morning" (Brunswick 463; recorded January 29, 1929, in New York City)

"Echoes of Shenandoah Valley"/"Mandolin Rag" (Brunswick 397; recorded January 29, 1929, in New York City)

[Title Unknown] (County 548; H.M. Barnes' Blue Ridge Ramblers perform "Mandolin Rag")

Early Mandolin Classics, Vol. 1 (Rounder 1050; released 1989; H.M. Barnes' Blue Ridge Ramblers perform "Echoes of the Shenandoah Valley")

AS JACK REEDY AND HIS WALKER MOUNTAIN STRING BAND

"Ground Hog"/"Chinese Breakdown" (Brunswick 221; recorded in Ashland, Kentucky, ca. February 15, 1928)

A Collection of Mountain Songs (County 504; released 1965; edited by David Freeman;

consists of commercial 78 rpm recordings made from 1927 to 1930; Jack Reedy and His Walker Mountain String Band perform "Groundhog")
Music from the Lost Provinces (Old Hat CD-1001; released 1997; produced, booklet notes and graphic design by Marshall Wyatt; Jack Reedy and His Walker Mountain String Band perform "Ground Hog" and "Chinese Breakdown")

AS THE SMYTH COUNTY RAMBLERS
"My Name Is Ticklish Reuben"/"Way Down in Alabama" (Victor 40144; recorded in Bristol, Tennessee, on October 27, 1927)
Music from the Lost Provinces (Old Hat CD-1001; released 1997; produced, booklet notes and graphic design by Marshall Wyatt; the Smyth County Ramblers are featured on "My Name Is Ticklish Reuben" and "Way Down in Alabama")

Larry Richardson

Bluegrass singer and banjoist Larry Richardson was born and raised in Mount Airy, N.C. Richardson began his professional music career as a Scruggs-style banjo picker, heavily influenced by the early recordings of Bill Monroe.

In the summer of 1949 Richardson picked and sang with Bobby Osborne on WPFB radio in Middletown, Ohio. After a dispute with the WPFB management they started working for WHIS in Bluefield, West Virginia. Richardson and Osborne (along with fiddler Ray Morgan) joined up with the Lonesome Pine Fiddlers in the fall of 1949, replacing brothers Charlie and Curly Ray Cline. Led by bassist Ezra Cline, the Fiddlers recorded two duets featuring the vocals of Richardson and Osborne, but for the most part Richardson played a purely instrumental role in helping the Fiddlers establish a full-fledged bluegrass sound. With Richardson the Fiddlers recorded four sides for Cozy in March 1950. One of the songs, "Pain in My Heart," was leased to Carol and subsequently covered by Flatt and Scruggs on Mercury.

In mid–1951 Richardson left the Fiddlers to develop his clear, high tenor and distinctive banjo picking with Carl Sauceman, a multi-label recording artist. Richardson was briefly reunited with the Lonesome Pine Fiddlers before performing on WCYB in Bristol, Tennessee, in the spring of 1951.

After several years of traveling (and working with Bill Monroe in 1954), Richardson returned to the Tar Heel State in 1955. He and banjoist Happy Smith made a couple of recordings on the now-defunct Blue Ridge label. In the mid–1960s Richardson joined the Blue Ridge Boys, and their recording *Blue Ridge Bluegrass* contains two original compositions by banjoist Richardson ("You Left Me So Blue" and "Pain in My Heart," cowritten by Bobby Osborne) and his classic arrangement of "Let Me Fall."

Richardson experienced a religious conversion in 1970 and subsequently performed only gospel music. In the 1990s he lived in Lakeland, Florida.

Discography

American Banjo Tunes & Songs in Scruggs Style (Smithsonian/Folkways CD SF 40037; originally issued as Folkways FA 2314 in 1957; rereleased 1990 with 16 previously unissued tracks; collected and recorded by Mike Seeger in 1956; four-page insert brochure by Ralph Rinzler and Mike Seeger; Richardson performs "Little Maggie," "Take Me Back to the Sunny South," and, only on the 1990 reissue, "Bucking Mule," "Dear Old Dixie" and "Lonesome Road Blues")

Galax Va. Old Fiddlers' Convention (Folkways FA 2435; released 1964; recorded by Lisa Chiera, Michael Eisenstadt, Alice Schwebke and Brian Sinclair in Galax, Virginia, 1961–63; six-page brochure by Lisa Chiera; Richardson joins Sonny Miller and Johnny Jackson on "Turkey in the Straw")

Blue Ridge Bluegrass (County 702; released 1966; with Red Barker and the Blue Ridge Boys; contains 12 tracks)

Springtime in the Mountains (County 749; released 1975; Larry Richardson performs "Larry's Ride," and, with Happy Smith, "I'm Lonesome," "Let Me Fall," "Lonesome Road Blues" and "Nashville Jail")

Windy Mountain (Bear Family Germany; released 1992; contains 26 tracks—the complete early 1950s Cozy and RCA/Victor masters of the Lonesome Pine Fiddlers)

Ric-O-Chet *see* Last Run

Enoch Rutherford

Old time fiddle and banjo player Enoch Rutherford was born on April 26, 1916, in the Gold Hill community near Independence, Virginia. His father was a fiddler and his cousin, Lee Hash, taught him to play the banjo. In his youth Rutherford played frequently with Dean Ward and Lester Anders. In addition to his skills on the fiddle and banjo, Rutherford also learned to play the piano, harmonica and guitar.

In 1944 Enoch followed his two brothers to Pennsylvania to work in the steel mills for a year. After the war, when the soldiers came back to their jobs, he was laid off and returned to Grayson County. Over the years he was a frequent winner at local fiddlers' conventions.

Rutherford played and recorded with the Gold Hill Band, whose members included, at various times, guitarist Dale Morris of Galax, fiddler Alice Gerrard of Galax, guitarist Carol Holcomb of Sparta, bassist Debbie Lawson, guitarist Dave Lawson and fiddler Wiley S. Mayo of Glade Spring, Virginia. Rutherford, Morris and Mayo were also members of the Iron Mountain

Enoch Rutherford (left) and the Gold Hill Band (left to right, Lynn Worth, Alice Gerrard, Dale Morris) perform at the Whitetop Molasses Festival in 1990 (photo by Amy Hauslohner/courtesy Dale Morris).

String Band, whose *Music from the Mountain* album was named to the Library of Congress' list of the best folk recordings of 1992. Other band members included bassist Nancy Bethel of Selma, Virginia, and guitarist Gene Hall of Elk Creek, Virginia.

Discography

Old Five String, Vol. 2 (Heritage 052; released 1991; Enoch Rutherford performs "Walking in the Parlor," "Sourwood Mountain," "Sugar Hill" and "Fall on My Knees")

WITH THE GOLD HILL BAND
Old Cap'n Rabbit (Heritage 080; released 1989; recorded by Bobby Patterson, Alice Gerrard and Hilary Dirlam; mastered by Patterson; mixed by Patterson, Gerrard and Dale Morris; liner notes by Gerrard)
Going Down This Road (Heritage HRC-C 110; released 1994; recorded and mastered by Bobby Patterson)

WITH THE IRON MOUNTAIN STRING BAND
Music from the Mountain (Heritage HRC-C 101; released 1992; recorded by Bobby Patterson; produced by Dale Morris; mixed by Patterson, Morris and W.S. Mayo on March 19–20, 1992)

The Shady Mountain Ramblers

Popular old-time traditional music group the Shady Mountain Ramblers were organized in 1971 by fiddler and luthier Whit (Big Howdy) Sizemore, who won first place in the old-time fiddle competition at the 1972 Galax Fiddlers' Convention. Bassist Audine Lineberry can also play the fiddle and guitar, and has been active in music since the 1950s. Also a songwriter, Lineberry captured many first places at fiddlers' conventions over the years.

Thomas Norman, a native of Surry County, N.C., and later a resident of Galax, Virginia, is left-handed and plays the banjo upside down and backwards, with his forefinger playing what would normally be the drop thumb notes of a right-handed player. Guitarist Chester McMillian was born in Carroll County, Virginia, and later lived in Pine Ridge, N.C. An active musician since 1950, McMillian recorded with Tommy Jarrell and played with Ernest East and the Pine Ridge Boys.

In addition to making multiple recordings and winning numerous prizes at fiddlers' conventions, the Shady Mountain Ramblers played at the Blue Ridge Folklife Festival in Ferrum, Virginia, the Smithsonian Festival of American Folklife, the Wolf Trap Center for the Performing Arts, and the 1977 National Folklife Festival near Washington, D.C. Other members of

Whit Sizemore (center) and the Shady Mountain Ramblers (left to right, Tom Norman, Mike Sizemore, Dale Morris, Dan Williams) at the 1977 Folklife Festival in Washington, D.C. (courtesy Dale Morris).

the group have included Dan Williams, Barbara Poole, and Whit's son Mike on guitar and mandolin.

Discography

Old Time Music from the Blue Ridge Mountains (Heritage II; released 1974; recorded by Bobby Patterson)

Nobody's Business (Heritage XXXI; released 1980; recorded and cover design by Bobby Patterson; produced by Fred Williams; photography by Dennis Kegley; jacket notes by Roger Wilson; consists of 18 tracks)

All Smiles Tonight (Heritage XXXIV; released 1981; recorded by Bobby Patterson; produced by Fred Williams; cover design by Andy Cahan; photography by Dennis Kegley; jacket notes by Blanton Owen; consists of 16 tracks; also features pianist Gary Patton of Galax, Virginia)

Best of Seedtime on the Cumberland (June Appal JA 0059C; released ca. 1985; Whit Sizemore and the Shady Mountain Ramblers perform "Ebenezer")

Jim Shumate

Both a member of Bill Monroe's Blue Grass Boys and Flatt & Scruggs's Foggy Mountain Boys, bluegrass fiddler Jim Shumate was born on Chestnut Mountain in northern Wilkes County. His uncle was a fiddler, and Shumate was also influenced by the "long-bow" technique and bluesy slides of the Grand Ole Opry's premier fiddler, Arthur Smith.

As a teenager Shumate played on a local radio program in Hickory, which was heard by Bill Monroe in 1944 as he drove through the Tar Heel State in his band's vehicle, the "Blue Grass Special" (a converted airport limousine). Soon after Monroe called up Shumate and invited him to join his band, the Blue Grass Boys, which was in need of a fiddler. With Monroe and the rest of the band in 1944 and 1945, Shumate played every Saturday night on the *Grand Ole Opry* program and spent the rest of the week performing at theaters, schoolhouses and ball parks across the South. (Shumate also played shortstop on Monroe's baseball team, which would take on local ball clubs before and after gigs.)

Earl Scruggs's audition with Bill Monroe was arranged by Shumate, who knew him from back home and thought highly of his three-finger banjo picking. However, Shumate did not get to play with Scruggs, because the next week fiddler Howdy Forrester returned from the Navy and, in accordance with draft regulations, was given his old job back.

In January of 1948 Earl Scruggs and Lester Flatt left Bill Monroe to form their own group, the Foggy Mountain Boys. They offered Shumate a spot in the band and soon started playing on radio programs in Danville, Virginia, Hickory, North Carolina, and Bristol, Tennessee. Shumate fiddled on the legendary band's first recording session. That same year, he won first place in the National Fiddlers' Convention in Richlands, Virginia.

Tired of life on the road, Shumate returned to Hickory in 1949 and took a job in retail furniture sales. However, he continued to perform on radio and television with his own band, and made three recordings on the Heritage label.

Shumate was a recipient of the 1995 North Carolina Folk Heritage Award, presented by the North Carolina Arts Council.

Discography

Jim Shumate: Bluegrass Fiddle Supreme (Country Road RSR-1152)
Up and at 'Em (Heritage 100)
Buckle Up the Backstrap (Heritage 106)
Whing-Ding (Heritage 112)
Going to Town (Heritage 122; released 1996)

WITH BILL MONROE AND THE BLUE GRASS BOYS
"Rocky Road Blues"/"Kentucky Waltz" (Columbia 20013; Columbia 36907; released January 14, 1946)
"True Life Blues"/"Footprints in the Snow" (Columbia 20080; Columbia 37151; released October 28, 1946)
Sixteen All-Time Greatest Hits (Columbia CS1065; released 1970)
The Classic Bluegrass Recordings, Vol. 1 (County CCS-104; released 1980)
The Classic Bluegrass Recordings, Vol. 2 (County CCS-105; released 1980)

WITH FLATT AND SCRUGGS & THE FOGGY MOUNTAIN BOYS
"God Loves His Children"/"I'm Going to Make Heaven My Home" (Mercury 6161; released January 15, 1949)
"We'll Meet Again Sweetheart"/"My Cabin in Caroline" (Mercury 6181; released April 1, 1949)
"Baby Blue Eyes"/"Bouquet in Heaven" (Mercury 6200; released July 1949)
"Down the Road"/"Why Don't You Tell Me So" (Mercury 6211; released October 1949)
Country Music (Mercury MG20359; released 1958)
Flatt and Scruggs (Mercury MG20542; released 1960)
Original Sound (Mercury MG20773; released 1963)
The Mercury Sessions, Vol. 2 (Rounder SS019)

Skeeter and the Skidmarks

The progressive old-time band Skeeter and the Skidmarks was formed in the early 1990s and consisted of clawhammer banjoist Edwin Lacey, mandolinist and fiddler Scott Freeman, guitarist Willard Gayheart and acoustic bassist Sandy Grover. All four members shared vocal duties.

Gayheart, a native of Hazard, Kentucky, was formerly a member of the Highlanders. His son-in-law Freeman was born in Mount Airy, N.C., and later relocated to Galax, Virginia. Freeman began playing as a youth with his brothers. Before joining the Skidmarks he played in Windy Hill, which placed in the top ten at a SPBGMA band contest in Nashville, Tennessee. Freeman's songwriting has been featured on recordings by IIIrd Tyme Out, Ric-O-Chet and Barry Barrier.

Skeeter and the Skidmarks made two recordings on the Hay Holler label and performed at major bluegrass festivals on both coasts, including the Merle Watson Festival in Wilkesboro, N.C., and the California Bluegrass Music Association's Grass Valley Festival.

In the late 1990s Gayheart and Freeman helped form the five-piece acoustic band Alternate Roots. Other members of the group, which released the acclaimed self-produced CD *Tales of Love and Sorrow* in 1998, are Dobroist Randy Pasley, guitarist-vocalist Katy Taylor and bassist Tony Testerman. Taylor and Testerman had previously played in Windy Hill with Freeman. Pasley was named Best All-Around Performer at the 1999 Galax Old-Time Fiddlers' Convention, as well as first-prize winner in Dobro.

A lighthearted publicity shot of Skeeter and the Skidmarks—that's mandolinist Scott Freeman about to share some "rapport" with banjoist Ed Lacey, as an amused Willard Gayheart and Sandy Grover look on (courtesy Scott Freeman).

Discography

Alternate Roots (Hay Holler HHH-CD-701; released 1994; recorded in March, July and August 1994 at Warehouse Recording in Galax, Va.; produced and mixed by Skeeter and the Skidmarks and Joseph C. Robins; executive produced by Kerry Hay; engineered and mixed by Allen Conner; liner notes by Rick Abrams)

Hubbin' It (Hay Holler HHH-CD-702; released 1996; recorded in November and December 1995 and January 1996 at Warehouse Recording in Galax, Va.; produced by Skeeter and the Skidmarks; executive produced by Kerry Hay; engineered by Allen Conner; mixed by Tim Austin; liner notes by Howard Parnes)

The Slate Mountain Ramblers

Formed in 1982, the Slate Mountain Ramblers is a Galax, Virginia–based band that carries on the traditions of old-time music into the 21st century.

The band was founded by banjoist Ray Chatfield, who moved from Colorado (where he worked at the Denver Folklore Center) to the Galax-Mount Airy area in 1980 to live near the apex of old-time music and learn from both Tommy Jarrell and Calvin Cole. On a recommendation from Jarrell, Chatfield got in touch with Richard Bowman, a fiddler from Ararat, Virginia, and a four-year veteran of the Pine River Boys. After Dan Williams of Pipers Gap—a guitarist who had played with the Shady Mountain Ramblers for seven years—and Buck Stockton from Slate Mountain (on bass) signed on, the Slate Mountain Ramblers began playing and winning at fiddlers' contests. (Bowman took top honors in old time fiddle at the 1997 Galax Old Fiddlers' Convention.)

Fiddler Richard Bowman shows his winning form at the 1999 Mount Airy Bluegrass and Old Time Fiddlers' Convention. On bass is his wife Barbara (photo by the author).

When Stockton left to play bluegrass gospel, Williams (who was born in Alleghany County in 1934) recruited Barbara Poole, an old Shady Mountain Rambler band mate of ten years past from Low Gap, N.C., to play bass. Poole's grandfather was old-time fiddler Norman Edmonds, and her brother is bluegrass fiddler Jimmy Edmonds. She also played for about eight years in Wade Ward's Buck Mountain Band. In the late 1990s Poole's musical partner was Larry Sigmon.

Chatfield left the band after four years to play with another old-time band, the Smokey Valley Boys, and later with Old Time Tradition (whose album *Jamboree* was released on Heritage in 1998). He was replaced by Bill Mansfield of Siloam in southern Surry County. Mansfield was born and raised in Raleigh, N.C. His clawhammer-style banjo playing was heavily influenced by Fred Cockerham. In the late 1990s the Slate Mountain Ramblers were in large part a Bowman family band, with Richard on fiddle, his wife Barbara on bass and teenaged daughter Marcia on banjo.

Discography

49th Annual Galax Old Fiddlers' Convention (Heritage 700; released 1985; the Slate Mountain Ramblers perform "Breaking Up Christmas")

51st Annual Galax Old Fiddlers' Convention (Heritage 703; released 1987; the Slate Mountain Ramblers are featured on "Sail Away Ladies")

Blue Ridge Mountain Holiday: The Breaking Up Christmas Story (County 2722; released 1997; produced by Paul Brown; production coordinated by Burgess Hurd; field recordings made by Paul Brown, Bob Carlin, Terri McMurray, Ray Alden and Dave Spilkia; the Slate Mountain Ramblers play "Ragtime Annie")

60th Annual Galax Old Fiddlers' Convention (Heritage 712; released 1997; the Slate Mountain Ramblers perform "Lost Indian"; Richard Bowman fiddles on "Sourwood Mountain")

The Smokey Valley Boys

Formed at the Marion (Va.) Fiddlers' Convention in 1971, the Smokey Valley Boys were originally made up of Benton Flippen on fiddle, Gilmer Woodruff on banjo, band organizer Paul Sutphin on guitar and vocals, Larry Flippen on bass and guitar, and Hoyle Jones on mandolin. All third or fourth generation musicians, they lived in and around Mount Airy, Surry County, all their lives.

The Smokey Valley Boys were one of the more dominant bands at area fiddlers' conventions, winning top prizes both as a group and individuals at Union Grove (where they took top band honors seven times), Galax, and many of the smaller festivals. From the 1950s through the early 1970s the

Members of the Smokey Valley Boys in the mid–1970s included (front row, left to right) Larry Flippen, Verlen Clifton, (back row, left to right) Paul Sutphin, Benton Flippen and Gilmer Woodruff (courtesy Paul Sutphin).

members of the Smokey Valley Boys played in bands with Kyle Creed (the Camp Creek Boys), Ernest East (and the Pine Ridge Boys) and Fred Cockerham. Well-known local musicians such as Charlie Lowe, Tommy Jarrell, Fred Cockerham, Kyle Creed and Rafe Brady were very influential in the music of the Smokey Valley Boys.

Fiddler James Benton Flippen was born in 1921. He started playing the banjo when he was 15, but soon followed the lead of his two brothers when he switched to the fiddle at age 18. He eventually joined and led several bands, including the Dryhill Draggers and Glen McPeak's Green Valley Boys, with whom he had a daily radio show on WPAQ in Mount Airy. In 1990, Flippen received the North Carolina Folk Heritage Award.

Woodruff was born in the Stuart's Creek township, near Mount Airy. He started playing the clawhammer banjo when he was 10 or 11 but put it down when he was 17 or 18. He took it up again around 1960 and played with the Pine Ridge Boys for several years.

Sutphin was born in the Round Peak community of Surry County on

October 1, 1918, and started playing guitar with Fred Cockerham and Kyle Creed when he was 14 years old. He subsequently joined the Round Peak Band, Ernest East's band, and the Camp Creek Boys before playing with the Smokey Valley Boys.

Hoyle Jones and Gilmer Woodruff eventually dropped out of the band, and mandolinist Verlen Clifton (born February 22, 1928) left for a time to play in G.F. Collins' Blue Ridge Entertainers. Curtis Spurlin handled mandolin duties for a short time. In the 1980s the Smokey Valley Boys included banjoists Carlie Marion, Ray Chatfield and Paul Brown (a noted disk jockey and historian), and guitarists Frank Bode of Toast, Mac Snow, Grady Largen and Foster Murray. The Smokey Valley Boys disbanded in 1985, after performing at such events as the 1982 Knoxville World's Fair, the final Brandywine Mountain Music Convention (1983) and the 1984 National Folk Festival.

In the 1990s Paul Sutphin, Paul Brown, Frank Bode and Verlen Clifton were members of the Toast String Stretchers, along with Terri McMurry and Ginger Bode, and produced *Wanted!* on their own label. Clifton and Sutphin were recipients of North Carolina Folk Heritage Awards in 1996.

Discography

The 38th Annual Galax Old Fiddlers Convention (Gazette 38; released 1973; the Smokey Valley Boys play "Richmond Cotillion")

The 50th Annual Old Time Fiddlers Convention at Union Grove (Union Grove SS-9; released 1974; the Smokey Valley Boys are featured on "Pole Cat Blues")

The Smokey Valley Boys (Rounder 0029; released 1974; recorded August 1973 in Pine Ridge, Surry County; produced by the Rounder Collective; back cover notes and interview by Bill Hicks; 14 traditional songs, mostly instrumental, including "Lost Indian," "Whoa Mule," Sally Ann," and "June Apple")

Visits (Heritage XXXIII; released 1981; collected, recorded and edited by Ray Alden; gatefold jacket notes by Ray Alden; the Smokey Valley Boys perform "Polecat Blues")

Appalachia—The Old Traditions—Vol. 2 (Home-Made Music LP002; released 1983; collected, recorded and edited by Mike Yates in Virginia and North Carolina, 1979-80 and 1983; three-page booklet by Mike Yates; the Smokey Valley Boys play "Cotton-Eyed Joe" and "Gary Dawson's Tune")

Brandywine '83: The 10th Anniversary Celebration of the Brandywine Mountain Music Convention (Heritage 054; released 1984; the Smokey Valley Boys perform "June Apple" and "Pole Cat Blues")

The Green Glass Cloggers: Through the Ears (Rounder 0228; released 1985; recorded in Asheville, N.C., by Steven Heller; the Smokey Valley Boys accompany the Green Glass Cloggers on "Bile Them Cabbage Down" and "Nobody's Business")

Old Time Music on the Air, Vol. 1 (Rounder 0331; released 1994; produced by Old Time Music on the Radio; the Smokey Valley Boys perform "Benton's Dream")

John Kilby Snow

Born in Grayson County, Virginia, on May 28, 1906, autoharpist John Kilby Snow and his family moved to North Carolina in 1908. Snow was introduced to the autoharp at the age of 4 (when his father traded a one-gallon ice cream freezer for a five-bar), and by the time he was 5 years old won the state autoharp championship (and a $20 prize) at Brown's Warehouse in Winston-Salem.

Snow made his first television appearance, alongside the Stanley Brothers, in 1948 on WHIS in Bluefield, West Virginia. Snow played at the Second Fret and Main Point clubs in Philadelphia and at various folk festivals, including the 1964 Philadelphia Folk Festival.

Snow developed unique brass fingerpicks and thumbpicks that allowed him to strum both up and down on the strings of the autoharp. A special index fingerpick used to pick out the melody allowed Snow, who was left-handed, to play twice as many notes as the conventional autoharpist. He played a standard 12-bar, modified autoharp and achieved a distinctive sound by "slurring" or "dragging" notes (playing two or three adjacent open strings upward in pitch very accurately with the chord bar released).

When he wasn't playing music, Snow worked primarily as a builder and carpenter. He raised four children, two of whom play autoharp and other instruments. His youngest son Jim (born 1942) plays with him on the Folkways album *Mountain Music Played on the Autoharp* and the self-produced *Father and Son* (released in 1994). After the former record was released Snow started playing at folk festivals at Philadelphia, Newport, Chicago, Mariposa, San Diego and Brandywine, among others. John Kilby Snow retired near Nottingham, Pennsylvania, and died on March 20, 1980.

In 1993 Snow was posthumously inducted into the Autoharp Hall of Fame at the Mountain Laurel Autoharp Gathering in Newport, Pennsylvania.

Discography

Mountain Music Played on the Autoharp (Folkways FA 2365; released 1965; recorded by Mike Seeger in Virginia in 1957 and 1961; eight-page booklet by Mike Seeger; Snow is featured on "May I Sleep in Your Barn Tonight, Mister?" "She'll Be Coming 'Round the Mountain" [with Wade Ward on banjo], "Flop-Eared Mule," "Ain't Going to Work Tomorrow," "John Henry," "Mule Skinner Blues," "Precious Jewel," "Red River Valley," "Tragic Romance" [with Ward] and "Wildwood Flower")

Kilby Snow: Country Songs and Tunes with Autoharp (Folkways/Asch AH 3902; released in the late 1960s)

Close to Home (Smithsonian/Folkways SF 40097; released 1997; recorded by Mike

Autoharp legend Kilby Snow could play twice as many notes as most players because of a special index fingerpick (photo by David Gahr/Southern Historical Collection, Wilson Library, The University of North Carolina at Chapel Hill).

Seeger at Wade Ward's home near Independence, Virginia, in August 1957; Kilby Snow performs "He Will Set Your Fields on Fire")

The Southern Mountain Boys
see Bob Paisley, Ted Lundy

Ernest V. "Pop" Stoneman

Ernest V. "Pop" Stoneman was born on May 25, 1895, in a log cabin on a small farm in Monarat (now Iron Ridge), Carroll County, Virginia. Left motherless at the age of 3, the youngster was reared by a stern old father with the help of three musically inclined cousins: Burton, George and Bertha Stoneman. By the age of 8 he was playing the autoharp; he would soon also learn to play the harmonica, guitar and banjo. In his youth he worked as a carpenter, on the railroad, and in nearby iron mines.

In November 1919 he married Hattie Foster (1900–1976), who like her husband came from a musical family. After their marriage, Ernest went to work in Bluefield, West Virginia. In early 1924 he heard, at a store, the debut recording of Henry Whitter, a singer, harmonica player and guitarist from Fries, Virginia, whom Stoneman knew quite well. Knowing he could outplay and outsing Whitter, Stoneman started practicing the autoharp and rack harmonica, and began saving his money for a train trip to New York City.

After making the trip and subsequently walking out of an appointment with Columbia, Stoneman recorded "The Titanic" and "The Ship That Never Returned" (recognized as the first recording with autoharp) for Ralph Peer and Polk Brockman at OKeh on September 3–4, 1924. The tracks, which subsequently had to be recut—at Stoneman's personal expense—because they were too fast, appeared, as OKeh 40288, in the spring of 1925. In May he cut more records in New York for OKeh, including a couple on which, for the first time, he was accompanied by another musician: his second cousin fiddler Emmett W. Lundy, also from Carroll County.

In 1926 Stoneman recorded for OKeh, Edison, Gennett and Victor. Ralph Peer, now with Victor, persuaded Stoneman to bring a group of musicians—the Blue Ridge Corn Shuckers—up to Camden, New Jersey, to record a group of sacred numbers and dance tunes during a lengthy session that lasted from September 21st to the 25th. The Corn Shuckers included in-laws Bolen and Erma Frost; kinfolk Hattie, George and Willie Stoneman; and neighbors such as Uncle Eck Dunford, fiddler Kahle Brewer (born 1904; died August 12, 1989), Walter Mooney and Tom Leonard. Band members later included Herbert and Earl Sweet, Frank and Oscar Jenkins, and Fields and Sampson Ward.

Stoneman was even busier in 1927, appearing at 11 sessions for six companies, chiefly in New York but also in Bristol, Tennessee (where Stoneman helped Peer conduct the now legendary sessions that led to the discovery of the Carter Family and Jimmie Rodgers), and Atlanta, Georgia. In the spring or early summer of 1927, Stoneman signed a contract with Victor that allowed him to continue making records for only Victor and Edison under his own name.

Stoneman logged five substantial sessions in 1928: two each for Victor and Edison and one for Gennett. In the summer of 1929 he played in a band with fiddler Frank Jenkins and banjoist Oscar Jenkins. That fall the trio recorded for Paramount and Gennett. In 1931 they landed roles on the radio soap *Irma and Ezra* that aired on WJSV in Mt. Vernon Hills, Virginia. Stoneman's final session was for Vocalion in 1934, by which time he had placed more than 200 sides on disc.

Falling on hard times midst the strafed textile-based economy of Carroll

Ernest V. (Pop) Stoneman and His Blue Ridge Corn Shuckers: (bottom row, left to right) George Stoneman, Pop Stoneman, Bolen Frost, (top row, left to right) Iver Edwards, Uncle Eck Dunford and Hattie Stoneman (Southern Historical Collection, Wilson Library, The University of North Carolina at Chapel Hill).

County, Ernest and his large family—he had 15 children, nine of whom survived—moved to Washington, D.C., in the fall of 1932. Struggling to stay above dire poverty, Stoneman worked at various skilled factory and carpentry jobs during the rest of the 1930s and most of the 1940s.

After World War II Stoneman's musical career began to ascend. The children became part of his band, and two of them—Roni and Scotty—would later establish themselves professionally. In 1947 the Stoneman Family won a talent contest at Constitution Hall, which gave them six months' exposure on local television.

In 1956, "Pop" (as he was now called) won $10,000 on the NBC television quiz program *The Big Surprise* and also sang on the show. That same year, the Blue Grass Champs, made up primarily of his children, won a talent contest on Arthur Godfrey's CBS show. In 1957 Mike Seeger recorded Pop and Hattie for the Folkways album *Old-Time Tunes of the South*.

The Stonemans (as they were now known) prospered even more during the folk music revival, recording albums for Starday in 1962 and 1963, on which Pop handled most of the vocal duties. About this time the family started appearing regularly on the Grand Ole Opry. In 1964 they cut an album for World Pacific, played on some network variety shows and appeared at several folk festivals. In November 1965 they went to Nashville, Tennessee, where they signed a contract with MGM Records and started a syndicated television show. The Stonemans won the Country Music Association's "Vocal Group of the Year" award in 1967.

Over the course of a long and distinguished career in entertainment, Stoneman introduced some of the most durable and legendary country songs—including "The Titanic" (his first recording) and "We Parted by the Riverside"—and was noted for his ability to pick out melodies note-by-note on the autoharp, a rare talent. Up until about two months before his death in Nashville on June 14, 1968, Stoneman continued to appear in concerts with his children, helping make the Stonemans one of the most enduring bluegrass bands of the modern period.

In 1994 Ernest V. (Pop) Stoneman was posthumously inducted into the Autoharp Hall of Fame.

Discography

"The Ship That Never Returned"/"The Titanic" (OKeh 40288; recorded in New York City, ca. January 8, 1925)

"Freckled Face Mary Jane"/"Me and My Wife" (OKeh 40312; recorded in New York City, ca. January 8, 1925)

"Uncle Sam and the Kaiser"/"Dixie Parody" (OKeh 40430; recorded in New York City on May 27, 1925)

"Jack and Joe"/"The Lightning Express" (OKeh 40408; recorded in New York City on May 27, 1925)

"Sinful to Flirt"/"Dying Girl's Farewell" (OKeh 40384; recorded in New York City on May 27, 1925)

"Piney Woods Gal"/"The Long Eared Mule" (OKeh 40405; recorded in New York City on May 27, 1925)

"The Sailor's Song"/"The Fancy Ball" (OKeh 45015; recorded in Asheville, N.C., on August 27, 1925)

"Blue Ridge Mountain Blues"/"All I Got's Gone" (OKeh 45009; recorded in Asheville, N.C., on August 27, 1925)

"The Kicking Mule" (OKeh 45036; recorded in Asheville, N.C., on August 27, 1925)

"The Wreck on the C&O"/"John Hardy" (OKeh 7011 [12-inch disc]; recorded in Asheville, N.C., on August 27, 1925)

"The Religious Critic"/"When My Wife Will Return to Me" (OKeh 45051; recorded in Asheville, N.C., in April 1926)

"Asleep at the Switch"/"The Orphan Girl" (OKeh 45044; recorded in Asheville, N.C., in April 1926)

"Kitty Wells"/"In the Shadow of the Pines" (OKeh 45048; recorded in Asheville, N.C., in April 1926)

"The Texas Ranger"/"Don't Let Your Deal Go Down" (OKeh 45054; recorded in Asheville, N.C., in April 1926)

"Bad Companions"/"When the Work's All Done This Fall" (Edison 51788; Edison 5188, 5201 [cylinders]; recorded in New York City on June 21, 1926)

"Wreck of the C&O"/"Sinking of the Titanic" (Edison 51823; Edison 5198, 5200 [cylinders]; recorded in New York City on June 21 and 22, 1926)

"Wild Bill Jones"/"John Henry" (Edison 51869; Edison 5196, 5194 [cylinders]; recorded in New York City on June 21, 1926)

"Watermelon Hanging on the Vine"/"The Old Hickory Cane" (Edison 51864; Edison 5191, 5241 [cylinders]; recorded in New York City on June 21, 1926)
"My Little German Home Across the Sea"/"Bury Me Beneath the Willow" (Edison 51909; Edison 5187 [cylinder]; recorded in New York City on June 23, 1926)
"Silver Bell"/"My Pretty Snow Dear" (OKeh 45060; recorded in New York City ca. August 1926)
"May I Sleep in Your Barn Tonight, Mister"/"The Old Hickory Cane" (OKeh 45059; recorded in New York City ca. August 1926)
"Are You Angry with Me, Darling?"/"Katie Kline" (OKeh 45065; recorded in New York City ca. August 1926)
"He's Going to Have a Hot Time By and By"/"The Old Go Hungry Hash House" (OKeh 45062; recorded in New York City ca. August 1926)
"May I Sleep in Your Barn Tonight Mister?"/"The Girl I Left Behind in Sunny Tennessee" (Gennett 3368; recorded in New York City on August 28, 1926)
"Silver Bell"/"Pretty Snow Dear" (Gennett 3369; recorded in New York City on August 28, 1926)
"Katy Cline"/"Barney McCoy" (Gennett 3381; Herwin 75528; recorded in New York City on August 28, 1926)
"May I Sleep in Your Barn Tonight Mister?"/"Silver Bell" (Challenge 153; Challenge 312; recorded in New York City on August 28, 1926)
"May I Sleep in Your Barn Tonight Mister?"/"Pretty Snow Dear" (Herwin 75530; recorded in New York City on August 28, 1926)
"The Girl I Left Behind in Sunny Tennessee"/"Katy Cline" (Challenge 151; recorded in New York City on August 28, 1926)
"Pretty Snow Dear"/"Barney McCoy" (Challenge 152; recorded in New York City on August 28, 1926)
"The Girl I Left Behind in Sunny Tennessee"/"Silver Bell" (Herwin 75529; recorded in New York City on August 28, 1926)
"The Fatal Wedding"/"The Fate of Talmadge Osborne" (OKeh 45084; recorded in New York City on January 29, 1927)
"Hand Me Down My Walking Cane"/"When the Roses Bloom Again" (Banner 1993; Domino 3964; Regal 8324; recorded in New York City ca. early May 1927)
"Bully of the Town"/"Pass Around the Bottle" (Banner 2157; Challenge 665; Conqueror 7755; recorded in New York City ca. early May 1927)
"Pass Around the Bottle"/"Sinful to Flirt" (Domino 3985; Regal 8346; Conqueror 7064; recorded in New York City ca. early May 1927)
"Bully of the Town"/"The Fatal Wedding" (Domino 3984; Regal 8347; recorded in New York City ca. early May 1927)
"Pass Around the Bottle" (Paramount 3021; Broadway 8054; recorded in New York City ca. early May 1927)
"Bully of the Town" (Paramount 3379; Perfect 12358; Supertone 32279; recorded in New York City ca. early May 1927)
"Pass Around the Bottle"/"Bully of the Town" (Cameo 8217; Romeo 597; Lincoln 2822; recorded in New York City ca. early May 1927)
"The Old Hickory Cane"/"Sinful to Flirt" (Pathe 32271; Perfect 12350; Conqueror 7064; recorded in New York City in May 1927)
"The Fatal Wedding"/"Sinful to Flirt" (Cameo 8220; Romeo 600; Lincoln 2825; recorded in New York City in May 1927)
"The Old Hickory Cane" (Domino 0187; Regal 8369; recorded in New York City in May 1927)

"The Fatal Wedding"/"Pass Around the Bottle" (Pathe 32287; Perfect 12357; Conqueror 7064; recorded in New York City in May 1927)
"Sinful to Flirt"/"The Fatal Wedding" (Challenge 666; Banner 2158; recorded in New York City in May 1927)
"The Poor Tramp"/"The Fate of Talmadge Osborne" (Victor 20672; recorded in New York City on May 19, 1927)
"The Old Hickory Cane"/"Till the Snowflakes Fall Again" (Victor 20799; recorded in New York City on May 19, 1927)
"The Story of the Mississippi Flood" (Victor 20761; reverse by Ernest Rodgers; recorded in New York City on May 21, 1927)
"In the Shadow of the Pine" (Pathe 32380; Perfect 12459; recorded in New York City in May 1928)

AS ERNEST V. STONEMAN AND HIS DIXIE MOUNTAINEERS

"The Poor Tramp"/"The Fate of Talmadge Osborne" (Victor 20672; recorded in New York City on September 21, 1926)
"In the Golden Bye and Bye"/"I Will Meet You in the Morning" (Victor 20223; recorded in New York City on September 21, 1926)
"The Great Reaping Day"/"I Would Not Be Denied" (Victor 20672; recorded in New York City on September 21 and 24, 1926)
"I Love to Walk with Jesus"/"Hallelujah Side" (Victor 20224; recorded in New York City on September 21, 1926)
"I'll Be Satisfied" (Victor 20533; recorded in New York City on September 24, 1926)
"West Virginia Highway"/"All Go Hungry Hash House" (Victor 20237; recorded in New York City on September 24 and 25, 1926)
"Peek-a-boo Waltz" (Victor 20540; recorded in New York City on September 24, 1926)
"When the Redeemed Are Gathered In"/"I Would Not Be Denied" (Victor 20532; recorded in New York City on September 24, 1926)
"Going Up Cripple Creek"/"Sugar in the Gourd" (Victor 20294; recorded in New York City on September 24 and 25, 1926)
"Sourwood Mountain"/"Little Old Log Cabin in the Lane" (Victor 20235; recorded in New York City on September 24, 1926)
"Little Old Log Cabin in the Lane" (Montgomery Ward 8305; recorded in New York City on September 24, 1926)
"Bright Sherman Valley"/"The Bully of the Town" (Edison 51951; recorded in New York City on January 24 and 29, 1927)
"Bright Sherman Valley" (Edison 5383; recorded in New York City on January 24 and 29, 1927)
"Once I Had a Fortune"/"Two Little Orphans—Our Mama's in Heaven" (Edison 51935; recorded in New York City on January 24 and 25, 1927)
"Once I Had a Fortune" (Edison 5357; recorded in New York City on January 24, 1927)
"The Long Eared Mule"/"Hop Light Ladies" (Edison 52056; recorded in New York City on January 25, 1927)
"Two Little Orphans—Our Mama's in Heaven" (Edison 5338; recorded in New York City on January 25, 1927)
"Kitty Wells"/"We Courted in the Rain" (Edison 51944; recorded in New York City on January 25 and 29, 1927)
"The Bully of the Town"/"Kitty Wells" (Edison 5341; recorded in New York City on January 25, 1927)

"Hand Me Down My Walking Cane"/"Tell Mother I Will Meet Her" (Edison 51938; recorded in New York City on January 28, 1927)

"Tell Mother I Will Meet Her" (Edison 5382; recorded in New York City on January 28, 1927)

"Hand Me Down My Walking Cane" (Edison 5297; recorded in New York City on January 28, 1927)

"We Courted in the Rain" (Edison 5308; recorded in New York City on January 29, 1927)

"Fate of Talmadge Osborne"/"The Fatal Wedding" (Edison 52026; recorded in New York City on May 10, 1927)

"Fate of Talmadge Osborne" (Edison 5369; recorded in New York City on May 10, 1927)

"The Fatal Wedding" (Edison 5355; recorded in New York City on May 10, 1927)

"The Orphan Girl" (Edison 52077; Edison 5367; recorded in New York City on May 10, 1927)

"The Dying Girl's Farewell"/"Tell Mother I Will Meet Her" (Victor 21129; recorded in Bristol, Tennessee, on July 25, 1927)

"The Mountaineer's Courtship"/"The Whip-poor-will Song" (Victor 20880; reverse issued as by Uncle Eck Dunford; recorded in Bristol, Tennessee, on July 25 and 27, 1927)

"Sweeping Through the Gates"/"Are You Washed in the Blood?" (Victor 20844; recorded in Bristol, Tennessee, on July 25, 1927)

"I Know My Name Is There"/"No More Goodbyes" (Victor 21129; recorded in Bristol, Tennessee, on July 25, 1927)

"Are You Washed in the Blood?" (Montgomery Ward 8136; recorded in Bristol, Tennessee, on July 25, 1927)

"The Resurrection"/"I Am Resolved" (Victor 21071; recorded in Bristol, Tennessee, on July 25, 1927)

"He Was Nailed to the Cross for Me"/"When the Redeemed Are Gathered In" (Edison 52290; recorded in New York City on April 24, 1928)

"When the Redeemed Are Gathered In" (Edison 5527; recorded in New York City on April 24, 1928)

"All Go Hungry Hash House"/"Sally Goodwin" (Edison 52350; recorded in New York City on April 24, 1928)

"All Go Hungry Hash House" (Edison 5528; recorded in New York City on April 24, 1928)

"There'll Come a Time"/"The Old Maid and the Burglar" (Edison 52369; recorded in New York City on April 24 and 25, 1928)

"There'll Come a Time" (Edison 5336; recorded in New York City on April 24, 1928)

"Sally Goodwin" (Edison 5529; Edison 0000 [special lateral cut development disc]; recorded in New York City on April 24, 1928)

"Careless Love"/"It's Sinful to Flirt" (Edison 52386; recorded in New York City on April 24 and 25, 1928)

"Careless Love" (Edison 5530; recorded in New York City on April 24, 1928)

"The East Bound Train"/"The Unlucky Road to Washington" (Edison 52299; recorded in New York City on April 25, 1928)

"The East Bound Train" (Edison 5548; recorded in New York City on April 25, 1928)

"The Unlucky Road to Washington" (Edison 5545; recorded in New York City on April 25, 1928)

"The Old Maid and the Burglar" (Edison 5531; recorded in New York City on April 25, 1928)

"Down on the Banks of the Ohio"/"We Parted at the River" (Edison 52312; recorded in New York City on April 25, 1928)

"We Parted at the River" (Edison 5635; recorded in New York City on April 25, 1928)

"It's Sinful to Flirt" (Edison 5547; recorded in New York City on April 25, 1928)

"Down to Jordan and Be Saved"/"There's a Light Up in Galilee" (Victor 40078; recorded in Bristol, Tennessee, on October 31, 1928)

"Goodbye Dear Old Stepstone"/"All I've Got's Gone" (Edison 52489; recorded in New York City on November 21, 1928)

"Fallen by the Wayside"/"The Prisoner's Lament" (Edison 52461; recorded in New York City on November 21, 1928)

"Fallen by the Wayside" (Edison 5686; recorded in New York City on November 21, 1928)

"The Prisoner's Lament" (Edison 5673; recorded in New York City on November 21, 1928)

"Midnight on the Stormy Deep" (Edison 5536; recorded in New York City on November 22, 1928)

"I Remember Calvary"/"He Is Coming After Me" (Edison 52479; Edison N-2004 [laterally cut disc]; recorded in New York City on November 22, 1928)

"I Remember Calvary" (Edison 5676; recorded in New York City on November 22, 1928)

Ernest V. Stoneman and His Dixie Mountaineers (Historical HLP-8004; released 1968; rereleased on CD 1991; consists of 10 tracks)

Folk Music in America, Vol. 7: Songs of Complaint and Protest (Library of Congress LBC-07; released 1987; Ernest V. Stoneman and His Dixie Mountaineers perform "All I've Got's Gone")

AS THE ERNEST V. STONEMAN TRIO
"Lonesome Road Blues"/"Round Town Gal" (OKeh 45094; recorded in New York City on January 27, 1927)

AS ERNEST V. STONEMAN AND HIS BLUE RIDGE CORN SHUCKERS
"Old Time Corn Shuckin' Part 1"/"Old Time Corn Shuckin' Part 2" (Victor 20835; recorded in Bristol, Tennessee, on July 27, 1927)

"Possum Trot School Exhibition, Part 1"/"Possum Trot Exhibition, Part 2" (Victor 21264; recorded in Atlanta, Georgia, on February 22, 1928)

"A Serenade in the Mountains"/"A Serenade in the Mountains" (Victor 21518; recorded in Atlanta, Georgia, on February 22, 1928)

"The Two Little Orphans"/"The Raging Sea, How It Roars" (Victor 21648; recorded in Atlanta, Georgia, on February 22, 1928)

"Sweet Summer Has Gone Away" (Victor 21578; recorded in Atlanta, Georgia, on February 22, 1928)

Ernest V. Stoneman and the Blue Ridge Corn Shuckers (Rounder 1008; produced by Mark Wilson; collection of 16 recordings [original 78s courtesy of the Archive of American Folk Song, the Library of Congress, and Joe Bussard] made from 1926 to 1928; 12-page annotated brochure by Tony Russell [*Old Time Music*])

AS ERNEST STONEMAN, WILLIE STONEMAN, AND THE SWEET BROTHERS
"My Mother and My Sweetheart"/"Falling by the Wayside" (Gennett 6655; recorded in Richmond, Indiana, on July 5, 1928)

"New River Train"/"John Hardy" (Gennett 6619; recorded in Richmond, Indiana, on July 9, 1928)

"Say, Darling, Say" (Gennett 6733; recorded in Richmond, Indiana, on July 9, 1928)
"I Got a Bulldog" (Gennett 6620; recorded in Richmond, Indiana, on July 10, 1928)
"East Tennessee Polka" (Supertone 9406; recorded in Richmond, Indiana, on July 10, 1928)

AS THE PINE MOUNTAIN RAMBLERS
"Rambling Reckless Hobo" (Champion 15610; recorded in Richmond, Indiana, on July 10, 1928)

AS ERNEST V. STONEMAN AND HIS GRAYSEN [SIC] COUNTY BOYS
"The Poor Tramp Has to Live"/"Kenny Wagner's Surrender" (Gennett 6044; Herwin 75535; recorded in New York City on February 5, 1927)
"Sweet Bunch of Violets"/"When the Roses Bloom Again" (Gennett 6065; Herwin 75541; recorded in New York City on February 5, 1927)
"Long Eared Mule"/"Round Town Gals" (Gennett 6052; recorded in New York City on February 5, 1927)

AS UNCLE JIM SEANY
"Sweet Bunch of Violets"/"The Poor Tramp Has to Live" (Champion 15233; recorded in New York City on February 5, 1927)
"The Poor Tramp Has to Live" (Challenger 324; Challenger 398; recorded in New York City on February 5, 1927)
"Kenny Wagner's Surrender"/"When the Roses Bloom Again" (Champion 15222; recorded in New York City on February 5, 1927)

AS UNCLE BEN HAWKINS (AND HIS GANG)
"When the Roses Bloom Again"/"The Poor Tramp Has to Live" (Challenger 244; Silvertone 5001; Silvertone 8155; Silvertone 25001; Supertone 9255; recorded in New York City on February 5, 1927)
"Sweet Bunch of Violets"/"Kenny Wagner's Surrender" (Silvertone 5004; Silvertone 25004; recorded in New York City on February 5, 1927)
"Long Eared Mule"/"Round Town Gals" (Silvertone 5003; Silvertone 25003; recorded in New York City on February 5, 1927)
"Round Town Gals" (Champion 15248; recorded in New York City on February 5, 1927)
"New River Train"/"Say, Darling, Say" (Supertone 9400; recorded in Richmond, Indiana, on July 9, 1928)

AS SIM HARRIS
"Pass Around the Bottle"/"Hand Me Down My Walking Cane" (Oriole 916; Homestead 16490; recorded in New York City ca. early May 1927)
"When the Roses Bloom Again"/"The Fatal Wedding" (Homestead 16498; Oriole 946; recorded in New York City ca. early May 1927)
"Bully of the Town"/"Sinful to Flirt" (Homestead 16500; Oriole 947; recorded in New York City ca. early May 1927)

AS MR. AND MRS. STONEMAN
"The Road to Washington"/"The Mountaineer's Courtship" (OKeh 45125; recorded in New York City on May 12, 1927)

Anthology of American Folk Music, Vol. 3: Songs (Folkways FA 2953; released 1952; reissued as Smithsonian/Folkways SFW 40090 in 1997; edited by Harry Smith; Ernest and Hattie Stoneman are featured on "Mountaineer's Courtship")
Close to Home (Smithsonian/Folkways SF 40097; released 1997; recorded by Mike Seeger at Ernest and Hattie Stoneman's home in Carmody Hills, Maryland, on June 22, 1962; Ernest and Hattie Stoneman perform "Gather in the Golden Grain")

AS THE ERNEST V. STONEMAN TRIO
"Lonesome Road Blues"/"Round Town Gal" (OKeh 45094; recorded in New York City on January 27, 1927)
Folk Music in America, Vol. 9: Songs of Death and Tragedy (Library of Congress LBC-09; released 1978; the Ernest V. Stoneman Trio are featured on "Wreck of Old Ninety-Seven")
Roots 'n' Blues: The Retrospective (1925-50) (Columbia Legacy 47911/47912-15; released 1992; brochure notes by Pete Welding and Lawrence Cohn; the Ernest V. Stoneman Trio perform "Untitled")

AS OSCAR JENKINS' MOUNTAINEERS
"Burial of Wild Bill"/"The Railway Flagman's Sweetheart" (Paramount 3240; Brunswick 8249; recorded in Chicago, Illinois, in August 1929)

AS FRANK JENKINS' PILOT MOUNTAINEERS
"The Railroad Flagman's Sweetheart"/"A Message from Home Sweet Home" (Conqueror 7269; recorded in Richmond, Indiana, on September 12, 1929)
"When the Snowflakes Fall Again"/"The Burial of Wild Bill" (Conqueror 7269; recorded in Richmond, Indiana, on September 12, 1929)
"Sunny Home in Dixie"/"Old Dad" (Gennett 7034; Supertone 9677; recorded in Richmond, Indiana, on September 12, 1929)

AS ERNEST STONEMAN AND EDDIE STONEMAN
"My Own Sweetheart"/"All I Got's Gone" (Vocalion 02901; recorded in New York City on January 8 and 9, 1934)
"There's Somebody Waiting for Me"/"Texas Ranger" (Vocalion 02632; recorded in New York City on January 8 and 9, 1934)
"Nine Pound Hammer"/"Broke Down Section Hand" (Vocalion 02655; recorded in New York City on January 8 and 9, 1934)
Cool Cowboy (Capitol 1230; released 1959)
Galax Va. Old Fiddlers' Convention (Folkways FA 2435; released 1964; recorded by Lisa Chiera, Michael Eisenstadt, Alice Schwebke and Brian Sinclair in Galax, Virginia, 1961–63; six-page brochure by Lisa Chiera; Stoneman plays "Sally Ann")
Mountain Music Played on the Autoharp (Folkways FA 2365; released 1965; recorded by Mike Seeger in Virginia in 1957 and 1961; eight-page booklet by Mike Seeger; Stoneman performs "All I Got's Gone," "Bile 'Em Cabbage Down," "The Great Reaping Day," "I'm Alone, All Alone," "Stoney's Wife," "Sweet Marie" and "Wreck of the Number Nine")
Old Time Fiddle Classics (County 507; released 1965; edited by David Freeman; consists of commercial 78 rpm recordings made in the 1920s and 1930s; Stoneman performs "Sunny Home in Dixie" with Frank and Oscar Jenkins; Stoneman's Dixie Mountaineers are featured on "Sugar in the Gourd" [with Kahle Brewer])

Mountain Sacred Songs (County 508; released 1965; edited by David Freeman; liner notes by Archie Green; consists of 12 commercial 78 rpm recordings made in the 1920s and 1930s; Ernest Stoneman's Dixie Mountaineers perform "Going Down the Valley")

Traditional Country Classics, 1927-1929 (Historical HLP 8003; released ca. 1968; edited by Joe Bussard, Jr.; liner notes by Richard Nevins; contains 14 commercial 78 rpm recorded from 1927 to 1929; Ernest Stoneman is featured on "Kenny Wagner Surrender")

Early Country Music, Volume 1 (Historical 8001 [originally issued as Historical BC 2433-1]; released ca. 1968; produced by Arnold S. Caplin; liner notes by Fields Ward and Arnold S. Caplin; 1929 recordings by Fields Ward's Buck Mountain Band hitherto unissued, rerecorded from test pressings cut at Richmond, Indiana, but never issued by Gennett because of contractual disagreements; features Ward on guitar and vocal, Ernest V. Stoneman on harmonica and autoharp, Eck Dunford on fiddle, and Sampson Ward on banjo; 5 of 16 tracks—"I Am Gonna Marry That Pretty Little Girl," "I Got a Bulldog," "John Hardy," "The New River Train" and "Say Darling Say"—were recorded at a different session, in 1928 as Ernest Stoneman and the Sweet Brothers)

Pop Stoneman Memorial Album (MGM 4588; released 1969)

Going Down the Valley: Vocal and Instrumental Styles in Folk Music from the South (New World Records NW 236; released 1977; edited by Norm Cohen; six-page sewn-in notes by Norm Cohen; consists of 18 studio recordings made from 1926 to 1938; Ernest V. Stoneman and His Dixie Mountaineers perform "Going Down the Valley")

Round the Heart of Old Galax, Vol. 1 (County 533; released 1980; edited by David Freeman; liner notes by Wayne Martin; consists of 14 commercial 78 rpm recordings made in the 1920s and 1930s; Stoneman is featured on "Buffalo Gals," "Flop Eared Mule," "I Am Resolved," "John Hardy," "Lonesome Road Blues," "New River Train," "No More Goodbyes," "Sweet Bunch of Violets," "Tell Mother I Will Meet Her," "There's a Light Lit Up in Galilee," "Too Late," "Two Little Orphans" and "The Old Hickory Cane")

Round the Heart of Old Galax, Vol. 2 (County 534; released 1980; edited and liner notes by Wayne Martin; consists of 14 songs, some commercial 78 rpm recordings made in the 1920s and 1930s, others from Library of Congress field recordings made by John Lomax; Dunford, Stoneman and Edwards perform "Ain't That Trouble in Mind" and "Skip to My Lou"; Fields Ward & the Grayson County Railsplitters perform "My Only Sweetheart," "Watch and Pray" and "Way Down in North Carolina)

Round the Heart of Old Galax, Vol. 3 (County 535; released 1980; liner notes by Wayne Martin; consists of 14 songs, some commercial 78 rpm recordings made in the 1920s and 1930s, others from Library of Congress field recordings of 1941; Stoneman is featured on "I've Got a Bulldog" and "Say Darling Say" [with the Sweet Brothers], and "Piney Woods Gal" [with Emmett Lundy])

A Rare Find (Stonehouse; released 1982; reissued as *Me and My Autoharp* on Old Homestead, 1993)

Ernest V. Stoneman with Family and Friends, Vol. 1 (Old Homestead 172; released 1986)

Ernest V. Stoneman with Family and Friends, Vol. 2 (Old Homestead 173; released 1986)

The Bristol Sessions: Historic Recordings from Bristol, Tennessee (Country Music Foundation CMF 011-L [2-LP set]; released 1987; edited by Bob Pinson; gatefold jacket notes by Charles K. Wolfe; consists of studio recordings made in Bristol, Tennessee, in 1927; Ernest V. Stoneman and His Dixie Mountaineers perform

"Are You Washed in the Blood?" and "The Resurrection"; Stoneman, Miss I. Frost and Eck Dunford are featured on "Midnight on the Stormy Deep" and "The Mountaineer's Courtship")

Sinking of the Titanic, Vol. III (Old Homestead; released 1991)

Virginia Traditions: Native Virginia Ballads and Songs (Global Village C 1004; released 1994; Ernest Stoneman performs "Fate of Talmadge Osborne")

Old-Time Mountain Ballads (County 3504; released 1995)

Ernest Stoneman: 1928 Edison Recordings (County 35102; released 1996; produced by Gary B. Reid; contains all 22 tracks that Stoneman recorded for Edison in 1928)

AS THE STONEMAN FAMILY

"The Broken-Hearted Lover"/"We Parted by the Riverside" (Victor 40030; recorded in Bristol, Tennessee, on October 30 and 31, 1928)

"Going Up the Mountain After Liquor Part 1"/"Going Up the Mountain After Liquor Part 2" (Victor 40116; recorded in Bristol, Tennessee, on October 31, 1928)

"The Spanish Merchant's Daughter"/"Too Late" (Victor 40206; recorded in Bristol, Tennessee, on October 31 and November 1, 1928)

Anthology of American Folk Music, Vol. 3: Songs (Folkways FA 2953; released 1952; reissued as Smithsonian/Folkways SFW 40090 in 1997; edited by Harry Smith; the Stoneman Family play "Spanish Merchant's Daughter")

Stoneman Family Old Time Songs (Folkways FA2315; released 1957; the Stoneman Family perform "Old Blind Dog" and "Wreck of Old Ninety-Seven")

Ernest V. Stoneman and the Stoneman Family (Starday; released 1962; repackaged and rereleased on Starday/Nashville)

The Great Old Timer at the Capitol (Starday; released 1964; repackaged and rereleased on Starday/Nashville)

Big Ball in Monterey (World Pacific; rereleased in shortened form on Sunset)

Those Singin' Swingin' Stompin' Sensational Stonemans (MGM; released 1966)

Stoneman's Country (MGM; released 1967)

All in the Family (MGM; released 1967)

The Great Stonemans (MGM; released 1968)

A Stoneman Christmas (MGM; released 1968)

The Sweet Brothers

Herbert and Earl Sweet, a fiddle and banjo duo from Washington County, Virginia, recorded with Ernest Stoneman in the summer of 1928. The Sweet brothers lived near Damascus and met Stoneman around 1926 at a fiddlers' convention in Elizabethton, Tennessee.

In the spring of 1928 Stoneman's regular band broke up, so he recruited the Sweet brothers to accompany him to Richmond, Indiana, to record for Gennett Records. On July 5 the Sweet brothers participated in what would be their only recording session, which produced 12 issued sides. The brothers lived in Grayson County for many years before moving to Pennsylvania.

Discography

AS WILLIE STONEMAN AND THE SWEET BROTHERS
"Katy Lee" (Gennett 6565; recorded in Richmond, Indiana, on July 5, 1928)

AS DAVE HUNT AND JOHN CLARK
"Prisoner's Lament"/"Katy Lee" (Champion 15565; recorded in Richmond, Indiana, on July 5, 1928)

AS ERNEST STONEMAN, WILLIE STONEMAN, AND THE SWEET BROTHERS
"My Mother and My Sweetheart"/"Falling by the Wayside" (Gennett 6655; recorded in Richmond, Indiana, on July 5, 1928)
"New River Train"/"John Hardy" (Gennett 6619; recorded in Richmond, Indiana, on July 9, 1928)
"Say, Darling, Say" (Gennett 6733; recorded in Richmond, Indiana, on July 9, 1928)
"I Got a Bulldog" (Gennett 6620; recorded in Richmond, Indiana, on July 10, 1928)
"East Tennessee Polka" (Supertone 9406; recorded in Richmond, Indiana, on July 10, 1928)

AS THE PINE MOUNTAIN RAMBLERS
"Rambling Reckless Hobo" (Champion 15610; recorded in Richmond, Indiana, on July 10, 1928)

AS HERBERT SWEET
"Prisoner's Lament" (Gennett 6567; Supertone 9184; Supertone 9305; recorded in Richmond, Indiana, on July 5, 1928)

AS THE SWEET BROTHERS
"Somebody's Waiting for Me" (Gennett 6620; recorded in Richmond, Indiana, on July 5, 1928)

AS THE CALDWELL BROTHERS
"Somebody's Waiting for Me" (Supertone 9323; recorded in Richmond, Indiana, on July 5, 1928)

AS THE CLARK BROTHERS
"Somebody's Waiting for Me"/"Falling by the Wayside" (Champion 15586; recorded in Richmond, Indiana, on July 5, 1928)

AS SAM CALDWELL
"Prisoner's Lament" (Supertone 9184; Supertone 9305; recorded in Richmond, Indiana, on July 5, 1928)
"Falling by the Wayside" (Supertone 9185; recorded in Richmond, Indiana, on July 5, 1928)

AS THE VIRGINIA MOUNTAIN BOOMERS
"Sugar Hill" (Gennett 6687; recorded in Richmond, Indiana, on July 5, 1928)
"Cousin Sally Brown" (Gennett 6687; recorded in Richmond, Indiana, on July 10, 1928)

"East Tennessee Polka"/"Rambling Reckless Hobo" (Gennett 6567; recorded in Richmond, Indiana, on July 10, 1928)

"Rambling Reckless Hobo" (Supertone 9305; recorded in Richmond, Indiana, on
July 10, 1928)

Early Country Music, Volume 1 (Historical 8001 [originally issued as Historical BC
2433-1]; released ca. 1968; produced by Arnold S. Caplin; liner notes by Fields
Ward and Arnold S. Caplin; March 12–16, 1929, recordings by Fields Ward's
Buck Mountain Band and Ernest Stoneman and the Sweet Brothers hitherto
unissued, remastered (by Paul Cady) from test pressings cut at Richmond, Indiana, but never issued by Gennett because of contractual disagreements; 5 of 16
tracks were recorded at a different session, in 1928 as Ernest Stoneman and the
Sweet Brothers)

Round the Heart of Old Galax, Vol. 1 (County 533; released 1980; edited by David Freeman; liner notes by Wayne Martin; consists of 14 commercial 78 rpm recordings
made in the 1920s and 1930s; the Sweet Brothers perform "John Hardy," and Herbert and Earl Sweet are featured on "New River Train" [both with E.V. Stoneman)

Round the Heart of Old Galax, Vol. 3 (County 535; released in 1980; liner notes by
Wayne Martin; consists of 14 songs, some commercial 78 rpm recordings made
in the 1920s and 1930s, others from Library of Congress field recordings of 1941;
the Sweet Brothers perform "I'm Going to Marry That Pretty Little Girl," "I've
Got a Bulldog" and "Say Darling Say" with E.V. Stoneman)

Robert Sykes and
the Surry County Boys

Robert Sykes was born February 25, 1914, the second youngest of ten
children to William Hilyard and Celie Lowe Sykes. When Robert was 7 his
family moved from the Mitchells River section of Surry County to the bank
of Stewarts Creek, three miles west of Mount Airy. Robert's father and an
uncle played the banjo and fiddle, and Robert was also exposed to old-time
music through Saturday night radio broadcasts of the *Grand Ole Opry*.

At the age of 12, Robert traded his 20-gauge shotgun for his older brother
Coy's fiddle. Along with Coy on guitar and banjo, Robert teamed up with
Edith Jarrell (Tommy Jarrell's younger sister) and Fern Ramey to play at local
dances, parties and school breakings all over Surry County in the 1930s.
Around this time Robert was offered a job at new Winston-Salem radio sta-
tion WSJS, but he had to decline.

Robert married Lucy Mosley in 1936, and the following year they moved
to be near Lucy's father, who had just been widowed. Over the next ten years
Sykes fiddled regularly with guitar-picking brothers Ernest and Ralph Creed
and banjoist Coy Bruner. The band drifted apart in the 1950s, and Sykes
stopped playing for what would be the next quarter century.

Robert Sykes (second from left) performs with Andy Cahan (banjo), Verlen Clifton (mandolin) and Frank Bode (guitar) in the late 1980s (courtesy Larry Clifton).

Sykes—a farmer, carpenter and factory worker—operated a couple of Farmers' Cooperative Exchange stores in the 1960s. Lucy died in 1971, and Robert retired the following year, returning to Surry County where he lived for the rest of his life. In 1975 he married his wife's first cousin, Lettie Venable, and the couple moved to the Toast community, on the outskirts of Mount Airy. Sykes' new neighbor, Tommy Jarrell, encouraged him to start fiddling again.

In the 1980s Sykes played frequently with friends and neighbors, including mandolinist Verlen Clifton, guitarist Frank Bode and banjoist Paul Brown. In the early 1980s Robert Sykes and the Surry County Boys were regular performers on WPAQ in Mount Airy. Robert Sykes died on November 7, 1994.

Discography

Appalachia—The Old Traditions—Vol. 2 (Home-Made Music LP002; released 1983; collected, recorded and edited by Mike Yates in Virginia and North Carolina, 1979-80 and 1983; three-page booklet by Mike Yates; Robert Sykes and the Surry County Boys perform "Black-Eyed Susie" and "Paddy on the Turnpike")

Robert Sykes and the Surry County Boys (Heritage 057; released 1986; recorded by Paul Brown and Lew Bode [12 of 14 tracks were recorded during radio sessions at WPAQ in Mount Airy, N.C.]; mastered by Bobby Patterson; jacket notes by Paul Brown; features Frank Bode on guitar and Paul Brown on banjo)

The Virginia Mountain Boys

Led by fiddler Glen Neaves, the Virginia Mountain Boys were an influential bluegrass band from southwestern Virginia whose repertoire and style were deeply rooted in old time, local musical traditions.

Formed in the early 1960s, the Virginia Mountain Boys recorded a number of albums for Folkways, performed on a popular radio program on WBOB in Galax, Virginia, and made good showings at local fiddlers' conventions, including Galax. The band consisted primarily of Neaves on fiddle and guitar, Cullen Galyean on banjo, Bobby Harrison on guitar, and Ivor Melton on mandolin. Also playing with the group were guitarist Jesse Neaves (Glen's wife), bassist Roger Dalton, fiddler Herman Dalton, mandolinist Mike Bedwell (Glen's grandson), fiddler Johnny Jackson and bassist Marvin Cockram (who has also played with the Snowy Mountain Boys, the Dixie Gentlemen and the Highlanders).

Glen Neaves was born in Ashe County, N.C., in 1910. His father was a clawhammer banjoist, and Glen began to play the fiddle when he was 9. Neaves was strongly influenced by the fiddling of the legendary G.B. Grayson, who lived nearby in Laurel Bloomery, Tennessee. Also noted for his excellent singing, Neaves frequently accompanied himself on the guitar, which he played "old style" with a flatpick. Glen and his wife Jesse lived in Fries, Virginia, where Glen was employed in factories and mills all his life.

Neaves, Galyean and Melton all played with the famed Mountain Ramblers in the late 1950s and early 1960s. Galyean, the group's three-finger style banjoist, was born in 1939 and raised in Low Gap, N.C. Both of his parents played the five-string banjo, and his father also fiddled. Cullen played fiddle and banjo for the Mountain Ramblers, and recorded three singles with Ed Vogler on M-K-B in the mid–1960s.

Galyean played guitar and sang lead with the Border Mountain Boys on Homestead Records, and he played guitar with Ralph Stanley briefly in the early 1970s, after Carter Stanley died. Cullen made frequent radio and television appearances out of Winston-Salem, N.C., and some years ago played on the Grand Ole Opry. In the 1980s Galyean played banjo with the Christian Quartet, a country bluegrass gospel group based in Ennice, N.C.

Guitarist Bobby Harrison was born in Galax in 1934. He was introduced to music as a young boy, when his father bought him an old, rare Martin

00-21 guitar. Harrison played with Galyean for most of his adult life; the pair recorded an album for County Records as the Foot Hill Boys, which was released after the death of the third member of the band, Wayburn Johnson.

The group's mandolinist, Ivor Melton, was born in 1927 near Galax. He played with Harrison and Galyean for more than 20 years, a good many of which as the Virginia Mountain Boys. Melton was employed as a mill worker and lived in Galax.

Discography

Glen Neaves and the Virginia Mountain Boys (Folkways Records FA 3830; released 1974; consists of 13 tracks)

The Virginia Mountain Boys, Vol. 2: A Bluegrass String Band (Folkways Records FA 3833; released 1977)

Virginia Mountain Boys: Old Time Bluegrass from Grayson and Carroll Counties, VA, Vol. 3 (Folkways Records FA 3839; released 1980; recorded by Eric Davidson, Lyn Davidson and Jane Rigg, from 1963 to 1974; contains 13 tracks)

Cullen Galyean, Bobby Harrison and the Virginia Mountain Boys, Vol. 4 (Folkways Records FS 3829; released 1983; also features fiddler Johnny Jackson)

49th Annual Galax Old Fiddlers' Convention (Heritage 700; released 1985; the Virginia Mountain Boys perform "I Hear a Choo-Choo Coming")

AS CULLEN GALYEAN AND BOBBY HARRISON

Let Me Fall: Old Time Bluegrass from the Virginia–North Carolina Border (Folkways Records FS 3910; released 1984; recorded by Eric H. Davidson in Woodlawn, Virginia, in August 1983; liner notes by Paul Newman, Paul Tyler and Eric Davidson)

AS GLEN NEAVES

Traditional Music from Grayson & Carroll Counties (Folkways FS 3811; released 1962; collected and recorded by Eric Davidson and Paul Newman in Virginia, 1958–61; eight-page booklet by Eric Davidson and Paul Newman; Neaves performs "Handsome Molly")

Ballads and Songs of the Blue Ridge Mountains: Persistence and Change (Asch AH 3831; released 1968; collected and recorded by Eric Davidson, Paul Newman and Caleb Finch in Virginia and North Carolina in the 1950s and 1960s; 12-page booklet by Paul Newman and Eric Davidson; Neaves is featured on "1809" and "Lawson Family Murder")

AS GLEN NEAVES AND THE GRAYSON COUNTY BOYS

Traditional Music from Grayson & Carroll Counties (Folkways FS 3811; released 1962; collected and recorded by Eric Davidson and Paul Newman in Virginia, 1958–61; eight-page booklet by Eric Davidson and Paul Newman; Neaves and the GCB perform "Devilish Mary" and "Tom Dooley")

28th Annual Galax Old Fiddlers Convention (Folk Promotions 825/Kanawha 302; released 1963; Neaves and the GCB play "White House Blues")

The Rich-R-Tone Story: The Early Days of Bluegrass, Vol. 5 (Rounder 1017; released 1975; Neaves and the GCB perform "Old Swinging Bridge" and "Black Mountain Rag")

Dock Walsh

Doctor Coble Walsh, the self-proclaimed "Banjo King of the Carolinas," was born July 23, 1901, in the Lewis Fork township of Wilkes County, to Lee and Diane Elizabeth (Gold) Walsh. Dock, born into a family of talented musicians (he had seven brothers and sisters), taught himself to play a fretless banjo at the age of 4. While in his teens, Dock started being hired to play at local parties and other functions. He received his teaching certificate at Mountain View in 1921, and taught public school for about four years.

Walsh quickly became well known for his unique "Hawaiian" or "bottleneck" banjo sound (made by placing pennies under the bridge and using a knife for fretting). Seeking to become a recording artist like Henry Whitter, Walsh wrote to OKeh and Columbia but was not invited to try out. Undaunted, he journeyed south to Atlanta and worked on a cotton plantation for six months before finally being auditioned by William Brown, local manager at Columbia. Walsh did his first recording on October 3, 1925, cutting four sides as a solo banjoist for Columbia, including two of his original compositions: "I'm Free at Last" and "Bull Dog Down in Sunny Tennessee."

Walsh returned to Atlanta to do some more recording for Columbia in April 1926. He added five more pieces to the catalog (one side was unissued), including the earliest known recording of "In the Pines," an original composition.

In the summer of 1926 Walsh met harmonica and guitar player Gwin Foster, who at the time was in his early twenties and working as a doffer in a Dallas, N.C., textile mill. The pair added a couple of Gaston County musicians—Dave Fletcher and Floyd Williams—to form a full string band, the Four Yellowjackets. The group was soon on their way to Atlanta for a Victor session for Ralph Peer on February 11, 1927. Peer, however, signed up only Walsh and Foster and called them the Carolina Tar Heels.

Walsh and Foster made three recording sessions as the Carolina Tar Heels before splitting up (due to

Dock Walsh, the "Banjo King of the Carolinas" (courtesy Drake Walsh).

the distance between their homes) in late fall of 1927. Walsh replaced Gwin Foster with old friend Garley Foster (no relation), a fellow Wilkes Countian who sometimes billed himself as "the Human Bird" because of his unique whistling and bird mimicry skills. Garley was born on a Lewis Fork farm on January 10, 1905, one and a half miles from the Walsh place. Garley's first instrument was the French harp, but he learned the fiddle and banjo from his father, Monroe Gilbert Foster. In his late teens he took up the guitar and mouth harp, playing with Walsh at square dance parties.

Banjoist and singer Clarence (Tom) Ashley, whom Walsh had met in 1925 at a fiddlers' convention in Boone, joined the band in the fall of 1928. They recorded eight numbers in October 1928 for Victor in Atlanta. In the spring of 1929 the trio traveled to Camden, New Jersey, to record eight more sides for Victor. Ashley left the band after these two sessions.

Walsh recorded six more sides (four of which were issued) for Victor in late September 1929, in Memphis, Tennessee. He married in December 1929, and Garley Foster followed suit in December 1931, but the Carolina Tar Heels' recording career did not end until early 1932. Ralph Peer recorded Walsh and Foster once in 1931 as the Pine Mountain Boys. Walsh enlisted the talents of original member Gwin Foster for his last studio session, in Atlanta in late February 1932. The duo was forced to bill themselves as "The Original Carolina Tar Heels" because an entirely separate band called the Carolina Tarheels were performing at the time over WSB radio in Atlanta.

In the 1940s and 1950s Walsh worked in the poultry and auto parts businesses. Later, in the early 1960s, he operated a small restaurant in Hudson, N.C., for a brief time. In 1962 researchers Eugene Earle and Archie Green discovered Walsh and Garley Foster and recorded them for release on a Folk Legacy album. This LP (FSA-24) also features Dock's son, Drake (born December 28, 1930), who had recorded earlier with the Church Brothers and the Radio Pals. Dock Walsh died on May 28, 1967.

Discography

"The East Bound Train"/"I'm Free at Last" (Columbia 15047-D; recorded in Atlanta, Georgia, on October 3, 1925)

"The Bull Dog Down in Sunny Tennessee"/"Educated Man" (Columbia 15057-D; recorded in Atlanta, Georgia, on October 3, 1925)

"Traveling Man" (Columbia 15105; reverse by Gid Tanner; recorded in Atlanta, Georgia, on April 17, 1926)

"Knocking on the Hen House Door"/"We Courted in the Rain" (Columbia 15075-D; Clarion 5426-C; Velvet Tone 2486; recorded in Atlanta, Georgia, on April 17, 1926)

"In the Pines"/"Going Back to Jericho" (Columbia 15094-D; recorded in Atlanta, Georgia, on April 17, 1926)

"Laura Lou"/"We're Just Plain Folks" (Victor V-40325; recorded in Memphis, Tennessee, on September 25, 1929)

Columbia *New Process* Records

"DOCK" WALSH

"Dock" Walsh

"**D**OCK" WALSH is hard to catch. So great is the demand for him at country dances and entertainments in the South, that it's mighty difficult to tell where he'll be next. However, when you do catch him, it's worth all the trouble. That's why "Dock" is recording for Columbia.

"Dock's" banjo work is as good as his singing. Consequently, he is able to play his own accompaniment. This is a big factor in making "Dock" Walsh one of the very greatest of Southern minstrels.

KNOCKING ON THE HEN HOUSE DOOR — Vocal with Banjo Accomp. WE COURTED IN THE RAIN — Vocal with Banjo Accomp.	15075-D 10-inch 75c

THE BULL DOG DOWN IN SUNNY TENNESSEE—Vocal with Banjo Accomp. EDUCATED MAN—Vocal with Banjo Accomp.	15057-D 10-inch 75c
THE EAST BOUND TRAIN—Vocal with Banjo Accomp. I'M FREE AT LAST—Vocal with Banjo Accomp.	15047-D 10-inch 75c

JACK PICKELL

WHEN THEY RING THE GOLDEN BELLS—Vocal with Piano and Violin Accomp. MEMORIES (MOTHERS' SONG)—Vocal with Piano and Violin Accomp.	15061-D 10-inch 75c
THE OLD RUGGED CROSS—Vocal with Piano and Violin Accomp. THAT'S WHY I LOVE HIM SO—Vocal with Piano and Violin Accomp.	15052-D 10-inch 75c

MINER HAWKINS

A COAL MINER'S DREAM—Vocal with Guitar Accomp. THE SONG OF THE SEA—Vocal with Guitar and Mouth Harp Accomp.	15067-D 10-inch 75c

THE *ONLY* RECORDS *WITHOUT SCRATCH*

‖ 10 ‖

A Columbia Records catalog from 1926 lists the solo efforts cut that year and the year before by Dock Walsh, "one of the very greatest of Southern minstrels" (courtesy Drake Walsh).

"A Precious Sweetheart from Me Is Gone"/"Bathe in That Beautiful Pool" (Victor V-40237; recorded in Memphis, Tennessee, on September 25, 1929)

Mountain Sacred Songs (County 508; released 1965; edited by David Freeman; liner notes by Archie Green; consists of 12 commercial 78 rpm recordings made in the 1920s and 1930s; Dock Walsh performs "Bathe in That Beautiful Pool")

Mountain Banjo Songs and Tunes (County 515; released 1968; liner notes by John Burke; consists of 12 commercial 78 rpm recordings made from 1925 to 1933; Dock Walsh is featured on "Going Back to Jericho")

The North Carolina Banjo Collection (Rounder 0439; 2-CD set released 1998; produced by Bob Carlin; Dock Walsh performs "Come Bathe in That Beautiful Pool")

WITH THE PINE MOUNTAIN BOYS (GARLEY FOSTER)

"She Wouldn't Be Still" (Victor 23582; recorded in Charlotte, North Carolina, on May 30, 1931)

"The Gas Run Out"/"Wild Woman Blues" (Victor 23592; recorded in Charlotte, North Carolina, on May 30, 1931)

"Roll On, Daddy, Roll On"/"The Apron String Blues" (Victor 23605; recorded in Charlotte, North Carolina, on May 30, 1931)

WITH THE CAROLINA TAR HEELS

"There Ain't No Use Workin' So Hard"/"I'm Going to Georgia" (Victor 20544; recorded in Atlanta, Georgia, on February 19, 1927)

"Bring Me a Leaf from the Sea"/"Her Name Was Hula Lou" (Victor 20545; recorded in Atlanta, Georgia, on February 19, 1927)

"When the Good Lord Sets You Free"/"I Love My Mountain Home" (Victor 20931; recorded in Charlotte, North Carolina, on August 15, 1927)

"Shanghai in China"/"The Bulldog Down in Sunny Tennessee" (Victor 20941; recorded in Charlotte, North Carolina, on August 11, 1927)

"My Mama Scolds Me for Flirting"/"Goodbye, My Bonnie, Goodbye" (Victor 21193; recorded in Charlotte, North Carolina, on August 11 and 15, 1927)

"Farm Girl Blues"/"Washing Mama's Dishes" (Victor 23516; recorded in Memphis, Tennessee, on November 19, 1930)

"The Hen House Door Is Always Locked"/"Your Low-Down Dirty Ways" (Victor 23546; recorded in Memphis, Tennessee, on November 19, 1930)

"Got the Farm Land Blues"/"Back to Mexico" (Victor 23611; recorded in Memphis, Tennessee, on November 19, 1930)

"Nobody Cares If I'm Blue"/"Why Should I Care" (Victor 23671; recorded in Atlanta, Georgia, on February 25, 1932)

"She Shook It on the Corner"/"Times Ain't Like They Used to Be" (Victor 23682; recorded in Atlanta, Georgia, on February 25, 1932)

"You're a Little Too Small"/"Peg and Awl" (Victor 40007; recorded in Atlanta, Georgia, on October 11, 1928)

"Lay Down Baby, Take Your Rest"/"Roll On, Boys" (Victor 40024; recorded in Atlanta, Georgia, on October 11, 1928)

"There's a Man Goin' Around Takin' Names"/"I Don't Like the Blues No-How" (Victor 40053; recorded in Atlanta, Georgia, on October 11, 1928)

"Rude and Rambling Man"/"Oh, How I Hate It" (Victor 40077; recorded in Camden, New Jersey, on April 3, 1929)

"Who's Gonna Kiss Your Lips, Dear Darling?"/"My Home's Across the Blue Ridge Mountains" (Victor 40100; recorded in Camden, New Jersey, on April 3, 1929)

"Somebody's Tall and Handsome"/"The Train's Done Left Me" (Victor 40128;
    recorded in Camden, New Jersey, on April 3 and 4, 1929)
"Hand in Hand We Have Walked Along Together"/"The Old Gray Goose" (Victor
    40177; recorded in Camden, New Jersey, on April 3 and 4, 1929)
"Can't You Remember When Your Heart Was Mine?"/"I'll Be Washed" (Victor 40219;
    recorded in Atlanta, Georgia, on October 11, 1928)
Anthology of American Folk Music, Vol. 1: Ballads (Folkways FA 2951; released 1952; reis-
    sued on CD as Smithsonian/Folkways SFW 40090 in 1997; edited by Harry
    Smith; the Carolina Tar Heels are featured on "Got the Farm Land Blues" and
    "Peg and Awl")
Old Time Music at Clarence Ashley's, Volume Two (Folkways 2359; released 1963; recorded
    July 1961 in Saltville, Virginia, February 1962 in Chicago, Illinois, and April 1962
    in Los Angeles, California, by Eugene Earle, Mike Seeger, Ed Kahn and Ralph
    Rinzler; edited by Richard and Ralph Rinzler; notes by Ralph Rinzler; discog-
    raphy by Eugene Earle and Ralph Rinzler; includes lyrics and bibliographic ref-
    erences; Ashley, Garley Foster and Dock Walsh combine their talents (along with
    Doc Watson) on the track "My Home's Across the Blue Ridge Mts." [written by
    Ashley])
The Carolina Tar Heels (Folk-Legacy FSA-24; released 1965; recorded by Archie Green
    and Eugene Earle in Taylorsville, N.C., in 1961-62; 33-page booklet by Green
    and Earle; the 17 songs feature Dock Walsh, Drake Walsh and Garley Foster)
A Collection of Mountain Songs (County 504; released 1965; edited by David Freeman;
    consists of commercial 78 rpm recordings made from 1927 to 1930; the Carolina
    Tar Heels perform "Your Low Down Dirty Ways")
The String Bands, Vol. 2 (Old Timey 101; released 1965; edited by Chris Strachwitz;
    liner notes by Strachwitz; consists of 16 commercial 78 rpm recordings made
    from 1922 to the 1950s; the Carolina Tar Heels perform "Lay Down Baby, Take
    Your Rest")
Southern Dance Music, Vol. 2 (Old-Timey LP 101; released 1965; the Carolina Tar Heels
    perform "Lay Down Baby, Take Your Rest")
The Railroad in Folksong (RCA Victor LPV 532; released 1966; edited by Archie Green;
    liner notes by Archie Green; consists of 16 studio recordings made from 1926 to
    1940; the Carolina Tar Heels are featured on "The Train's Done Left Me")
Mountain Blues (County 511; released ca. 1966; edited by David Freeman; consists of
    12 commercial 78 rpm recordings made in the 1920s and 1930s; the Carolina Tar
    Heels are featured on "Farm Girl Blues")
Early Rural String Bands (RCA Victor LPV 552; released 1968; edited by Norm Cohen;
    liner notes by Norm Cohen; consists of 14 studio recordings made from 1922 to
    1949; the Carolina Tar Heels perform "Bring Me a Leaf from the Sea")
The Carolina Tar Heels (GHP [West Germany] LP 1001; released 1969; reissued as
    Old Homestead OH 113 in 1978; edited by Gerd Hadeler; consists of 14 com-
    mercial 78s recorded from 1927 to 1931; liner notes by Norm Cohen; the first Tar
    Heels reissue, on the now long-defunct German label GHP)
Can't You Remember the Carolina Tar Heels? (Bear Family [West Germany] BF 15507;
    released 1975; edited by Richard Weize; comprised of 16 commercial 78s recorded
    from 1927 to 1931; annotated brochure by Richard Weize)
Folk Music in America, Vol. 2: Songs of Love, Courtship... (Library of Congress LBC-
    02; released 1978; the Carolina Tar Heels perform "You Are a Little Too Small")
Folk Music in America, Vol. 13: Songs of Childhood... (Library of Congress LBC-13;
    released 1978; the Carolina Tar Heels contribute "Go Tell Aunt Rhody")

Fields Ward

Old-time singer and guitarist Fields Mac Ward was born January 23, 1911, in Buck Mountain, Grayson County, Virginia. Fields was influenced by a musically rich family: Father Crockett (ca. early 1880s–mid–1960s) was a noted fiddler and banjoist, mother Perlina (Linie) was a ballad singer, and his four siblings were all musically inclined. When Fields was 10 his family moved to the Ballard Branch community, just west of Galax. At the age of 12 Fields learned guitar runs by listening repeatedly to Riley Puckett's 78s, and local fiddler-guitarist Alec (Eck) Dunford taught Fields several finger-style guitar pieces and the basics of backup guitar.

In 1927 the 16-year-old Fields (lead singer and guitarist), his father Crockett (fiddle), and brothers Curren (autoharp) and Sampson (banjo) cut several sides in New York for the OKeh label, four of which were released as by Crockett Ward and His Boys. Fields, Samp, Dunford and Ernest V. Stoneman then formed the Grayson County Railsplitters and cut 15 sides in 1929 for the Gennett Record Company, although the material was never released until around 1968 on Historical Records. Fields took home test pressings of the entire session, and refused to deal with another record company for almost 40 years.

In the 1930s Fields played with the Buck Mountain String Band, led by his uncle Wade Ward, the area's top banjo picker. Around 1934 Fields formed a family band, the Ballard Branch Bogtrotters, which included Dr. W.P. Davis—a local chiropractor and the Wards' family doctor—Crockett, Samp, and Eck (and later Uncle Wade). The Bogtrotters swept the top prizes at the 1935 Galax fiddlers' convention and recorded over 150 songs for John Lomax at the Library of Congress between 1937 and 1942. On January 9, 1940, the band traveled to Roanoke, Virginia, to broadcast over WDBJ for the nationally televised CBS *American School of the Air.* Fields was offered a solo contract by John Lair to perform on the *Renfro Valley Barn Dance,* but he balked at leaving his bandmates and forcing his wife and family to live on the road.

By 1942 Crockett and Eck had decided they were too old to lead the lives of professional musicians, and the Bogtrotters disbanded. Fields moved to Hartford County, Maryland, in 1947 to manage a dairy farm. Over the next several years he worked at several jobs, eventually becoming a painter, the trade he was to follow the rest of his life. There he was "discovered" by the folk revival audience in the 1960s, and played at colleges and folk festivals. As a result Ward recorded albums for Biograph and Rounder. An unauthorized recording made by he and his Uncle Wade for the Parsons Auction Company in Virginia was released on a Folkways album, adding to his mistrust of record companies.

Despite a variety of health problems (including hypertension, diabetes, emphysema and arthritis), Ward continued to perform in public into the 1980s. He died on October 26, 1987, at his home in Bel Air, Maryland.

Discography

AS CROCKETT WARD AND HIS BOYS

"Sugar Hill"/"Deadheads and Suckers" (OKeh 45179; recorded in Winston-Salem, N.C., on September 26, 1927)

"Love's Affections"/"Ain't That Trouble in Mind" (OKeh 45304; recorded in Winston-Salem, N.C., on September 26, 1927)

Early Country Music, Volume 1 (Historical 8001 [originally issued as Historical BC 2433-1]; released ca. 1968; produced by Arnold S. Caplin; liner notes by Fields Ward and Arnold S. Caplin; recordings made on March 5 and 7, 1929, by Fields Ward's Buck Mountain Band hitherto unissued; remastered [by Paul Cady] from test pressings cut at Richmond, Indiana, but never issued by Gennett because of contractual disagreements; features Ward on guitar and vocal, Ernest V. Stoneman on harmonica and autoharp, Eck Dunford on fiddle, and Sampson Ward on banjo; features three original compositions by Fields Ward: "Way Down in North Carolina," "Ain't That Trouble in Mind" and "Those Cruel Days of Slavery"; 5 of 16 tracks were recorded at a different session, in 1928 as Ernest Stoneman and the Sweet Brothers)

Fields and Wade Ward (Biograph RC-6002; released 1968; collected and recorded by Richard Nevins in Galax, Virginia, in 1968; produced by Arnold S. Caplin; liner notes by Richard Nevins; vocals and guitar by Fields, banjo by Wade; with Jimmy Edmonds [fiddle on "John Hardy"] and John Rector [fiddle on "Riley and Spencer"])

The Original Bogtrotters (Biograph RC-6003; released 1968; produced by Arnold S. Caplin; liner notes by Richard Nevins; Library of Congress recordings made by John Lomax, Alan Lomax and others from 1937 to 1942 in Galax, Virginia; most of these recordings were made by John Lomax at the Galax Old Time Fiddlers' Convention in October 1937; "Deadheads and Suckers" and "Sugar Hill" are commercial 1927 recordings for the OKeh label by Crockett Ward and His Boys [Fields and Sampson Ward]; also features Eck Dunford, Dr. W.P. Davis, Walter Alderman, Marvin Evans and Dr. W.E. Dalton)

Bury Me Not on the Prairie (Rounder 0036; released 1974; recorded in Bel Air, Maryland, in 1973; produced by Mark Wilson; liner notes by Mark Wilson; Ward plays both guitar and banjo on this album, which also features Nancy Ward, Jerry Lundy [on fiddle] and Burt Russell)

Oh My Little Darling: Folk Song Types (New World NW 245; released 1977; edited by Jon Pankake, who provides a six-page insewn brochure; comprised of commercial 78s and field recordings made from 1923 to 1939; Fields Ward performs "Sweet William"; Mr. and Mrs. Crockett Ward [Fields' parents] are credited with "King William Was King George's Son")

Folk Music in America, Vol. 3: Dance Music, Breakdowns and Waltzes (Library of Congress LBC-03; released 1978; the Bogtrotters perform "Days of Forty Nine")

Folk Music in America, Vol. 5: Dance Music, Ragtime, Jazz... (Library of Congress LBC-05; released 1978; the Bogtrotters perform "California Cotillion")

Folk Music in America, Vol. 6: Songs of Migration and Immigration (Library of Congress LBC-06; released in 1978; the Bogtrotters perform "Barney McCoy")

Folk Music in America, Vol. 9: Songs of Death and Tragedy (Library of Congress LBC-09; released 1978; Fields Ward performs "Lexington Murder")

Round the Heart of Old Galax, Vol. 2 (County 534; released 1980; edited and liner notes by Wayne Martin; consists of 14 songs, some commercial 78 rpm recordings made in the 1920s and 1930s, others from Library of Congress field recordings made by John Lomax; Fields Ward performs "Sweet William," and, with the Grayson County Railsplitters, "My Only Sweetheart," "Watch and Pray" and "Way Down in North Carolina"; Crockett Ward & His Boys perform "Ain't That Trouble in Mind" and "Sugar Hill")

Traditional Music on Rounder: A Sampler (Rounder SS-0145; released 1981; collected and recorded by Jim Carr, et al.; produced by Mark Wilson; liner notes by Mark Wilson; Fields Ward performs "Riley and Spencer")

Rural String Bands of Virginia (County CD-3502; released 1994; notes by Kinney Rorrer; remastered by Dave Glasser; Crockett Ward & His Boys perform "Sugar Hill")

Wade Ward

Benjamin "Uncle" Wade Ward, born on October 15, 1892, near the town of Independence in Grayson County, Virginia, was known for his frailing or clawhammer style of banjo playing. He also had an equally personal fiddle style.

Ward began to pick the banjo when he was 11 years old, and began fiddling at the age of 16. Wade learned how to play from his brother Davy Crockett Ward, 20 years his senior and already an accomplished musician. When Wade was 14 he traveled to Tennessee and saw for the first time "chording" and picked up the tune "Chilly Winds" from local musicians there. By the age of 18 Ward had become well known in the area, playing for a variety of local social and economic events alongside Crockett.

On August 6, 1913, Wade married 19-year-old Lelia Mathews. (Lelia died on May 10, 1951, at the age of 63; Wade's second wife, Mollie Yates, died on August 4, 1961.) Ward's first real band, formed in 1919, was called the Buck Mountain Band. The band was composed of Wade, his brother Crockett, well known local fiddler Van Edwards, and Van's son, Earl Edwards, a guitar player. The Buck Mountain Band was briefly recorded for OKeh Records.

Wade, who soon became widely known for both his fiddling and banjo playing, was hired in 1919 by the Parsons Auction Company to provide the music for their Saturday sales. He continued in this capacity for 51 years, well into the 1960s. Besides dances and land sales, Ward also played at local Republican party meetings and events.

Ward did his first solo banjo recording in Asheville, North Carolina, on August 31–September 1, 1925, but the four songs he cut—"Fox Chase," "A Married Man's Blues," "Chilly Winds" and "Brother Ephram"—were not issued by OKeh. Wade picked the banjo with his nephew Fields (who handled a majority of the vocal duties) and brother Crockett (fiddle) in the Galax

One of the finest to ever frail on the banjo—Uncle Wade Ward (Blue Ridge Heritage Archive).

string band known as the Ballard Branch Bogtrotters in the 1930s and early 1940s. The Bogtrotters were led by autoharp player Doc Davis, and the other member of the band was fiddler Uncle Alec (Eck) Dunford.

After John Lomax and Pete Seeger recorded Wade and the Bogtrotters for the Library of Congress starting in 1937, the band appeared on a nationwide CBS radio program, originating in Roanoke, Virginia, on January 9, 1940. Not long after this famed radio broadcast, the Bogtrotters started gradually breaking up due to illness and death. The final blow to the band was when Fields moved to Maryland in 1947.

Wade suffered a severe heart attack in 1942, and over the succeeding couple of decades played occasionally with the nearby Lundy family, Galax fiddler Charlie Higgins, guitarist Dale Poe, or just by himself. In the late 1950s interest in his music was renewed by urban folk music enthusiasts. Young banjo pickers began to make the pilgrimage to Independence to visit Ward, and soon he enjoyed a nationwide reputation as one of the premier clawhammer banjo players of his generation. He also toured extensively (playing at the Smithsonian Festival in Washington, D.C., in 1967) before his death at his Peach Bottom Creek farm on May 29, 1971.

Discography

Anglo-American Shanties, Lyric Songs, Dance Tunes and Spirituals (Library of Congress AFS L2; released 1943 [78 rpm] and 1956 [LP reissue]; collected and recorded by Alan Lomax [with Elizabeth Lomax or Pete Seeger], Charles Todd, Robert Sonkin and Herbert Halpert; recordings made from 1937 to 1941; 13-page booklet by Alan Lomax, with an introduction by Wayne Shirley; Ward performs "Chilly Winds" and "Old Joe Clark")

Sounds of the South (Atlantic SD-1346; released 1960; recorded by Alan Lomax with Shirley Collins in 1959; four-page booklet by Lomax; Ward, Charlie Higgins and Charley Poe play "Paddy on the Turnpike")

Blue Ridge Mountain Music (Atlantic SD-1347; released 1960; recorded by Alan Lomax with Shirley Collins in 1959; four-page booklet by Lomax; Ward plays "Chilly Winds")

Ballads and Breakdowns from the Southern Mountains: Southern Journey 3 (Prestige International INT 25003; released 1961 [rereleased as Rounder 1702 *Southern Journey, Vol. 2: Ballads and Breakdowns* in 1997]; collected and recorded by Alan Lomax with Shirley Collins and Anne Lomax in 1959 and 1960; produced by Kenneth S. Goldstein; annotated by Alan Lomax; Ward performs "Uncle Charlie's Breakdown" and "Willow Garden" with Charlie Higgins and Dale Poe)

Banjo Songs, Ballads, and Reels from the Southern Mountains: Southern Journey 4 (Prestige International INT 25004; released 1961; collected and recorded by Alan Lomax with Shirley Collins and Anne Lomax in 1959 and 1960; produced by Kenneth S. Goldstein; eight-page booklet by Alan Lomax; Ward plays "Cluck Old Hen," "The Fox Chase," "June Apple," "Old Joe Clark" and "Piney Woods Gal")

The Music of Roscoe Holcomb and Wade Ward (Folkways 2363; released 1962; edited by John Cohen and Eric H. Davidson; recorded in New York City and Independence, Virginia; eight-page brochure by John Cohen and Eric H. Davidson; includes lyrics; the last two of the 26 selections are Bogtrotters tunes recorded in 1937 by John A. Lomax: "Cluck Old Hen" and "Waterbound"; the remaining Ward songs were recorded by Eric Davidson or Mike Seeger between 1956 and 1961)

Traditional Music from Grayson & Carroll Counties (Folkways FS 3811; released 1962; collected and recorded by Eric Davidson and Paul Newman in Virginia, 1958–61; eight-page booklet by Eric Davidson and Paul Newman; Ward performs "Ida Red," "Cripple Creek" and "Sourwood Mountain")

28th Annual Galax Old Fiddlers Convention (Kanawha 302; released 1963; Wade Ward is featured on "Little Maggie")

Galax Va. Old Fiddlers' Convention (Folkways FA 2435; released 1964; recorded by Lisa Chiera, Michael Eisenstadt, Alice Schwebke and Brian Sinclair in Galax, Virginia, 1961–63; six-page brochure by Lisa Chiera; the Buck Mountain Band [Ward, Charlie Higgins and Dale Poe) perform "Blackberry Blossom")

Clawhammer Banjo (County 701; released 1965; Wade Ward performs "John's Lover's Gone" and "June Apple")

Mountain Music Played on the Autoharp (Folkways FA 2365; released 1965; recorded by Mike Seeger in Virginia in 1957 and 1961; eight-page booklet by Mike Seeger; Wade Ward is featured on "Stoney's Waltz")

Bluegrass from the Blue Ridge (Folkways FA 3832; released 1967; recorded by Eric H. Davidson, Paul Newman and Caleb Finch in Grayson and Carroll counties, Virginia, ca. 1958–67; 16-page booklet by Davidson and Newman; Ward, with Glen Smith, is featured on "John Lover Is Gone," "Ragtime Annie," "Sally Ann," "Sally Goodin'," "Soldier's Joy," "Walkin' in the Parlor" and "Western Country"; Wade Ward, Fields Ward and Glen Smith play "Don't Let Your Deal Go Down," "John Hardy," "Jesse James" and "Train on the Island")

Ballads and Songs of the Blue Ridge Mountains: Persistence and Change (Asch AH 3831; released 1968; collected and recorded by Eric Davidson, Paul Newman and Caleb Finch in Virginia and North Carolina in the 1950s and 1960s; 12-page booklet by Paul Newman and Eric Davidson; Ward performs "Barbry Allen" with Granny Porter)

More Goodies from the Hills (Union Grove SS-3; released 1969; Wade Ward and Jimmy Edmonds perform "Sally Goodin")

Uncle Wade: A Memorial to Wade Ward, Old Time Virginia Banjo Picker, 1882–1971 (Folkways 2380; released 1973; contains recordings made from 1957 to 1970 by Eric H. Davidson and Jane Rigg, plus a selection from his 1938 Library of Congress field recordings made by John A. Lomax; edited and annotated [six-page booklet] by Eric H. Davidson and Jane Rigg; Ward plays the banjo and fiddles, as does Glen Smith; ten of the twenty-three songs are banjo-fiddle duets by Ward and Smith; includes reminiscences of Ward's niece, Mrs. Katy Hill)

High Atmosphere (Rounder 0028; released 1974; collected and recorded by John Cohen in Virginia and North Carolina in 1965; produced by Mark Wilson and John Cohen; nine-page booklet by Cohen and Wilson; Ward plays "Half Shaved," "High Atmosphere" and "Shady Grove")

Clawhammer Banjo, Vol. 3 (County 757; released 1978; most recordings by Charlie Faurot and Richard Nevins, made in North Carolina, Virginia and West Virginia; edited by Charlie Faurot; liner notes by Blanton Owen; Ward performs "Hollyding" and "Johnson Boys")

Round the Heart of Old Galax, Vol. 2 (County 534; released 1980; edited and liner notes by Wayne Martin; consists of 14 songs, some commercial 78 rpm recordings made in the 1920s and 1930s, others from Library of Congress field recordings made by John Lomax; Wade Ward performs "Die in the Field of Battle," "Lost Indian" and "A Married Man's Blues")

Round the Heart of Old Galax, Vol. 3 (County 535; released 1980; liner notes by Wayne Martin; consists of 14 songs, some commercial 78 rpm recordings made in the 1920s and 1930s, others from Library of Congress field recordings of 1941; Ward is featured on "Chilly Winds" and "Fox Chase")

Rounder Old-Time Music (Rounder 11510; released 1988; Ward performs "Shady Grove")

Close to Home (Smithsonian/Folkways SF 40097; released 1997; recorded by Mike Seeger at Wade Ward's home near Independence, Virginia, in August 1957 and April 12, 1961; Ward performs "Lone Prairie" and "Molly, Put the Kettle On")

A Treasury of Library of Congress Field Recordings (Rounder 1500; released 1997; selected, annotated and produced by Stephen Wade)

Southern Journey, Vol. 1: Voices from the American South—Blues, Ballads, Hymns, Reels,

Shouts, Chanteys and Work Songs (Rounder 1701; released 1997; recorded and produced by Alan Lomax with Shirley Collins; Uncle Charlie Higgins, Wade Ward and Dale Poe are featured on "Interview/Cripple Creek")

WITH FIELDS WARD
Fields and Wade Ward (Biograph RC-6002; released 1968; collected and recorded by Richard Nevins in Galax, Virginia, in 1968; produced by Arnold S. Caplin; liner notes by Richard Nevins; vocals and guitar by Fields, banjo by Wade; with Jimmy Edmonds [fiddle on "John Hardy"] and John Rector [fiddle on "Riley and Spencer"])

AS THE BUCK MOUNTAIN BAND
"Yodeling Blues"/"Don't Let the Blues Get You Down" (OKeh 45428; Clarion 5292 [as by Art, Andy, Bert, and Dave]; Velvet Tone 2361 [as by Art, Andy, Bert, and Dave]; recorded in Richmond, Virginia, on October 16, 1929)

Doc Watson

Legendary flat-top guitar picker Arthel Lane (Doc) Watson was born March 3, 1923, in Deep Gap, N.C., one of nine children to General Dixon and Annie Greene Watson. He grew up listening to ballads and songs sung by his parents and grandmother; later, when Doc was 6 years old, he started listening to such early country artists as the Carter Family, Gid Tanner and His Skillet Lickers, Clarence Ashley, the Carolina Tar Heels and Jimmie Rodgers on the family's wind-up Victrola.

From the age of 6 Doc received a new harmonica every Christmas, and when he was 11 his father made him his first banjo (fretless with a catskin head). A few years later, after his second year at the Governor Morehead School for the Blind in Raleigh, a friend, Paul Montgomery, introduced Doc to the guitar. Doc's father bought him a $12 Stella guitar after Doc learned, in one day, to play "When the Roses Bloom in Dixieland," an old Carter Family tune he had heard on a 78 rpm record. Within months Doc and his older brother Linney were playing their guitars and harmonizing on street corners, performing the songs of the Carter Family, the Monroe Brothers and the Delmore Brothers.

Doc's father encouraged him to be independent and to carry his own weight around the family farm (like putting him at the end of a crosscut saw) despite his blindness, which struck him as an infant from a condition that restricted the flow of blood to his eyes. As a teen Watson learned how to finger pick the guitar from his neighbor Olin Miller. When he was 17 Watson graduated to a Silvertone, then a Martin D-28, and played at a fiddlers' convention in Boone, N.C. The following year he joined Paul Greer and R.G.

Doc Watson (left), Gaither Carlton, Blackie, and 11-year-old Merle Watson in Deep Gap, N.C., on Labor Day 1960 (photo by Eugene Earle/Southern Historical Collection, Wilson Library, The University of North Carolina at Chapel Hill).

Watson, who had a regular live radio program in Lenoir, N.C. It was during one of these shows that one of the announcers referred to the guitarist as "Doc"—a nickname that stuck.

A few years later, in 1947, Watson married Rosa Lee Carlton (born February 5, 1931), and from her father—mountain fiddler Gaither W. Carlton (February 3, 1901–June 24, 1972)—Watson picked up a number of traditional tunes such as "Georgie" and "The Old Man Below." Doc and Rosa Lee had two children: son Eddy Merle was born in 1949, and daughter Nancy Ellen was born in 1951.

In the forties and fifties Watson performed mostly country and western tunes, playing his beloved traditional songs only for his own amusement. He also earned money as a piano tuner. Watson was almost 30 years old before landing his first professional gig in 1953 as an electric guitar player in the band of Jack Williams, which performed a wide variety of music, including country and western, rock, pop, and old square dance tunes. Watson played with Jack Williams and His Country Gentlemen for seven years.

Determined to earn his living as a musician, Watson traveled by himself in the early sixties, playing the coffeehouse circuit and picking for change on street corners. In 1960, spurred by the growing folk revival, Ralph Rinzler and Eugene Earle came south to record Clarence (Tom) Ashley, and in the process heard some of the best local musicians, including Watson. Rinzler and Earle decided to record the duo (later released as *Old Time Music at Clarence Ashley's* in two volumes), and in March of 1961 Watson went to New York with the Clarence Ashley String Band (which also included Gaither Carlton, Fred Price and Clint Howard) and played on a "Friends of Old-Time Music" bill. Watson was so well-received that he was soon booked at Gerde's Folk Club in Greenwich Village, New York, where he made his first solo appearance in December 1962.

Watson—who was now playing the acoustic guitar exclusively—got his big break in May 1962, when he played with old friend and neighbor Ashley for nearly a month at the Ash Grove in Los Angeles, California. In 1963 Watson performed at the Newport Folk Festival and at Town Hall, New York, with Bill Monroe and His Blue Grass Boys.

Now in the limelight of the sixties' folk revival, Watson started making several solo recordings for Folkways. On *The Doc Watson Family* and *The Watson Family Tradition* he played with his wife Rosa Lee, son Merle, father-in-law Gaither on fiddle, and brother Arnold on banjo.

Eddy Merle—named for country greats Merle Travis and Eddy Arnold—was born February 8, 1949, and was taught to play by his mother. After first playing with his father in front of 12,000 people at Berkeley, California, in June of 1964, Merle developed into an accomplished banjoist and guitarist in his own right, playing alongside Doc on nearly a dozen albums on the Vanguard label. Merle's playing was laced with the blues; meeting (and later playing with) 72-year-old Mississippi John Hurt at the 1964 Newport Folk Festival had a profound impact on the young guitarist, and he was inspired by Duane Allman to learn how to play the slide in 1973.

Doc and Merle's career received a considerable boost after the release of the Nitty Gritty Dirt Band's *Will the Circle Be Unbroken* (1972), on which Doc played alongside other country and bluegrass legends such as Mother Maybelle Carter, Merle Travis, Roy Acuff, Earl Scruggs and Jimmy Martin. For a year or two Doc and Merle put together the Frosty Morn Band with Bob Hill, T. Michael Coleman and Joe Smothers. After that group disbanded Doc and Merle began playing as a trio, with Coleman on bass, in 1974.

With Merle playing backup guitar and serving as manager and driver, the father-son team performed frequently, often spending up to 300 nights

(From left) Merle Watson, Jack Lawrence, T. Michael Coleman and Doc Watson as depicted in Willard Gayheart's "Reunion in Wilkesboro" (courtesy Willard Gayheart).

a year on the road, and consequently expanding their audience nationwide. Doc and Merle played in 48 of the 50 states and also performed in Africa, Japan, Canada, Mexico and most of the European countries. (It has been estimated that Merle, during his 21-year career, drove over 4 million miles while touring with Doc, and flew many more thousands of miles.) In 1985 Merle was named "Best Finger Picking Guitarist—Folk/Blues or Country" by *Frets* magazine. Merle died in a tragic farm tractor accident on October 23, 1985, but his memory lives on through the annual MerleFest (started in 1988) on the campus of Wilkes Community College, Wilkesboro, site of one of the largest acoustic and American roots music festivals on the East Coast.

A five-time Grammy Award winner, Doc Watson received honorary degrees from Appalachian State University in Boone and the University of North Carolina at Chapel Hill in 1997. In 1975 the Brown-Hudson Folklore Award was presented by the North Carolina Folklore Society to Doc and Merle Watson for "in special ways contributing to the appreciation, continuation, or study of North Carolina folk traditions." Doc played for President Jimmy Carter at the White House in the late 1970s. In 1983 he received the third annual North Carolina Prize awarded by North Carolina newspapers owned by the New York Times Company. Watson received the North Carolina Award in Fine Arts in 1986, and the North Carolina Folk Heritage Award in 1994 (along with the rest of his family). He was also awarded the National Medal for the Arts by President Bill Clinton in 1997. In 1999 Watson was named North Carolinian of the Year by the N.C. Press Association.

The first Doc Watson Appreciation Day concert was held July 18, 1998, in Sugar Grove, Watauga County, during which Doc received proclamations of appreciation from local and state government, and even the White House. In the 1990s Doc played almost exclusively with Merle's immensely talented son, Richard Eddy Watson (born 1966), Jack Lawrence and Charles Welch.

Discography

Old Time Music at Clarence Ashley's (Folkways 2355; released 1961; edited and annotated by Ralph and Richard Rinzler; discography by Eugene Earle; includes lyrics and bibliographic references)

Old Time Music at Clarence Ashley's, Volume Two (Folkways 2359; released 1963; recorded July 1961 in Saltville, Virginia, February 1962 in Chicago, Illinois, and April 1962 in Los Angeles, California, by Eugene Earle, Mike Seeger, Ed Kahn and Ralph Rinzler; edited by Richard and Ralph Rinzler; notes by Ralph Rinzler; discography by Eugene Earle and Ralph Rinzler; includes lyrics and bibliographic references)

The Doc Watson Family (Smithsonian/Folkways 31021; released 1963; Watson's debut album features musical support from fiddler Gaither Carlton and other family members)

The Watson Family (Folkways FA 2366; released 1963; reissued as Smithsonian Folkways 40012, with 11 previously unreleased tracks, in 1990; collected and recorded by Ralph Rinzler, Eugene Earle, Archie Green and Peter Siegel; edited by Ralph Rinzler and Jeff Place; recorded in Deep Gap, N.C., 1960–65, 1976; descriptive insert notes by Jeff Place; also features Rosa Lee Watson ["Your Long Journey" is her own composition], Arnold Watson, Mrs. Annie Watson, Gaither Carlton, Sophronie Miller Greer, Dolly Greer and Merle Watson)

Country Music and Bluegrass at Newport, 1963 (Vanguard 79146; released 1963; Watson plays "Doc's Guitar (Ticklin' the Strings)," "The Girl I Loved in Sunny

Tennessee," "Maggie Walker Blues" and "Way Downtown" with Fred Price, Clint Howard and Clarence Ashley)

Jean Ritchie and Doc Watson at Folk City (Folkways FA 2426; released 1963; reissued in 1990 as Smithsonian/Folkways CD SF 40005, with four bonus tracks; recorded on location at Folk City, New York, by George Pickow)

Old Time Music at Newport (Vanguard VRS-9147/VSD-79147; released 1964; recorded at Newport, Rhode Island, in 1963; liner notes by Stacey Williams; Watson plays "Groundhog," "Little Orphan Girl," "Rambling Hobo" and "The Train That Carried My Girl from Town"; Watson, Clint Howard, Fred Price and Clarence [Tom] Ashley perform "Amazing Grace" [with Jean Ritchie] and "The Old Account Was Settled Long Ago")

Doc Watson (Vanguard VRS-9152/VSD-79152; recorded November 25–26, 1963, in New York City; released 1964; Watson's first Vanguard album is highlighted by "Country Blues," "Black Mountain Rag," "Omie Wise," "Doc's Guitar" and "Tom Dooley"; also features John Herald on 2nd guitar; liner notes by Ralph Rinzler)

Treasures Untold (Vanguard CV 77001; released 1964; rereleased 1992; contains 17 previously unreleased performances recorded at the 1964 Newport Folk Festival; features four duets with Clarence White)

Friends of Old Time Music (Folkways 2390; released 1964; live performances from concerts staged in New York by the Friends of Old-Time Music; edited by Peter Siegel and John Cohen; notes by Siegel; recorded by Siegel, Cohen, Ralph Rinzler, Michael Seeger, Jerry Goodwin and Ed Kahn; Watson plays "Double File" and "Hicks' Farewell" with Gaither Carlton, "Dark Holler Blues" with Clarence Ashley, and "He's Coming in Glory Some Time" with Clint Howard and Fred Price)

Folk Box (Elektra EKL-9001; released 1964; Watson performs "Amazing Grace" and "Cripple Creek")

Doc Watson and Son (Vanguard VRS-9170/VSD-79170; recorded November 4–5, 1965, in New York City; released 1965; produced by Ralph Rinzler; liner notes by Ralph Rinzler; recording debut of Merle Watson)

Traditional Music at Newport 1964, Part I (Vanguard VRS-9182/VSD-79182; released 1965; collected, recorded and edited by Ralph Rinzler with Jack Lothrop at Newport, Rhode Island, in 1964; liner notes and four-page brochure by Ralph Rinzler; Watson performs "Cripple Creek" and "Muskrat" with Gaither Carlton and Arnold Watson)

Southbound (Vanguard VRS-9213/VSD-79213; recorded January 27, 1966, in New York City; released 1966; liner notes by Doc Watson; with Merle Watson, John Pilla [guitar] and Russ Savakus [string bass])

Strictly Instrumental (Columbia CL-2643; rereleased as CS 9443; recorded in December 1966; released 1967; 11 tracks with Flatt & Scruggs)

Home Again (Vanguard VRS-9239/VSD-79239; recorded January 10–11, 1966; released 1967; produced by Ralph Rinzler; liner notes by A.L. Lloyd; with Merle Watson and Russ Savakus [string bass])

Good Deal! Doc Watson in Nashville (Vanguard 79276; recorded March 20–21, 1968, in Nashville, Tennessee; released 1968; features Merle Watson and eight Nashville studio players, including banjoist Don Stover, pianist Floyd Cramer and bassist Junior Huskey)

Progressive Bluegrass and Other Instruments, Vol. 1 (Folkways 2370; recorded in February 1968; released 1968; features Roger Sprung on banjo)

Bill and Doc (Sonyatone FEN-210; released ca. 1970; 12 tracks also feature Bill Monroe)

Folk Go-Go (Verve/Folkways FV 9011; released ca. 1970; Watson performs "Skillet Good and Greasy")

Doc Watson on Stage (Vanguard VSD 9/10; released 1970; recorded by Ed Friedner and Claude Karczmer at Cornell University and Town Hall, New York, in 1968; brief annotations by A.L. Lloyd; live double album featuring Merle Watson)

Ballads from Deep Gap (Vanguard VSD-6576; released 1971; recorded in New York City in 1971; produced by Jack Lothrop; liner notes by Bill Vernon; with Merle Watson and Eric Weissberg; 12 traditional songs and ballads)

Will the Circle Be Unbroken (with the Nitty Gritty Dirt Band) (United Artists 9801; released in 1972; Watson is featured on "Black Mountain Rag #2," "Down Yonder," "Late Last Night [When Willie Came Home]" and "Tennessee Stud")

Greatest Folksingers of the Sixties (Vanguard 17/18; released 1972)

The Essential Doc Watson (Vanguard VSD/VCD 45/46; LP issued in 1973, CD in 1986; double album drawn from performances at the 1963 and 1964 Newport [R.I.] Folk Festivals, plus traditional country and folk songs from 1960s studio sessions)

Then and Now (Poppy/United Artists LA022-F; released 1973; Grammy Award winner for Best Ethnic or Traditional Recording; features Merle Watson on lead and slide guitar, Vassar Clements on fiddle, and Norman Blake on Dobro)

Two Days in November (Poppy/United Artists LA210-G; recorded November 1–2, 1973; released in 1974; Grammy Award winner for Best Ethnic or Traditional Recording; features Merle Watson on guitar and banjo)

Doc Watson—Memories (Sugar Hill/United Artists UA-LA423-H2; released 1975; produced by Merle Watson)

Doc and the Boys (United Artists LA601-G; released 1976; features Merle Watson and Frosty Morn)

The Watson Family Tradition (Topic 12TS336; released 1977; collected and recorded by Ralph Rinzler and Daniel Seeger in Deep Gap, N.C., 1964–65; edited by Peter Siegel, Ralph Rinzler and A.L. Lloyd; annotations by A.L. Lloyd and Ralph Rinzler; features Annie Watson, Rosa Lee Watson, Gaither Carlton, Arnold Watson, Merle Watson, Dolly Greer and Tina Greer)

Old Timey Concert (Vanguard VSD-107/108; released 1977; recorded in Seattle, Washington, in 1967; engineered by Fritz Richmond from tapes made by Phil Williams; produced by Manny Greenhill; two-record set also features Fred Price and Clint Howard)

Lonesome Road (United Artists LA725-G; released 1977; features Merle Watson)

Look Away (United Artists LA887-H; released 1978; features Merle Watson)

Live and Pickin' (United Artists LA943-H; released 1979; features Merle Watson; Grammy Award winner for Best Country Instrumental Performance—"Big Sandy/Leather Britches")

Reflections (with Chet Atkins) (RCA AHL 1-3701; released 1980)

Red Rocking Chair (Flying Fish 252; released 1981; features Merle Watson; guest artists include Herb Pedersen and T. Michael Coleman)

Telluvlive (Flying Fish; released in early 1980s)

Out in the Country (Intermedia/Quicksilver QS 5031; released 1982; Watson is featured on 12 tracks)

Doc Watson Favorites (Liberty LN 10201; released 1983; features Merle Watson)

Doc & Merle Watson's Guitar Album (Flying Fish FF 301; released 1983)

Down South (Sugar Hill SH-3742/Rykodisc; released 1984; produced by Merle Watson; recorded at North Star Productions in Todd, N.C.; engineered by Carl Rudisill; mixed by Carl Rudisill and Merle Watson; also features T. Michael Coleman on bass, Buddy Davis on bass, and Sam Bush on fiddle)

Pickin' the Blues (Flying Fish FF-352; released 1985; with Merle Watson)

Riding the Midnight Train (Sugar Hill 3752; released 1986; Grammy Award winner for Best Traditional Folk Recording; features Sam Bush on mandolin, Mark O'Connor on fiddle, and Belà Fleck on banjo; last recordings of Merle Watson)

Arthel Doc Watson: Portrait (Sugar Hill SH-3759; released 1987; Watson is joined by Sam Bush and Mark O'Connor)

Favorites of Clint Howard, Doc Watson and the Blue Ridge Mountain Boys (Rutabaga RR-3010; released 1988)

Rounder Old-Time Music (Rounder 11510; released 1988; Doc, Arnold Watson and Gaither Carlton perform "Reuben's Train")

On Praying Ground (Sugar Hill SH-CD-3779; released 1990; recorded in Nashville, Tennessee; produced by T. Michael Coleman; accompanied by Jack Lawrence, Alan O'Bryant, Stuart Duncan, Jerry Douglas, Sam Bush, Roy Huskey, Jr., and T. Michael Coleman; Grammy Award winner for Best Traditional Folk Recording; gospel songs)

Doc Watson Sings Songs for Little Pickers (Sugar Hill SH-CD-3786; Alacazam! 1005; released 1990; recorded in Newport, Rhode Island, in 1988, Atlanta, Georgia, in 1990, and other venues; produced by Mark Greenberg and Mitch Greenhill; eight-page insert by Doc Watson)

My Dear Old Southern Home (Sugar Hill SH-CD-3795; released 1991; recorded in Nashville, Tennessee; produced by T. Michael Coleman, who also handles electric bass chores; also features Jack Lawrence on guitar, Stuart Duncan on fiddle, Jerry Douglas on Dobro and Sam Bush on mandolin, Alan O'Bryant, Roy Huskey, Jr., and Mark Schatz)

Sugar Plums: Holiday Treats from Sugar Hill (Sugar Hill SH-CD-3796; released 1991)

The Stained Glass Hour: Bluegrass and Old Timey Gospel Music (Rounder 11563; released 1991; compiled by Ken Irwin; the Watson Family perform "And Am I Born to Die")

Remembering Merle (Sugar Hill 3800; released 1992; as Doc & Merle Watson; all tracks recorded live between 1970 and 1976; also features Frosty Morn)

Elementary Doctor Watson (Sugar Hill/Poppy 5703; rereleased 1993)

Doc Watson and Clarence Ashley: The Original Folkways Recordings: 1960–1962 (Smithsonian/Folkways CD SF-40029/30; 2-CD set released 1994; produced and annotated by Ralph Rinzler; reissue of Folkways 2355 and 2359, with 20 additional unreleased selections)

Young Fogies (Rounder 0319; released 1994; Doc Watson performs "Raincrow Bill [Goes Up Cripple Creek]" with David Holt)

Songs from the Southern Mountains (Sugar Hill; released 1994; features the Doc Watson Family)

Then and Now/Two Days in November (Sugar Hill SH-CD-2205; released 1994; reissue of two Grammy Award winning albums on one compact disc)

Docabilly (Sugar Hill SHCD-3836; released 1995; includes covers of such 1950s rockabilly tunes such as "Shake, Rattle and Roll," "Heartbreak Hotel," "Bird Dogs" and "Walking After Midnight"; features Marty Stuart on electric guitar, Duane Eddy on electric guitar, Junior Brown on guit-steel guitar, Larry Knetchel on piano, and Roy Huskey, Jr., on bass)

The Vanguard Years (Vanguard 155/58-2; released 1995; produced and annotated by Mary Katherine Aldin; four–CD, 64-song collection draws primarily from the Vanguard releases of the 1960s and early 1970s, his solo albums, and his performances at the 1963 and 1964 Newport Folk Festivals; features 17 previously unreleased live tracks)

The Vanguard Years Sampler (Vanguard 711; released 1995; produced and liner notes by

Mary Katherine Aldin; engineered by Captain Jeff Zaraya; guest musicians include Clarence White, Merle Travis, Clint Howard, Gaither Carlton, Merle Watson and Fred Price)

Blue Ribbon Guitar (Easydisc 7006; released 1996; various artists and producers; Norman Blake, Tony Rice and Doc Watson pick "Salt Creek"; Doc & Merle Watson perform "Fisher's Hornpipe/Devils' Dream")

Crossroads: Southern Routes: Music of the American South (Smithsonian/Folkways SF CD 40080; released 1996; produced by Anthony Seeger and Amy Horowitz; notes by Anthony Seeger and Kip Lornell; Doc Watson with Merle Watson perform "Southbound")

Watson Country (Flying Fish 651; released 1996; produced, arranged and annotated by Mitch Greenhill; engineered by Hank Cicalo, Ernie Winfrey and Carl Rudisill; guest musicians include Sam Bush, Tom Scott, Byron Berline, T. Michael Coleman, Pat McInerney, Mark O'Connor, Herb Pedersen, Al Perkins, Joe Smothers, Ron Tutt and Merle Watson)

Doc [Watson] & Dawg [David Grisman] (Acoustic Disc ACD-25; released 1997; produced by David Grisman; also features Jack Lawrence on guitar)

Elementary Doctor Watson/Then & Now (Collectables 5839; released 1997; produced by Jack Clement; liner notes by Mark Marymont; guest musicians include Norman Blake, Joe Allan, Vassar Clements, Ken Lauber and Merle Watson)

Classic Railroad Songs, Vol. 1: Steel Rails (Rounder 1128; released 1997; compiled by Michael Hyatt; David Grisman, with Doc Watson and Alan O'Bryant, perform "Nine Pound Hammer")

Home Sweet Home (Sugar Hill 3889; released 1998; produced and annotated by T. Michael Coleman, who also plays bass; also features Marty Stuart, Sam Bush, Alan O'Bryant and Merle Watson)

The North Carolina Banjo Collection (Rounder 0439; 2-CD set released 1998; produced by Bob Carlin; Doc Watson performs "Reuben's Train"; Arnold Watson is featured on "Biscuits"; Gaither Carlton plays "Rambling Hobo")

Mac [Wiseman], Doc [Watson] & Del [McCoury] (Sugar Hill SHCD-3888; released 1998; produced by Scott Rouse for Groovegrass Recordings; also features Ronnie McCoury [mandolin], Jason Carter [fiddle], Terry Eldridge [guitar], Alison Krauss [harmony vocals], Jerry Douglas [Dobro], Jack Lawrence [guitar], Mike Bubb [bass], Gene Wooten [Dobro] and Byron House [bass])

The Best of Doc Watson: 1964–1968 (Vanguard 79535; released 1999; consists of 24 tracks)

WITH RICHARD WATSON
Third Generation Blues (Sugar Hill 3893; released 1999; consists of 14 tracks)

Ephraim Woodie and the Henpecked Husbands

Colonel Ephraim (Eef) Woodie was born on May 7, 1907, and raised in Furches (also known as Cranberry), N.C., which straddles the Ashe-Alleghany county line. Eef's mother, Leona, sang old English ballads around the house. As a child Eef had cataracts on both eyes and spent 14 years at the N.C. School for the Blind in Raleigh. After returning home in 1927, he was given a guitar by his mother and formed a string band with some neighbors.

The Henpecked Husbands (so named because they were older and married while Woodie was still a bachelor) consisted of fiddler John Clay Reed and banjoist Wilborn Edison Nuckolls (both of whom went by their middle name). Reed (who was born on April 24, 1900) was a farmer who grew up in Laurel Springs and had played music for years with Donald Thompson of the Carolina Night Hawks. Nuckolls (born March 11, 1985) operated a sawmill near Furches and raised corn and tobacco.

In the fall of 1929 the trio decided to audition for the Columbia Phono-graph Company in John-

Ephraim Woodie in Furches, N.C., circa 1929 (courtesy Marshall Wyatt).

son City, Tennessee. In what would be their only recording session, they cut two songs (for which they received $50): "Last Gold Dollar" and "The Fatal Courtship."

Edison Nuckolls soon moved a few miles north to the community of Scottsville. He then started a musical association with guitarist Charlie Cox and fiddler Bill Williams that would last more than thirty years—the trio even cut their own records on Nuckolls' own disc recording machine. Nuckolls died of a heart attack on August 22, 1975.

Clay Reed and his sons Ray and Howard played together for fun at local events in the 1940s. Howard and his wife, Josephine Crouse, formed a singing duo in 1954 and performed together well into the late 1990s. Clay Reed died of heart disease in 1965.

Eef Woodie later recorded two songs for Victor on May 29, 1931, with his older brother Lawton Woodie. Lawton was born near Furches on February 9, 1900, and pursued a career in education. He taught at various schools in Ashe and Alleghany counties before moving with his family to Surry County in 1951. There he was a math and science teacher at Mount Airy High School. Lawton retired from teaching in 1965, and died two years later of an aneurysm.

Ephraim Woodie married Effie Tilley of Laurel Springs on November 29, 1937. They lived in the Furches community of Alleghany County, operating a country store and a post office in the front part of their house. The couple's abode turned into a gathering spot of sorts for local musicians such as guitarist Charlie Cox and fiddler Bill Williams. In later years he lived near Laurel Springs in Alleghany County. Eef Woodie died on April 19, 1978.

Lawton Woodie (the elder member of the Woodie Brothers), pictured circa 1930 (courtesy Marshall Wyatt).

Discography

"Last Gold Dollar"/"The Fatal Courtship" (Columbia 15564-D; recorded in Knoxville, Tennessee, on October 23–24, 1929; released 1930)

Old-Time Southern Dance Music: Ballads and Songs (Old Timey 102; released 1965; edited by Chris Strachwitz; liner notes by Toni Brown; consists of 16 commercial 78 rpm recordings made from 1925 to 1939; Ephraim Woodie and the Henpecked Husbands perform "The Fatal Courtship")

Music from the Lost Provinces (Old Hat CD-1001; released 1997; produced, booklet notes and graphic design by Marshall Wyatt; Ephraim Woodie and the Henpecked Husbands are featured on "Last Gold Dollar" and "The Fatal Courtship")

AS THE WOODIE BROTHERS

"Likes Likker Better Than Me"/"Chased Old Satan Through the Door" (Victor 23579, Zonophone 4348; recorded in Charlotte, North Carolina, on May 29, 1931; released August 28, 1931)

Clay Reed, pictured with his sons Howard (on his right) and Ray, played fiddle with Ephraim Woodie and the Henpecked Husbands. This photo was taken in Laurel Springs, N.C., in 1949 (courtesy Marshall Wyatt).

The Cold-Water Pledge, Vol. 1: Songs of Moonshine and Temperance Recorded in the Golden Age (Marimac 9104 [cassette]; released 1984; edited by Pat Conte; contains brief insert leaflet; booklet by W.K. McNeil sold separately; consists of 19 commercial 78 rpm recordings made from 1925 to 1937; Woodie Brothers perform "Likes Likker Better Than Me")

Music from the Lost Provinces (Old Hat CD-1001; released 1997; produced, booklet notes and graphic design by Marshall Wyatt; the Woodie Brothers play "Likes Likker Better Than Me" and "Chased Old Satan Through the Door")

Art Wooten

Old time and bluegrass fiddler Art Wooten was born on February 4, 1906, in Sparta (Alleghany County), N.C., and always made his home there. Wooten first gained notoriety as a member of Bill Monroe's Blue Grass Boys, the unquestioned pioneers of bluegrass music. In early 1939—soon after Bill Monroe and his brother Charlie had split up—Bill Monroe and Cleo Davis advertised for other musicians, and Art Wooten was the first hired. In addition to his fiddle, Wooten played a one-man band contraption that was part organ, banjo and guitar. Since his mandolin was tuned the same as the fiddle,

Monroe personally tutored Wooten on how he wanted the notes bowed. Wooten also sang baritone with the group, which joined the Grand Ole Opry in 1939.

Wooten left the Blue Grass Boys in 1940 and was replaced by Tommy Magness, who had been working with Roy Hall and His Blue Ridge Entertainers since 1938. However, in the summer of 1941 Magness returned to Roy Hall and Wooten rejoined Bill Monroe. Wooten's second stint with the Blue Grass Boys was short-lived as well, though, as he left in early 1942 and was replaced by Howdy Forrester of west Tennessee.

In the summer of 1948, Wooten joined the Stanley Brothers' Clinch Mountain Boys after Leslie Keith left to form his own group, the Lonesome Valley Boys. Wooten brought a faster tempo and drive to the Stanley Brothers' music, evident in their recording of "Molly and Tenbrook," the first bluegrass copy of Bill Monroe's song (which was recorded earlier but would not be released until nearly a year after the Stanleys' single came out on Rich-R-Tone).

In 1948 Wooten and the Stanley Brothers singed a contract with Columbia, for which they recorded from 1949 until 1952. During these sessions they cut some of their classic numbers, such as "The White Dove," "The Lonesome River" and "The Fields Have Turned Brown." It was Wooten who suggested they form a high baritone vocal trio, with Pee Wee Lambert and Ralph Stanley singing above Carter Stanley's lead. After the final Columbia session in 1952, Wooten left the band and was replaced by Art Stamper.

Art Wooten died on October 6, 1986.

Discography

WITH THE STANLEY BROTHERS AND THE CLINCH MOUNTAIN BOYS
"Molly and Tenbrook"/"The Rambler's Blues" (Rich-R-Tone 418; recorded at radio station WOPI in Bristol, Virginia, in the summer of 1948)
"The White Dove"/"Gathering Flowers for the Master's Bouquet" (Columbia 20577; released April 4, 1949)
"Little Glass of Wine"/"Let Me Be Your Friend" (Columbia 20590; released June 20, 1949)
"Angels Are Singing in Heaven Tonight"/"It's Never Too Late" (Columbia 20617; released September 26, 1949)
"Vision of Mother"/"Have You Someone (in Heaven Awaiting)" (Columbia 20647; released December 5, 1949)
"Old Home"/"The Fields Have Turned Brown" (Columbia 20667; released February 13, 1950)
"I Love No One But You"/"Too Late to Cry" (Columbia 20697; released May 15, 1950)
"We'll Be Sweethearts in Heaven"/"Drunkard's Hell" (Columbia 20735; released August 21, 1950)
"Hey, Hey, Hey"/"Pretty Polly" (Columbia 20770; released December 18, 1950)

"The Lonesome River"/"I'm a Man of Constant Sorrow" (Columbia 20816; released
  May 7, 1951)
"Sweetest Love"/"Wandering Boy" (Columbia 20953; released June 7, 1952)
The Stanley Brothers, Their Original Recordings (Melodean MLP 7322; released 1965)
The Rich-R-Tone Story: The Early Days of Bluegrass, Vol. 5 (Rounder 1017; released
  1975)
The Stanley Brothers and the Clinch Mountain Boys, 1949–1952 (Bear Family BCD
  15564; released 1994; notes and discography by Gary Reid; complete reissue of
  the Columbia sessions, including two previously unissued takes)
Stanley Brothers Earliest Recordings: The Complete Rich-R-Tone 78s (1947–1952) (Rich-
  R-Tone/Revenant 203; released 1997; liner notes by Gary B. Reid; consists of 14
  tracks)

WITH BILL MONROE AND THE BLUE GRASS BOYS
"Blue Yodel No. 7"/"In the Pines" (Bluebird B8861; recorded October 1941 in Atlanta,
  Georgia)
"Orange Blossom Special"/"The Coupon Song" (Bluebird B8893; recorded October
  1941 in Atlanta, Georgia)
The Father of Bluegrass Music (RCA Camden CAL 719; released 1962; contains all of
  the 1940-41 Monroe recordings except for "The Coupon Song")
The Music of Bill Monroe (MCA 11048; released 1994; four CD boxed set that covers
  Monroe's entire career from 1936 to 1994)

AS A SOLO PERFORMER
Fiddlin' Art Wooten: A Living Legend (Homestead 104; released 1976)
Fiddlin' Art Wooten: A Living Bluegrass Legend (Dominion Records A-116; recorded at
  JRM Studios in Salem, Virginia; engineered by Rick Mullins; produced by Jack
  Mullins; jacket notes by Jim Eanes; also features Ray Cline and Herb Green on
  guitar, L.W. Lambert on banjo, Herb Lambert on mandolin and Danny Camp-
  bell on bass)

Bibliography

Alden, Ray. "Music from Round Peak." *Old Time Music* 19 (Winter 1975-76): 10–16.

Allen, Bob. "Lonesome River Band: Overcoming the Odds in the Long Pursuit of Musical Excellence." *Bluegrass Unlimited* Vol. 33, No. 2 (August 1998): 30–39.

Baggelaar, Kristin, and Donald Milton. *Folk Music: More Than a Song*. New York: Thomas Y. Crowell, 1976.

Bolle, Mary Jane. "Merle: The Silent Watson." *Bluegrass Unlimited* Vol. 8, No. 6 (December 1973): 9–12.

Brown, Caleb. "Clarence Greene: Mitchell County's Master Musician." *Bluegrass Unlimited* Vol. 20, No. 2 (August 1985): 15–21.

_____. "Eric Ellis: Elite Banjo." *Bluegrass Unlimited* Vol. 30, No. 9 (March 1996): 33–36.

_____. "The Lincoln County Partners: Traditional Bluegrass in Carolina." *Bluegrass Unlimited* Vol. 29, No. 3 (September 1994): 58–61.

Brown, Paul. "Through the Flippen Filter: The Life, Times, & Tunes of Benton Flippen." *The Old-Time Herald* Vol. 5, No. 1 (Fall 1995): 16–22+.

Carlin, Bob. "L.W. Lambert: True Banjo Picker." *Bluegrass Unlimited* Vol. 33, No. 9 (March 1999): 38–42.

Coats, Art. "Flat-Pickin' with Doc Watson, Norman Blake and Dan Crary." *Pickin'* Vol. 2, No. 1 (February 1975): 4–16.

Coffey, John. "Fields Ward, 1911–1987." *The Old-Time Herald* Vol. 1, No. 4 (Summer 1988): 12–16.

Cohen, Norm. *Traditional Anglo-American Folk Music: An Annotated Discography of Published Sound Recordings*. New York: Garland, 1994.

_____, and Eugene Earle. "An Ernest Stoneman Discography." *JEMF Quarterly* Vol. 16, No. 57 (Spring 1980): 36–49.

Correll, Ginger. "Willard Gayheart: A Credit to Bluegrass Music." *Bluegrass Unlimited* No. 12, Vol. 3 (September 1977): 24–27.

Cotton, Cay. "Albert Hash: Fiddle Master, Fiddle Maker." *Bluegrass Unlimited* Vol. 13, No. 10 (April 1979): 88–92.

Daniel, Wayne W. "Lulu Belle and Scotty: 'Have I Told You Lately That I Love You?'" *Bluegrass Unlimited* Vol. 20, No. 9 (March 1986): 70–76.

Davis, Stephen F., and Robert E. Nobley. "Norman Edmonds: Mountain Fiddler." *Old Time Music* 9 (Summer 1973): 22–23.

Docks, L.R. *American Premium Record Guide, 1915–1965*, 2d ed. Florence, Alabama: Books Americana, 1982.

Erlewine, Michael, ed., et al. *All Music Guide to Country*. San Francisco: Miller Freeman, 1997.

Fenton, Mike. "The Mountain Ramblers of Galax, Part 1: 1953–58." *Old Time Music* 21 (Summer 1976): 12–16.

_____. "The Mountain Ramblers of Galax, Part 2: 1959–1975." *Old Time Music* 22 (Autumn 1976): 12–16.

_____. "30 Years of the Mountain Ramblers." *Bluegrass Unlimited* Vol. 20, No. 4 (October 1985): 42–44.

Fetrow, Alan G. *Feature Films, 1940–1949: A United States Filmography.* Jefferson, N.C.: McFarland, 1994.

Gerrard, Alice. "Otis Burris: Galax Breakdown Fiddler." *The Old-Time Herald* Vol. 1, No. 7 (Spring 1989): 15–20.

Green, Archie. "Hillbilly Music: Source and Symbol." *Journal of American Folklore* LXXVII, No. 309 (July–September 1965): 204–28.

Greene, Clarence H. "The Church Brothers." *Bluegrass Unlimited* Vol. 22, No. 6 (December 1987): 18–24.

_____. "Dock Walsh and the Carolina Tar Heels." *Bluegrass Unlimited* Vol. 23, No. 12 (June 1989): 50–54.

_____. "Gwin Foster: Marvel of the Mouth Harp." *Bluegrass Unlimited* Vol. 33, No. 2 (August 1998): 64–68.

_____. "Ricochet: Band on the Move." *Bluegrass Unlimited* Vol. 25, No. 10 (April 1991): 58–60.

_____. "Steve Kilby: The Gentle Giant." *Bluegrass Unlimited* Vol. 26, No. 10 (April 1992): 52–55.

Hauslohner, Amy Worthington. "Twenty-Nine Hours: A Day (and More) in the Life of the Konnarock Country Critters." *Bluegrass Unlimited* Vol. 25, No. 9 (March 1991): 38–45.

Heier, Uli, and Rainer E. Lotz, eds. *The Banjo on Record: A Bio-Discography.* Westport, Connecticut: Greenwood, 1993.

Holland, Dave. "'Country My Eye, It's Hillbilly Where I Come From'—Ola Belle Reed." *Pickin'* Vol. 4, No. 1 (February 1977): 18–19.

Hunsucker, Lucy. "Ted Lundy, Bob Paisley & the Southern Mountain Boys." *Bluegrass Unlimited* Vol. 13, No. 1 (July 1978): 16–19.

Hutchens, Doug. "The Easter Brothers." *Bluegrass Unlimited* Vol. 18, No. 5 (November 1983): 42–44.

Johnson, Craig. "Remembering Kahle Brewer." *The Old-Time Herald* Vol. 2, No. 2 (Winter 1989-90): 18–19.

Kahn, Si, and Kathy Kahn. "Rediscovering Eef Woodie." *Old Time Music* 8 (Spring 1973): 11–13.

Kerr, Janet. "Lonnie Austin/Norman Woodlief." *Old Time Music* 17 (Summer 1975): 6–10.

Lair, John. "High Jinks on White Top!" *Old Time Music* 2 (Autumn 1971): 16–17.

Leiser, Roland. "Senator Robert C. Byrd: The Fiddling Politician." *Pickin'* Vol. 5, No. 8 (September 1978): 30–33.

Lightfoot, William E. "Belle of the Barn Dance: Reminiscing with Lulu Belle Wiseman Stamey." *Journal of Country Music* Vol. XII, No. I (1987): 2–15.

Lornell, Kip. "The Hills: Alive with the Sound of Music." *Old Time Music* 44 (Winter 1987-88): 12–15.

_____. "A Talk with Walter Frank Blevins." *The Devil's Box* 21 (Spring 1987): 3–12.

_____. *Virginia's Blues, Country, & Gospel Records, 1902–1943: An Annotated Discography.* Lexington: The University Press of Kentucky, 1989.

McCloud, Barry, et al. *Definitive Country: The Ultimate Encyclopedia of Country Music and Its Performers.* New York: Perigee, 1995.

Mallett, Carol. "Made by Hand: A Visit with Award-Winning Luthier and Guitarist Wayne Henderson." *Acoustic Guitar* Vol. 9, No. 9 (March 1999): 54–63.

Malone, Bill C. *Country Music, U.S.A.: A Fifty-Year History*. Austin, Texas: The University of Texas Press, for the American Folklore Society, 1968.

_____, and Judith McCulloh, eds. *Stars of Country Music: Uncle Dave Macon to Johnny Rodriguez*. Urbana: University of Illinois Press, 1975.

Mansfield, Bill, et al. "The Slate Mountain Ramblers." *The Old-Time Herald* Vol. 1, No. 1 (Fall 1987): 3–8.

Martin, Judy. "A Banjo Pickin' Girl: The Life and Music of Ola Belle Campbell Reed." *The Old-Time Herald* Vol. 3, No. 6 (Winter 1992-93): 17–22.

Martin, Len D. *The Republic Pictures Checklist: Features, Serials, Cartoons, Short Subjects and Training Films of Republic Pictures Corporation, 1935–1959*. Jefferson, N.C.: McFarland, 1998.

Miller, Dan. "Doc Watson." *Flatpicking Guitar Magazine* Vol. 2, No. 6 (September/October 1998): 4–10.

Norris, Cindy. "Jim Brooks: Bluegrass Picker and Instrument Builder." *Bluegrass Unlimited* Vol. 26, No. 12 (June 1992): 51–53.

Parker, Ray. "G.B. Grayson: A Short Life of Trouble." *Old Time Music* 35 (Winter 1980-Spring 1981): 10–13.

Pate, Jason D. "Ted Lundy, Bob Paisley & the Southern Mountain Boys." *Pickin'* Vol. 5, No. 6 (July 1978): 50–51.

Prouty, Clarke. "'Getting Where You Want to Be'—Wayne Henderson." *The Old-Time Herald* Vol. 6, No. 2 (Winter 1997-98): 17–21+.

Rhodes, Don. "Doc Watson." *Bluegrass Unlimited* Vol. 12, No. 7 (January 1978): 10–13.

Rosenberg, Neil V. *Bluegrass: A History*. Urbana, Illinois. University of Illinois Press, 1985.

Russell, Tony. "H.M. Barnes' Blue Ridge Ramblers." *Old Time Music* 17 (Summer 1975): 11.

Sandberg, Larry, and Dick Weissman. *The Folk Music Sourcebook*. New York: Alfred A. Knopf, 1976.

Seeger, Mike. "John Kilby Snow: May 28, 1906–March 20, 1980." *Bluegrass Unlimited* Vol. 14, No. 12 (June 1980): 7.

Smythe, Willie. *Country Music Recorded Prior to 1943: A Discography of LP Reissues*. JEMF Special Series, No. 13, n.d.

Steiner, Alan J. "Bob Paisley & the Southern Grass." *Bluegrass Unlimited* Vol. 18, No. 5 (November 1983): 10–14.

Strickland, Rhonda. "Ola Belle Reed: Preserving Traditional Music Without Killing It." *Bluegrass Unlimited* Vol. 17, No. 12 (June 1983): 40–46.

Tallmadge, William H. *A Selected and Annotated Discography of Southern Appalachian Mountain Music*. Berea, Kentucky: Berea College Appalachian Center, 1985.

Warner, Anne, and Frank Warner. "Frank Noah Proffitt: Good Times and Hard Times on the Beaver Dam Road." *Appalachian Journal* 1 (1973): 163–193.

Watson, Doc. *The Songs of Doc Watson*. New York: Music Sales, 1993.

Watson, Nancy E. "A Memorial for Merle." *Bluegrass Unlimited* Vol. 23, No. 7 (January 1989): 16–22.

_____. "Doc Watson: A Closer Look." *Bluegrass Unlimited* Vol. 19, No. 2 (August 1984)· 8–11.

Weston, Frank. "Albert Hash: Fiddler & Fiddle-maker." *Old Time Music* 39 (Spring 1984): 12–18.

_____. "E.C. Ball." *Old Time Music* 30 (Autumn 1978): 5–8.

_____. "Pickin' and Buildin': Wayne Henderson." *Old Time Music* 41 (Spring 1985): 5–7.

Whittaker, H. Lloyd "Stretch." "Doc Watson." *Bluegrass Unlimited* Vol. 5, No. 5 (November 1970): 4–7.

Wickham, Graham, and Eugene Earle. *The Early Recording Career of Ernest V. 'Pop' Stoneman: A Bio-discography*. JEMF Special Series No. 1, 1968.

Wolfe, Charles. "Legends—No. 8: Grayson & Whitter." *The Old-Time Herald* Vol. 3, No. 7 (Spring 1993): 7–8.

_____. "Robert Byrd: Fiddler in the Senate." *Bluegrass Unlimited* Vol. 14, No. 5 (November 1979): 28–31.

_____. "Up North with the Blue Ridge Ramblers: Jennie Bowman's 1931 Tour Diary." *Journal of Country Music* Vol. VI, No. III (Fall 1975): 136–142.

Worth, Lynn. "An Old-Time Life on Whitetop Mountain." *The Old-Time Herald* Vol. 3, No. 7 (Spring 1993): 18–23.

_____. "Old-Time Music in Laurel: New River Mountain Music Jamboree." *The Old-Time Herald* Vol. 3, No. 3 (Spring 1992): 41–42+.

Wyatt, Marshall. "'Governor Al Smith for President': The Story of the Carolina Night Hawks." *The Old-Time Herald* Vol. 3, No. 6 (Winter 1992-93): 26–30.

_____. "'I Ain't Never Heared Such a Rattlin' Bunch!': The Story of Frank Blevins and His Tar Heel Rattlers." *The Old-Time Herald* Vol. 2, No. 7 (Spring 1991): 14–20+.

_____. "Music from the 'Lost Provinces': Part One." *The Old-Time Herald* Vol. 5, No. 3 (Spring 1996): 38–47.

_____. "Music from the 'Lost Provinces': Part Two." *The Old-Time Herald* Vol. 5, No. 4 (Summer 1996): 26–35.

Index

"Washington and Lee Swing" 18, 74
"Wasn't She Dandy" 88
"Watch and Pray" 166, 180
"Waterbound" 182
"Watermelon Hanging on the Vine"
    160
Watson, Annie Greene 184, 188, 190
Watson, Arnold 188, 189, 190, 191, 192
Watson, Doc 5, 6, 10, 15, 17, 44, 69, 81,
    82, 112, 137, 184–92
Watson, General Dixon 184
Watson, Harvey 137
Watson, Linney 184
Watson, Merle 6, 185–92
Watson, Nancy Ellen 185
Watson, Peco 128, 129
Watson, R.G. 184–85
Watson, Richard 6, 188, 192
Watson, Rosa Lee (Carlton) 185, 186,
    188, 190
Watson Country 192
The Watson Family 188
Watson Family 191
The Watson Family Tradition 186, 190
"Waves on the Ocean" 119
"Way Down in Alabama" 144
"Way Down in North Carolina" 166,
    179, 180
"Way Down in Ole Caroline" 49
"Way Downtown" 189
"Wayfaring Stranger" 21
Wayne Henderson and Ray Cline Guitar
    Pickin' with Herb Key 82, 103
Wayne Henderson and Robin Kesinger:
    Contest Favorites 82
Wayne Henderson and Steve Kaufman:
    Not Much Work for Saturday 82
"We Courted in the Rain" 161, 162,
    174
"We Parted at the River" 163
"We Parted by the Riverside" 60, 159,
    167
Webb, Frill 91
"Weeping Willow Tree" 137, 139, 141
Weissberg, Eric 190
Weize, Richard 45, 177
Welch, Charles 113, 188
Welding, Pete 75, 165
"We'll Be Sweethearts in Heaven" 196
"We'll Meet Again Sweetheart" 149
"We'll Meet Up There" 49

Wells Fargo 112
We're Going Home 63
We're Gonna Make It 63
"We're Just Plain Folks" 174
West Jefferson, N.C. 19, 25, 28, 39, 40,
    77, 80, 112
"West Virginia Gals" 88
"West Virginia Highway" 161
West Virginia Hotfoots 14
"Western Country" 183
Weston, Don 124
"What Will I Do, for My Money Is
    All Gone" 58
"What Will I Do, for My Money's All
    Gone" 59
"What You Gonna Do with the Baby"
    70, 71
"When I Get Home (I'm Gonna Be
    Satisfied)" 21
When I Was a Cowboy, Vol. 2 98
"When Jesus Calls You Home" 49
"When My Time Has Come to Go"
    134
"When My Wife Will Return to Me"
    159
"When Pa Was Courtin' Ma" 117
"When the Good Lord Sets You Free"
    44, 176
"When the Redeemed Are Gathered
    In" 161, 162
"When the Roses Bloom Again" 160,
    164
"When the Roses Bloom in Dixieland"
    184
"When the Snowflakes Fall Again" 98,
    165
"When the Work's All Done This
    Fall" 159
"When You Ask a Girl to Leave Her
    Happy Home" 93
"Where Are You Going, Alice?" 70
Whing-Ding 149
"The Whip-poor-will Song" 59, 162
Whisnant, David 37
White, Clarence 189, 192
White, Helen 82, 104
White Country Blues, 1928–36: A
    Lighter Shade of Blue, Vol. 1 17
"The White Dove" 196
"White House Blues" 172
White Spirituals 21, 125